"Harry S. Truman was commander in chief at one of the critical moments in American—and global—military history: when the decision had to be made to drop the atomic bomb. As to his military credentials, however, Truman is often dismissed as little more than a National Guard hack and a Kansas City haberdasher with no real military acumen. Yet nothing could be further from the truth, as D. M. Giangreco makes clear in *The Soldier from Independence*."
  —Military Book Club

"With his customary thoroughness, D. M. Giangreco has given us a splendid account of Harry Truman's military career."
  —Alonzo L. Hamby, Distinguished Professor Emeritus of History at Ohio University

"Reading Truman's account of events is very powerful, and Giangreco has skill-fully constructed a narrative with these sources that makes it possible for readers to experience the war as if they were on the battlefield with Harry Truman and Battery D."
  —Jon E. Taylor, *Missouri Historical Review*

"Going into combat in the Meuse-Argonne offensive of 1918, Captain Truman's actions as recounted by Giangreco will engage readers drawn to the formative experiences of future presidents."
  —Gilbert Taylor, *Booklist*

"Giangreco not only gives us a look at one of the millions of ordinary Ameri-cans who served in the Great War, giving us a soldier's-eye view of the AEF and the trenches as well as a brief treatment of the army's mismanagement of the National Guard, but also discusses how Truman's time in uniform shaped his business and political life."
  —A. A. Nofi, Center for Naval Analysis, Naval War College, and senior editor of StrategyPage.com

"To this reviewer, an artilleryman, the single most useful part of this work is the detailed description of the inner workings of a light (75-millimeter) field artil-lery battery in combat. The details will likely be lost on many readers, but they are the best single source of 'how it really worked.' Everything except specific firing calculations is there—encrusted in mud, surrounded by chaos, compro-mised by lack of sleep, and, naturally, punctured throughout by enemy action. It really does not matter who is the focus of the story; Giangreco's detailed descriptions are so well provided."
  —Douglas V. Johnson II, *Parameters*

"Giangreco's book illuminates the combat experience neglected in studies of the thirty-third President of the United States. . . . Giangreco's military biography of Truman is a study in command and proper and successful employment of authority."

    —David O. Whitten, *On Point*

"D. M. Giangreco has done a valuable service here in undermining one of the more persistent myths—that Harry Truman had a minimal understanding of strategy or war. This is a biography of the military side of Truman's life . . . and it is high time. . . . [Giangreco's] careful and detailed scholarship is to be savored and enjoyed."

    —John T. Kuehn, General William Stofft Professor of Military History at the U.S. Army Command and General Staff College

The Soldier from
INDEPENDENCE

The Soldier from
INDEPENDENCE

A Military Biography of Harry Truman, Volume 1, 1906–1919

D. M. GIANGRECO

Foreword by **ALONZO L. HAMBY**

Potomac Books
An imprint of the University of Nebraska Press

Table of Contents

You know, the battery commander is the man to whom "the buck" is passed both going up and going down, and he's got to watch his P's and Q's mighty smartly [so] they don't succeed in getting something on him.

—Captain Harry S. Truman,
letter to Bess Wallace,
"Somewhere in France," October 30, 1918

Foreword

HARRY TRUMAN FREQUENTLY REMARKED that his political career was based on his military experience. At first glance, the declaration strikes one as an extreme exaggeration: six years of service with the Missouri National Guard as a young man; two years of active duty in the U.S. Army, three months of them in actual combat situations; a decade or so of what at first glance appears to be only brief summer outings in the Officers' Reserve Corps?

One grasps instantly how a Dwight D. Eisenhower could be shaped by four decades that took him to the pinnacle of American military achievement, but could Truman's sporadic involvement really be so important? In fact, it was.

As a boy, whether studying Julius Caesar or Robert E. Lee, Truman came to see military leadership as essential training for political leadership. Prevented from seeking appointment to the U.S. Military Academy by his myopic eyesight, he joined the National Guard at the age of twenty-one, trained diligently, and valued the comradeship he found there. Pressed into full-time work on the family farm, he had to decline reenlistment at the end of his second three-year term; nevertheless, he maintained contact with his guard friends and attended their social events.

What, the reader asks, could have motivated him to reenlist just weeks short of his thirty-third birthday as war with Germany loomed? It is tempting to say that he was trying to restart his life after a major business failure in lead and zinc mining, but he had moved beyond that to involvement in a speculative oil and gas venture that seemed to possess real possibilities. It seems fair to say that he, like most of his fellow officers, was primarily motivated by a sense of duty and patriotism too easily discounted by today's cynics. Several of his comrades were prominent businessmen and professionals beyond draft age who left comfortable and successful lives in pursuit of service to their country.

Winston Churchill, himself a soldier at the beginning of a long political career, once remarked that nothing was more exhilarating than being shot at without effect. Harry Truman knew the feeling. It is worth remembering that while eleven of the eighteen twentieth-century American presidents from William McKinley to William Jefferson Clinton had military service, only four actually led men in close-combat situations: Theodore Roosevelt, Harry Truman, John F. Kennedy, and George H. W. Bush. This was the most successful and satisfying experience of Truman's first thirty-five years. He demonstrated to himself both an inner courage and an ability to lead other men. The memories of war surely provided confidence and resolution in his later life.

Associations that came out of the conflict were important and lasting also, among them Capt. John Miles, later the Republican marshal of Jackson County, who dispatched deputies to guard a key ballot box in Truman's first campaign for the county court; Maj. Marvin Gates, the Yale-educated real estate developer who backed him throughout his career; Sgt. Eddie Jacobson, his friend, business partner, and advocate for the state of Israel; Lt. James Pendergast, his link to Kansas City's dominant political boss; and Lt. Harry Vaughan, oafish and indiscreet, but nonetheless a close and valued friend over Truman's long career. For the rest of his life he considered the men who worked under him to be his charges and would do what he could to help them out, often with patronage jobs.

Truman's years in the Officers' Reserve Corps would also provide him with new and lasting associations, most notably his future secretary of the treasury, John W. Snyder. It also brought him into contact with such notables as Jonathan Wainwright, George S. Patton Jr., Henry

"Hap" Arnold, Omar Bradley, and more than a dozen other future general officers.

Truman's military career, whether as National Guardsman or reserve officer, profoundly affected his policy outlook as president. Deeply believing in the ideal of the citizen soldier, he doggedly pushed the politically no-win issue of universal military training. Skeptical of the hidebound professional officer corps he had seen in World War I, he slashed the standing armed forces and cut defense spending to the bone. He believed that in a national emergency, young men could be trained and equipped as he had been for eventual battle overseas. The result would play out unhappily in the Korean War.

Harry Truman's assessment of the importance of his own career as a soldier was thus accurate in ways both positive and negative. No scholar has examined it with the depth and creativity that D. M. Giangreco displays in *The Soldier from Independence*.

—Alonzo L. Hamby

Preface

HARRY S. TRUMAN CERTAINLY DIDN'T NEED to reenlist in April 1917 and become a buck private at the age of thirty-three. He was too old to be drafted, and the army would soon classify him as being functionally blind in his left eye. And, as the owner of a farm that, despite its ups and downs, was larger and more prosperous than most in his home state, he was already involved in an occupation that President Wilson himself said was critical to victory. But Harry Truman always wanted to be a soldier. Twice before, he had signed up for three-year hitches in the Missouri National Guard, and though he had been a private citizen for nearly six years when the United States declared war on Germany, he signed up a third time. Truman earned two stripes before leaving the guard after his second stint, and having maintained close ties with the citizen soldiers in his old unit, he believed that he had a good shot at being appointed as one of the unit's sergeants.

Today, most Americans know this soldier from Independence, Missouri, as the man who, when president of the United States in 1945, ordered that atomic bombs be dropped on Hiroshima and Nagasaki in the hopes of forestalling a bloody invasion of Imperial Japan. Many are also aware of his service as the commander of an artillery battery during the First World War. Yet, it always struck me as curious that for all the words that have been written about Truman, his time leading men in combat had not been seriously examined—although much has been written about his managing of the regimental canteen—and that his postwar service has remained invisible in biography after biography. This, the first of two volumes on Harry S. Truman's military career, is the product of that curiosity.

Truman knew his business, and after the war he rose quickly within the ranks to become a fairly senior member of the select between-wars club that was the United States Army. He achieved the rank of colonel in the Officers' Reserve Corps, commanding an exceptionally well-trained National Guard artillery regiment long before his election to the U.S. Senate in 1934, and was given command of another regiment in 1936. Truman was a founder of the Reserve Officers Association immediately after the war, attended classes at the Command and General Staff School at Fort Leavenworth, Kansas, organized regular lectures for reserve and guard officers in Kansas City (his first lecturer was a bright young major named Omar Bradley), and was a familiar figure at the Fort Riley artillery range.

During both his time as a reserve officer and as the junior senator from Missouri, Truman came to know an extremely large number of the officers who would lead the army in World War II. On one occasion, he humorously wrote home to his wife, Bess, that he'd just left a promotion party for George S. Patton early because "it was too rough for me." Later, with his wife and daughter living back in Independence and he in Washington, Truman became a frequent visitor at the Reserve Officers Association headquarters in Washington, which, ironically, was then located in the Blair-Lee House, where Truman would reside during most of his second term as president. As the successful Berlin Airlift wound down, three decades after his return from the battlefields of France, he would write that if fate had played out differently, he might have ended his career as a two-star general in the Regular Army.

This volume of *The Soldier from Independence* follows Truman's life as a citizen soldier from his 1905 enlistment in Battery B of the Missouri Field Artillery's 1st Battalion through the multiple recommendations in the spring of 1919 that he be given the opportunity to become a major in the organization of his choosing, either the reserves or the Regular Army.

Little has been written of Truman's first six years as a part-time soldier, and probably for good reason, since his brief notes on this period were set down some three decades later during his first term in the U.S. Senate. Although the newly minted artilleryman soon proved to be proficient as a swing driver, handling the center pair of the six-horse team that pulled gun and caisson, he was best known within the unit as the battalion's ultra-efficient clerk. And if we are to believe Truman's own writings and the recollections of his very sober longtime army friend, Ted Marks, the young Corporal Truman was a bit of a cutup as well. (Marks, like Truman, would rise through the ranks to command a four-gun battery in the costly Meuse-Argonne fighting and be best man at his buddy's wedding.) Beyond Marks, however, there are no substantive accounts of Truman in Battery B. Little concrete information exists in Truman's letters to his then girlfriend Bess, either, and the valuable military-related oral histories conducted by his presidential library during the 1950s and 1960s were with the soldiers who served with him much later in France, but who knew something of his early days in the guard "through the grapevine."

This fuzzy picture comes into focus when materials from these sources are examined in conjunction with Missouri National Guard records and newspaper accounts of his unit's activities, providing an invaluable framework for the scattered bits of information. Similarly, oral histories were not conducted with the Battery F soldiers who were in contact with Truman from the time of his third enlistment in Kansas City and Camp Doniphan at Fort Sill, Oklahoma, when he was that unit's executive officer and ran the regimental canteen, a sort of post exchange, with Pvt. Eddy Jacobson. By this point, however, he was now an officer and a gentleman—Lieutenant Truman—and was writing chatty yet richly detailed letters to Bess. An added bonus to history was that his tent mate, Lt. Jay Lee, was to later become the regimental historian, and Truman's untapped personnel records as well as other military records were available for the writing of this book.

The letters to Bess are a particularly interesting story. With the exception of periods of combat and certain stretches of intense training, her devoted letter writer produced two, three, even four letters—

sometimes of significant length—every week. The raw quantity of verbiage was so great that Robert Ferrell, editor of the marvelous *Dear Bess: The Letters from Harry to Bess Truman, 1910–1955*, felt free to excise nearly every one of her captain's accounts of the rigorous training at Fort Sill and France, as well as his detailed descriptions of the fighting and the battery's movements to contact with the Germans. *Dear Bess* didn't suffer in the least from Ferrell's lumberjack deletions of material that, frankly, most readers would certainly consider extraneous. He provided just enough material on army life to provide context, and thus allowed the five-hundred-plus-page work to stay clearly focused on the Harry-and-Bess narrative. Naturally, *The Soldier from Independence* benefits greatly from this material remaining unpublished until now, and when I remarked to Ferrell that he had left a remarkable amount of the military material undisturbed, he said with a twinkle in his eye, "Well, I must have known that you'd be needing it."

Truman's November 23, 1918, letter recounting his very recent combat operations was particularly helpful, especially when used in conjunction with his "Soldier's Diary and Note Book," a sporadically annotated pocket-agenda for 1918 (frequently referred to in my text as Truman's "calendar book"). Truman had written the November 23 letter, more than four thousand words in length, as soon as he was at liberty to do so, and he explained to Bess that "Since the censorship was eased up somewhat today I am going to try and tell you from beginning to end just what happened to me." Understandably, though, he did not tell Bess everything, and he may never have mentioned to her that the very spot where his battery had fought for several days during the Meuse-Argonne offensive was referred to within his regiment's parent unit, the 35th Division, made up of Missouri and Kansas Guardsmen, as "a cemetery of unburied dead."

The Soldier's Diary and Note Book was in fact only one of several pocket-sized books Captain Truman used. He maintained another during his artillery training and yet another to keep track of his personal loans while he managed the canteen, most of which went to members of his own Battery F, and who, with some rare exceptions, all paid him back. The Harry S. Truman Library and Museum also holds numerous other notebooks of larger page sizes, such as, to name just a few, the "Gun Books" for each of Battery D's four cannons, a French ledger book that he labeled "Fire & Orientation," and the notebook "Agenda, Souvenir Journalier, 1919." Of particular value to this work were the "Roster and Reference Book—Battery D" and "Roster, Extra Duty—Battery D," both of which Truman maintained, as well as the battery's Correspondence Books maintained by Sgt. Leo P. Keenan until his death in January 1919, and subsequently by Sgt. Harold J. Bowman. Much of the battery's paperwork, particularly that having to do with the daily tracking and reporting of ammunition expenditures by gun, was handled by the executive officer, Lt. Victor Housholder, who also left behind his very heavily annotated copy of *Provisional Drill Regulations for Field Artillery, 75mm Gun,* and a monograph on Battery D's operations.

After the war, but while Truman was still in uniform, he produced a superb series of longhand drafts of his battery's operations once they reached the Meuse-Argonne. The draft written by a visibly unsteady hand and containing numerous cross-outs is presumably the first, and has a partially retyped and edited version associated with it. Another draft displays handwriting that is more uniformly and carefully set down. Both closely parallel each other, and while they agree in nearly every respect on times, dates, and places, each contains a variety of interesting details missing in its twin, and some structural differences. Written soon after the fighting, they are a more dependable account of his time in combat than the writings set down at different times between roughly fifteen and thirty-five years after the war, such as the well-known, handwritten, seventy-three-page manuscript titled "The Military Career of a Missourian," which Truman is believed to have penned during his first senatorial term, as well as lengthy notes he set down during stays at the Hotel Pickwick in Kansas City. These later accounts suffer from, among other problems, the fact that they contain incorrect dates and times, but become much more useful when matched against Truman's three lengthy, no-frills operations reports, battery and battalion records, including some very useful after-action reports by his battalion commander, Maj. Marvin H. Gates, as well as his observations in the "calendar notebook."

What emerges is a rich portrait of Truman's time in combat when he and the tough Irishmen of "Dizzy D" destroyed two batteries of German field artillery while emerging almost miraculously unharmed, even though their 27,000-man division suffered some 7,300 casualties during six—really four days—of fighting in the Meuse-Argonne. As for Truman's time in battle, experiencing air and artillery attacks on his positions, directing fire, setting up his antiaircraft machine guns for use against infantry during a German counterattack, all this may lead some readers to expect to find on these pages a questionable psycho-analysis of how it must have affected his later thinking on the atom bomb. They will not find it here. I think I'm on safe ground, however, in making two simple observations: first, that Truman's activities during the war were far more interesting and complex than previously realized, and second, the man who later ordered the invasion of Japan in the face of massive casualty estimates understood exactly what he was asking of our soldiers, sailors, and marines, and he understood it at a level that most Americans today would find unfathomable. Truman understood as only one who had lived and fought for six days in a "cemetery of unburied dead" could.

A note on unit designations and ranks: Readers exploring primary sources will find that unit designations within the Missouri National Guard of the late nineteenth and early twentieth centuries were often spelled out, as in First Brigade, Third Infantry, etc., while Regular Army units used numeric designations. All unit designations in this book are expressed numerically and readers should note that units of the same number, presented differently in the primary sources, are one and the same as those in this account. Readers will also find that some soldiers make their appearance with several different ranks. In each case, the soldier's rank is appropriate to the time frame of the event portrayed.

Acknowledgments

I WOULD LIKE THE THANK the many people whose kind assistance made *The Soldier from Independence* possible. Chief among them is my old Red-Leg boss, Col. (Ret.) Philip W. Childress, who more than two decades ago prodded me to do this book. Beyond my lovely wife and frequent coauthor, Kathryn Moore, those who lent assistance or encouragement—and sometimes a considerable amount of both—include Maj. (Ret.) Chris J. LeBlanc, Maj. (Ret.) Larry Seefeldt, Maj. (Ret.) Jeffrey L. Wingo, Lt. Col. (Ret.) George L. Humphries, Lt. Col. (Ret.) Dallas Van Hoose Jr., Lt. Col. (Ret.) Thomas E. Conrad, Lt. Col. (Ret.) Lester W. Grau, Lt. Col. (Ret.) Albert N. Garland, Lt. Col. (Ret.) Michael I. Roddin, Col. (Ret.) Jerry D. Morelock, Col. (Ret.) Frederick W. "Col. T" Timmerman Jr., Col. (Ret.) David Decker, Col. (Ret.) Steven F. Rausch, Gen. (Ret.) Frederick M. Franks Jr., Gen. (Ret.) Robert William RisCassi, and Col. Jonathan J. Smidt (who, as of this writing, is definitely *not* retired).

Several of my previous coauthors have also been a big help: Maj. (Ret.) Terry Griswold, Donald L. Gilmore, and "Dr.-Commander-Jet Jockey" John T. Kuehn (U.S. Navy, Ret.), all of whom are old colleagues from the Command and General Staff College at Fort Leavenworth, Kansas, as were JoAnne Knight and Betty Bohannon at its Combined Arms Research Library.

Others who have lent their assistance include Dr. Graham H. Turbiville; Dr. Edgar F. Raines Jr.; Maj. J. W. Timbers (Royal Artillery);

Maj. Simon J. Hulme (Royal Engineers); Ian V. Hogg (Royal Artillery, Ret.); Col. Michael L. Castillon (French Army); Dr. Boyd L. Dastrup, Command Historian, U.S. Army Field Artillery Center at Fort Sill, Oklahoma; Dick Shepherd of the Fort Sill Field Artillery Half Section; Holly Reed and John Taylor at the National Archives and Records Administration (College Park); James Parker of Archival Research International; and Glenn McAnarney of the Midwest Genealogy Center. Gene Norwood and Melissa Worthington provided steadfast assistance with document transcription and reproduction, as did Andrea M. Giangreco who also performed myriad clerical tasks. The staff at the Harry S. Truman Library and Museum, particularly Erwin Muller, Dennis Bilger, Pauline Testerman, Liz Safly, and Randy Sowell, were always cheerful and helpful, as were Doran Cart, Jonathan R. Casey, and Lynn M. Ward at the Liberty Memorial Museum in Kansas City, Missouri. The superb battlefield map showing the movements of Truman, Battery D, and their targets during the Meuse-Argonne offensive was produced by Kevin Ullrich. George M. Elsey, who worked with Truman for many years, offered valuable insights into how Truman viewed the military and made my research at the National Archives much less of a financial strain by graciously putting me up at his club, as did Maj. Gen. Donald S. Dawson (U.S. Air Force, Ret.) from Truman's staff who made similar arrangements during another research seige. And, finally, there's Robert H. Ferrell, who never failed to find and turn over to me documents useful for this study during his many trips to the Military History Institute at Carlisle Barracks, Pennsylvania, when researching his own books.

To these fine people and all the others I have inexcusably forgotten: "Cannoneers, yoh!"

Chapter 1

The Life of Napoleon

W HAT IN HELL is he waiting for?"[1] Sergeant Ed "Squatty" Meisburger, the section chief for No. 1 Gun, nervously watched the crews manning a neighboring pair of French-made 75mm cannons. He and his men were perhaps a little envious when Lt. Victor H. "Vic" Housholder had ordered No. 2 and No. 3 Guns "muzzles left" and pointed across the river at the small French town of Montblainville. Meisburger's own cannon and No. 4 remained oriented north to support the 129th Infantry, which was preparing to take a second lunge at Charpentry, but both crews watched down the gun line in keen antic- ipation and wondered what the target was. Long minutes had ticked by since Housholder had called the men to action and barked out firing data on the unseen enemy, yet nothing had happened. Was the battery going to come up short again?

Although the artillerymen had blasted German positions for more than three hours the previous morning—firing at such a blistering pace that they poured buckets of water hissing and steaming down the barrels to cool them—Battery D's "75s" so far had done little work that day. Last-minute orders to support a dawn attack were impossible to carry out from the ground where the battery had been directed to bivouac after its grueling passage north through no man's land. With that mission aborted, they were sent forward again. The men had passed through "a cemetery of unburied dead"[2] where Americans lay singly and in gruesome clusters where they were cut down, but arriving at their current position, the artillerymen found that they could not yet exact their revenge.

While the batteries to their right had unobstructed fields of fire and were able to go into action almost immediately, the soldiers of Battery D had been sent into a peach orchard, where they had to hack several rows of trees to the ground and drag them out of the way before their relatively flat-trajectory weapons could come into play. A low-flying German aircraft heading back to its own lines had machine-gunned and dropped a bomb on the unit, killing two horses, destroying some telephone equipment (including a phone set blown off the head of one soldier), and causing further delay. By the time the men got off their first rounds at 2:30, the other batteries had been banging away for an hour.

Unfortunately, neither Battery D nor the other batteries could do more than conduct an intermittent harassing fire on Charpentry and its environs. Communications with the infantry to their front were practically nonexistent, and the few calls for fire support that did make it back were uselessly vague and lacking coordinates: "We need a barrage at once. . . . They're coming over the top of the hill."[3] What hill? Without a clear idea of precisely where the infantry were located and what was happening along the line of contact, Battery D and the other gunners of the 2nd Battalion, 129th Field Artillery Regiment, could only use map coordinates to fire sight-unseen at the areas thought likely to benefit the assault.

Immediately after laying the guns, an eight-man reconnaissance party led by Battery D's captain was sent forward to do what they could to coordinate the battalion's activities with the infantry and observe the unit's shell fire. No sooner had they disappeared beyond the gun line, trailing a telephone wire behind them, than the men were seemingly swallowed up in the smoke and confusion to the north. The buzzer on the field telephone near Lieutenant Housholder, the battery's executive officer, would occasionally come alive, signaling a call, but almost as quickly as communications were established, Sgt. George Brice or 2nd Lt. William L. Eagleton would have to report that the line had gone dead. The battery, on orders from battalion, would periodically throw a few rounds in the direction of Charpentry, but it was frustrating to see that a great battle was in progress all around them and that they were being forced practically to sit it out.

Finally, as darkness neared, the connection was restored yet again. This time it held, and the call to action was not long in coming. The gunners knew from the firing data called out by Housholder that a target must be near at hand—less than two miles distant. "At my command," shouted Housholder. The crews were tense and ready, with loaders cradling fused shells. In seconds would come the order to fire the first round, maybe two, from which range and other corrections would be made, then a punishing bombardment unleashed on the enemy.

Each man stood silently at his station as the sounds of artillery and machine guns drifted over them. The seconds stretched torturously into minutes. Furtive glances back toward Brice huddled over the field telephone and the imposing, erect figure of Housholder vainly scanning to the northwest through his binoculars were met with stern rebukes from each gun's section chief. What was the matter? Were communications broken again? Was the wire broken?

The two could be seen exchanging some words. Still there were no orders. All eyes in the battery were on them, except those of some unlucky cannoneers with the No. 2 and No. 3 Guns facing the opposite direction. Housholder's attention returned to the northwest. What was he trying to see? Brice suddenly looked up and passed something on to the lieutenant. Damn him—he was speaking too low for anyone else to hear! Housholder turned fully to the guns and, raising his right arm high over his helmet, barked again, "At my command!" The arm seemed to hang there forever before a wide-eyed Brice passed another message and then slammed to the lieutenant's side as he shouted, "Fire!"

Forty-nine rounds later, an elated Housholder called out to his left-flank guns to suspend fire and announced to the artillerymen that they had just destroyed an entire battery of *Boche* cannons poised to begin lobbing shells into American lines. The gun crews performed "just like clockwork," said Cpl. Harry Murphy. "It was just—it was a sight, they were just perfect. They just got those rounds off so fast—unbelievable. And those marvelous French 75s!"[4]

Whoops and cheers rose along the guns, and Sergeant Brice may have even left the line open for the captain and his reconnaissance party to hear. Battery D's 75s were kept trained on the German position, ready to give it another going over if the Huns attempted to salvage their battered and broken 77mm field guns, but the approaching darkness soon made it impossible to observe the area.

The good work of 2nd and 3rd Sections was a satisfying end to a hard day, and the battery's confidence in their commander, Capt. Harry S. Truman, soared when they learned what was behind the nerve-wracking delay after "muzzles left." "The Germans had brought a battery of artillery up," said Pvt. Vere C. "Pup" Leigh, who had watched events unfold from Meisburger's 1st Section. "It would have been enfilading us, [as] it would have been firing off from our side. Truman didn't panic, [but] he let them take their horses away from the guns, which was exactly what he should have done. If it had been me, I would have probably hollered for D Battery to start firing as soon as I saw them. He didn't do that, [but] he let them get into position, get all set to fire, with their horses by this time a couple of miles away. Then he had his firing data exact. . . . We knocked all four of those guns out."[5]

THE MASONIC LODGE AND WOODMEN OF THE WORLD fraternal organizations, the Farm Bureau, Grandview Commercial Club, and Kansas City Athletic Club, even the town band of Grandview, where he briefly (*very* briefly) played the clarinet—Harry Truman joined them all as a young man in rural Jackson County, Missouri. He certainly wasn't content to just be a farmer even if, at 598 acres, the concern of J. A. Truman and Son, Farmers, was one of the largest in the state.

Truman, like both of his parents, was born and raised on a farm, growing up surrounded by many siblings and cousins. His family moved to the county seat of Independence so that the children could receive a better education, but while he also had many friends, Truman was always something apart. As a youngster he was "blind as a stump." The need to keep his fragile glasses from breaking kept him out of the rough and tumble enjoyed by other boys, and he was not only an extremely avid reader of history, but energetically pursued training as a classical pianist from the age of eleven through his high school years—hardly common for a youth in small-town Missouri. Truman's outgoing personality saved him from the ostracism that could easily have dogged him, and it didn't hurt that he was also a fine horseman.

At the age of eighteen in 1902, Truman got a job as timekeeper and paymaster for a construction company refurbishing a stretch of the Santa Fe Railroad near Kansas City. For six months, he lived and worked in a rough, track-side camp where he was exposed to a side of life somewhat different from the close-knit world of his family and neighbors. Here young Truman heard "all the cuss words in the English language"[6] and kept close tabs on the diverse assortment of foremen, blacksmiths, teamsters, farmers, cooks, and the down-and-out hobos who made up the muscle of the labor gangs.

Truman's domain encompassed three camps, spread along ten miles of track that he traveled along twice a day in a hand-pumped tricycle car. At thirty-five dollars per month, he actually earned a little less than the hobos who, at fifteen cents an hour during six, back-breaking, ten-hour days per week, could clear forty dollars over the same period (only to drink their money away after he paid them every Saturday evening). In addition to learning the colorful language that he occasionally unleashed on his artillerymen, Truman earned the respect of his boss on the line, who said, "He's all right from his asshole out in every direction."

When the construction job ended early in 1903, Truman took employment for the same pay at the National Bank of Commerce in Kansas City as a clerk. The taskmasters at the firm appreciated Truman's diligence, rewarding him with both a small raise and increased respon-sibilities. By April of 1905, however, Truman moved on to the First National Bank with a starting salary of $60. As before, he rose quickly within the firm and was soon earning a tidy $100 per month. It was here that Truman made what later turned out to be a pivotal decision when he and other young employees at Kansas City's banks were encouraged to join a new National Guard outfit being formed.

BATTERY B HAD FALLEN ON HARD TIMES. When various militia companies in the Kansas City area, the Marmaduke Guards, Scott Rifles, and Bullene Guards, organized a regiment, the 3rd Missouri Infantry, in 1886, Battery B did not follow suit. Whether this was a decision on the part of the civilian artillerymen or they simply lacked enough members to meet the minimum requirements to receive federal recognition, the unit only seemed to sputter along. In 1891, Battery B paraded through the city with the 3rd Missouri Infantry on the occasion of a reunion of the ex-Confederate veterans held at the Fairmont amusement park, and the following year the battery organized a band. But although the unit was recognized as part of the state's 1st Brigade during this period and continued on the rolls through 1897, it had apparently disbanded or become purely a cere-monial organization by the following year, when each of Missouri's infantry regiments and Battery A in St. Louis were accepted intact into federal service for the Spanish-American War.

That the city of St. Louis not only had its own contingent of artillery (led by some of its "foremost citizens"),[7] but also built and maintained a well-stocked armory for its battery, was galling to some Kansas City notables on the opposite side of the state. Local financier George R. Collins was determined to rectify this unsatisfactory situation. Collins, then commander of H Company in the 3rd Missouri, began organizing a new Battery B with the intent of creating a National Guard artillery unit completely up to U.S. Army standards, and with all the subsequent benefits that would entail—training with Regular Army units and other state guards as well as access to any resources that could be squeezed out of the federal and Missouri governments.

Battery B, 1st Battalion, Missouri Field Artillery was formally incor-porated into the Missouri National Guard on April 24, 1905, although the battery lacked the minimum of forty-eight members necessary for official status. There was apparently little concern that this would take long to rectify, and it didn't, as sixty men had passed the physical examination and were inducted during its first organizational meeting, held at the venerable Coates House Hotel on Flag Day, June 14, 1905.

It is tempting to speculate that when Collins and his associates began to comb the city's banking houses for steady, upright young men like Truman, they were aware of the sea change then taking place in army field artillery doctrine, which was beginning to abandon direct, or line-of-sight, fire in favor of indirect fire. This new method required gunners used to working with figures because they now had to shoot at distant, unseen targets located at any number of map coordinates. What better place to start than among the budding bankers in downtown Kansas City? The army, in fact, would greatly increase its efforts to recruit or train soldiers in mathematics for this very reason over the next decade, but, at this point, it was more likely just a happy coincidence that financial institutions made up one of the orbits in which Collins traveled.

Truman and his roommate, Hugh Urie, were excited at the prospect of joining the new outfit, and he later wrote that "We both got ambitious to become a part of that battery and at once began searching for Mr. Collins." A teller at the Union National Bank, Charlie Harling, who doubled as a recruiter, was only too happy to bring them to a doctor who performed cursory examinations, inquired about their families' medical histories, and declared them fit for military service. The fact that Truman's poor eyesight was quietly passed over (later, he would matter-of-factly state that "they needed recruits"),[8] leads one to suspect that the friendly doctor was J. Thomas Pittam, who, within a matter of days, would be appointed a first lieutenant and Battery B's surgeon. They were told to report to the Coates House on Wednesday night.

One by one, Truman and the assembled recruits stepped up to the table, where Lt. Valentine M. Porter, a member of the St. Louis battery and writer of military history, "got our names on the dotted line" under the watchful eyes of Collins and attorney Fred A. Boxley and were duly sworn in as soldiers in the Missouri National Guard for the next three years. As was the practice among militia formations of the day, all officers were elected to their positions by votes of the men. The officers included four lieutenants of varying grades, with Boxley as senior first lieutenant and Collins as battery captain. Collins was a young book-keeper in 1887 when he joined the original Battery B (Boxley was but ten years old at the time; Truman a toddler of three), and his election to captain was accompanied by rousing cheers. The rebirth of Battery B was viewed as a significant event, with one reporter describing its personnel as "superior" and noting that "it is well officered."[9]

"At last I was a military man," wrote Truman. "Drills began over at the Warwick Club's dance hall. I became acquainted with some mighty fine men in old Battery B. Urie, Tom McGee (afterwards Major McGee in the Big War) and I were initiated into the mysteries of Squads right and left, about face, salute, and various other things military. Tom and I got into the rear rank in the drill formations, and when the hard-boiled sergeant in charge put us in the front rank, we thought we'd been promoted."[10] Collins had not been able to secure dependable access to the city's few heavily used armories for regular training. Consequently, the requirement that "everybody had to deposit 25 cents" apiece to help defray the hall's rental meant that the men were spending a dollar per month, a significant amount of money in 1905, "to pay for the privilege of drilling" and "keep the thing running."[11]

Truman had long dreamed of being a soldier. By the time he was thirteen he had "read all the books in his home town library including the International and Britannica encyclopedias," and readily admitted that his "favorites were of soldiers and statesmen," with "Cyrus the Great, Alexander, Caesar, Hannibal, Genghis Khan, Tamerlane, Gustavus Adolphus and Charles XII of Sweden, Napoleon, Richelieu, Marlborough, Washington, Robert E. Lee, and Stonewall Jackson all down in his head as 'the heroes.'"[12] He also studied Latin and, with his future White House Press Secretary Charlie Ross and friend Elmer Twining, even spent weeks building a scale model of a Roman legion bridge across the Rhine River from details provided in Julius Caesar's *Commentaries on the Gallic War*. But while Truman may have done more reading than most of his peers, they all had one thing in common:

Most young Americans at some period or other between the ages of infancy and discretion have a strong desire to be soldiers, preferably Indian fighters. When I was about fourteen, the Spanish American War came on and every boy from ten to sixteen was either in a company of would-be soldiers or wanted to be in one. The one I was a member of consisted of about ten or twelve neighborhood boys in the Woodland College end of Independence. We had rifles and our principal occupation was shooting stray chickens and cooking them in the woods out north of town known as Idle Wild. We elected a Captain and a Lieutenant about every other day because one day or at most two was as long as any one boy could remain popular enough to be a captain.

After the war was over, most of us quit being soldiers and spent our time going to school in winter and doing odd jobs in summer. I worked at Clinton's Drug Store. That is I pretended to work. I ate ice cream and candy, and usually failed to show up when windows were to be washed. . . . I spent most of my odd moments and many that belonged to my employer reading the *Life of Napoleon* always hoping that in the end he'd win the Battle of Waterloo. Hannibal was another one of my heroes along with Alexander, Caesar, and Robert E. Lee. I hoped for a chance to go to West Point or Annapolis and perhaps imitate one of 'em when I was old enough.[13]

Truman's family, however—particularly the womenfolk—were against his joining the army. Although it was true that he was allowed to enter into special tutoring immediately after graduating high school in the hope that he might earn the privilege of wearing West Point gray, this was principally looked upon by families as a means to a free college education. In any event, he had reluctantly quit when informed that he had no chance of passing the strict eye examination. That his cousin Ralph Truman, who lived with the family after Uncle William moved to Texas, had been grievously wounded when fighting the Spanish in Cuba, might have also been a factor in the family's withholding their consent. But deeper issues were also involved, and Truman noted on several occasions that he could not join up until "I was twenty-one in May of that year and could do as I pleased.[14]

The calling of both northern and southern boys to the colors during the Spanish-American War (and judicious appointment of former Confederate officers to positions of high command) had gone a long way toward washing away the animosities of the Civil War. But for Truman's mother, Martha Ellen Truman, and grandmother, Harriet Louisa Young, this was not quite enough. Till their dying days, these women held an unbridled hate for all things Yankee. During the vicious, confused fighting along the Missouri-Kansas border before and during the Civil War, they suffered through a frightening series of raids on the Youngs' large, prosperous farm. The waves of destruction and theft culminated in the family's banishment from Jackson County, Missouri, in August 1863 under the infamous Orders No. 11, which depopulated much of western Missouri's border in an effort to deprive the southern guerrillas of supplies and create what a later generation of Americans would call a free-fire zone.

Truman's grandfather, Solomon Young, was leading a wagon train across Kansas to Santa Fe at the time, and it fell to Truman's grandmother Louisa to gather up her six children still on the farm and the single ox cart of food and possessions that they were allowed to take with them to a Union post near Kansas City. From there, they crossed the wide Missouri to the relative safety of Platte County, where the slave-holding but Unionist Truman family lived. Little Martha Ellen was eleven then and forever remembered the stark vision of smoke blotting out the sun and the burned, looted properties as they made their long, dusty trek north.

The all-too-common irony was that Solomon Young, a Kentuckian, was neither a slave owner nor a secessionist, and had publicly sworn allegiance to the Union. While this apparently did not make him a target of the various pro-South elements (likely because neighbors knew that his oldest son had joined the Confederate Army and that his "unsavory" son-in-law rode with Quantrill's raiders), it didn't protect his family and property from the Union cavalry—Regular Army or Jayhawker irregular—either. During one of Young's long, dangerous journeys hauling supplies and goods to Union-held New Mexico, Gen. James H. Lane's blue-coated "Red Legs," an abolitionist militia outfit from Kansas, descended on his farm, shooting the chickens "out of sheer cussedness," while Louisa was compelled to bake pan after pan of biscuits "until her fingers blistered."[15]

The Red Legs killed some four hundred Hampshire hogs and cut their hams off while torching the hay and stock barns. The raiders ominously demanded to know where "the man of the place" was hiding, and when Truman's then fifteen-year-old uncle Harrison (for whom he was named) honestly said that his father was out west, he was repeatedly hung by the neck and dropped to the ground choking until the blue-clad ruffians tired of trying to make him change his answer.

Harrison survived to become young Harry's favorite uncle. Receipts were provided for confiscated property on three of the five "visits" paid to the farm before the family's exile. Decades later, after Congress passed a law allowing loyal citizens to request compensation, the family filed for every loss they believed that they could prove: 1,200 pounds of bacon; forty-four head of hogs; one thousand and five hundred bushels of corn in separate raids; thirty thousand and thirteen thousand fence rails, again, in separate raids; 150 head of cattle; as well as two horses (one with bridle and saddle). However, there were no receipts for the family silverware which disappeared west, and whenever Truman would return from a trip across the state line to Kansas, his stern mother, Martha Ellen, would chide him, "Did you see your grandmother's silver?"[16]

No, the Truman women didn't forgive. And young Harry, bursting with pride over his new uniform, really should have known better than to waltz into the old homestead to parade it before Grandmother Louisa and Uncle Harry. Although the blue-dyed wool that U.S. soldiers wore from the Revolution through the Indian Wars had in recent years been replaced by a neutral brown during normal duty and in the field, the Missouri Guard's dress uniform was still very much a Yankee blue. And it was a particularly unhappy coincidence that the identifying red trim traditionally worn by "Red Leg" cannoneers of the Missouri Guard was eerily reminiscent of the bright accouterments—such as the large handkerchiefs worn around the neck and reddish sheepskin leggings— of the Kansas Red Legs as well. Truman likely anticipated that the uniform's color would generate some mild disapproval, but he learned almost instantly that he had made a big mistake:

> I went out one weekend to show [Grandmother Louisa] my new Guard uniform—beautiful blue with red stripes down the trouser legs and red piping on the cuffs, and a red fourragère over the shoulder. She looked me over and I knew that I was going to catch it. "Harry, this is the first time since 1863 that a blue uniform has been in this house. Don't bring it here again." I didn't.[17]

CHAPTER 2

Corporal Harry S. Truman

WHAT LITTLE IS KNOWN of Truman's first six years as a part-time soldier comes from his own notes, most of which were written three decades later during his first term in the U.S. Senate, and oral histories conducted with him and former battery members during the 1950s and 1960s. Thankfully, Missouri National Guard records provide a useful framework for the faded memories of the artillerymen.

The new Battery B, bereft of artillery, went into the summer brigade camp outside Saint Joseph at Camp Folk, Lake Contrary, where it trained with the 2nd and 3rd Missouri Regiments from July 5 to 17. Although it had inherited several Civil War–era cannons, recruits not already familiar with the antiquated weapons received little or no instruction on their use. Nearly all of the unit's training, in camp and in its weekly sessions at the Warwick Club, was oriented around just getting the men used to following orders and drilling together. Attendance was apparently not mandatory for the handful of guardsmen who transferred over from the 3rd Missouri, like Captain Collins, but new recruits were "ordered to report each Friday night until given written release showing proficiency."[1] Collins also owned some property in the Sugar Creek area between Independence and the Missouri River, and "he used to take his detachment down there"[2] for what must have been mounted drill for Truman and the other men who already knew how to ride and owned their own horses.

Truman took National Guard service seriously, and his diligence plus perfect attendance at battery meetings (an absolute prerequisite for promotion) quickly earned him a second stripe. He was presented with a certificate of promotion dated March 19, 1906, and wrote of his excitement at receiving it, adding that no other commission—and he'd received "a dozen of them, one signed by President Wilson himself"— ever gave him "the thrill of that warrant." Speaking to members of the National Guard Association during his presidency, he said, "I had that certificate framed, and I consider it one of the best certificates that I have had in my whole life."[3]

Truman mentions little more about his first year in the guard other than his promotion and being "initiated into the mysteries of Squads right and left,"[4] but the 1906 summer training left a profound impression. Held near the Mississippi River town of Cape Girardeau, across the state and far south of St. Louis, it included the 1st Regiment, 6th Separate Battalion, and, much to the delight of the Kansas City battery, their well-appointed sister unit, Battery A. Working with the generous St. Louis guardsmen was a gratifying and exhilarating experience that Truman remembered well. Taking a leaf from Caesar's *Commentaries*, he wrote of it in the third person:

On [July] 15th his outfit went to camp way down in the southeast corner of the State at Cape Girardeau. The trip was made from Kansas City to St. Louis by train and from St. Louis down the river by boat. The boys sang "Adeline," "Blue Bell," the "Spanish Cavalier," "Hot Time in the Old Town" and such other songs as were popular in the Spanish War. Some of the officers had been volunteers in that war and were looked upon by most of the boys in the battery as heroes even if they had only been to Tennessee and Florida.

They had a grand time on the encampment[,] and by doubling up with Battery A from St. Louis they had target practice and learned to ride horses and caissons across potato rows the wrong way. They also acted as gunners and Nos. 1, 2, & 3 [the crew positions that handled the ammunition, with Truman as a No. 2] in firing the pieces into the Mississippi River from a bluff. A salute was fired for the Governor[,] and when the outfit returned to Kansas City, they were real veterans.[5]

The unit moved into a well-tailored—and permanent—home at the corner of 17th and Highland, the Battery B Armory. Located across the street from a spacious, new park aptly named "The Parade," they had ample room now to conduct both indoor and outdoor foot drills at their own convenience. Yet, the battery still didn't have modern equipment. Then they arrived: four glistening, factory-fresh, M1902 3-inch guns courtesy of the War Department. Within just ten years, the weapon would be looked upon as something of an antique, but with its panoramic sights, hydrospring recoil system, and ability to rapid-fire either shrapnel or high-explosive shells out to a range of nearly three and a half miles, the M1902 was widely proclaimed as marking a "new era" in American field artillery. And now the National Guard units were beginning to receive their fair share.[6] Morale in the battery, already high, soared as the guns, caissons, and limbers were put through their paces out on Captain Collins's rural property, and a satisfied Truman observed that "some real drilling was done by the men."[7]

The new guns were Battery B's pride and joy, and, two long years after the unit's rebirth, it was anxious to show them off. Near the Sugar Creek land where the men practiced was a large picnic area adjacent to the Fairmont amusement park. At "1400 hours," or 2 p.m., on the weekend of June 8–9, 1907, every cannon, old and new, that the battery could muster was paraded through the park and set up for a demonstration of Mizzou firepower for the awed spectators. In all, seven cannons were used during the thundering exhibitions, and next to the round lines and comparatively bulbous barrels of the Civil War–era weapons, the long, sleek, 3-inch guns must have looked like something out of an H. G. Wells novel. How many of the gunners and their audience perceived that they were witnessing history as the nineteenth-century field pieces, perhaps in their last hurrah with the battery, were fired alongside artillery that well represented the dawning the twentieth century?

For the August 1907 brigade camp two months later, the artillerymen returned to Camp Folk in the Saint Joseph area, but this time they marched in battery formation, with six-horse teams pulling limbers, caissons, and their prized 3-inch guns. Getting enough horses for the column had, in fact, been a major obstacle to the movement, but arrangements were made with the Lemon Brothers Circus, then performing in Kansas City, to borrow some of the animals that normally pulled their gaily painted wagons from town to town.

Truman was the corporal of the battery's 6th Section under the command of yet another bank teller, Sgt. Arthur J. Elliott. He had known Elliott since joining the battery but did not hold a high opinion of him (as Dr. Pittam's private at the Cape Girardeau camp the previous year, Truman found him "a large fat individual whose military ability was shown by his adroitness in escaping duty of any nature").[8] Truman by now "had advanced to be a swing driver," handling the pair of horses making up the middle row of a team. Although this is the least complex of the three horseback positions (lead, swing, and wheel, with the wheel driver handling the first pair of horses to the front of the wooden limber having the most difficult task), it is certainly not an easy job and takes on added importance during tight turns and such things as movements across very uneven ground. Truman explained that "he could do right and left face and squads right if he were in the middle of the squad somewhere, so when he became a horseman on a gun, he considered himself rather well along on his proposed emulation of Napoleon and Marse Robert."[9]

Unfortunately for the guard units who had converged on Camp Folk, the period between August 11 and 19 saw considerable rainfall, and Truman "had the sorest saddle seat in the Bty. both going and coming."[10] Practical military training was greatly curtailed but, still writing in the third person, he related that the men found ways to amuse themselves:

The principle diversion during that wet week was to dig holes in front of tents where the water was a foot deep over all and let unsuspecting sergeants and second lieutenants fall into them. The ride home was not so pleasant as the one going up. A great many were suffering from saddle sores and an inability to sit down comfortably. While he was on guard duty one night on this trip, the Captain called him into his tent and asked him to help him off with his boots. He, the Captain, made it a request and stated that if someone didn't help him he'd have to sleep with them on. The young man was glad to help and felt very much pleased that so high an officer should notice him.[11]

At the expiration of Truman's term of service in June 1908 he reenlisted for another three years, but not before signing up a newcomer to the United States who would become a life-long friend and best man at his wedding, Theodore "Ted" Marks. A tailor like his father, Marks was born in Liverpool, England, in 1882, and thus was senior to Truman by two years. He had formerly been a soldier in the Grenadier Guards, where he rose to corporal. Although Marks quickly found employment in Kansas City and joined the Merchant Tailors' Association, he listened with keen ears when a member of the battery told him of the unit's high standards and good fellowship.

"I was very much interested in the military and I wanted to get acquainted with the fellows here," said Marks. "So, one night [I] went down to the battery at 17th and Highland where I met a corporal. I was told to go upstairs to the battery clerk's office. Upon arriving there I saw a corporal sitting at the desk who wore glasses. He said, 'What can I do for you?' I said, 'I'd like to enlist, sir.'"

Intrigued by the recruit's profoundly British diction, Truman asked, "How long have you been in this country?"

"About six months, sir."

Truman playfully quipped, "You speak pretty good English for the time you've been here."

Marks didn't immediately realize that the Missourian was having a little fun with him. Momentarily taken aback, he kept his lips zipped but thought to himself, "What kind of country is this to come to?" Truman brought Marks back downstairs to Captain Collins, who was observing drills. "He introduced me to the battery members," said Marks, "and I was one of them."[12]

Truman went back upstairs to the orderly room, and, for the next three years, Battery B's newest member saw relatively little of him, at least at the battery's evening drills. Marks later explained, "He would come down once in a while for drill, but there was quite a number of things to do in an office when fellows were enlisting—keeping records, making out papers for them. So he didn't have too much time; but he did drill occasionally on the first floor."[13]

This was not at all to Truman's liking, but it was only a matter of time before the skills that had made him such a desirable employee at various banks would come to the attention of his uniformed superiors. Ostensibly now the supply clerk under portly Sergeant Elliott, Truman experienced an exponential growth in his clerical duties. Although the summer training in 1908 should have been something that he could sink his teeth into—maneuvers that included Regular Army troops at Fort Riley, Kansas—Truman would later write that, although he "had a great time, . . . [he] didn't do much work or learn a lot of military duties."[14]

Truman was also finding it much more difficult to keep up his National Guard obligations. Several years earlier, a series of poor decisions and a disastrous flood had set the family on hard times, and Truman believed it his duty to help out. He quit his promising job at First National Bank and gave up the life he greatly enjoyed in the city, moving to the Grandview farm before the 1906 summer training camp at Cape Girardeau. For several years, his attendance at guard meetings barely wavered, as he willingly spent long hours riding Kansas City Southern passenger trains every week on a roundabout twenty-three miles to the Union Depot in the West Bottoms, and from there, cable and street cars across town to Battery B's armory. And he would have to retrace the route the following day.

The crush of farm work made it more and more difficult to attend every guard meeting. Although his promotion to corporal had occurred within nine months of his enlistment, that had been at a time when Truman had easy access to the weekly meetings at the Warwick Club on East Eighth Street off McGee, a quick walk from his boarding house at 1314 Troost Avenue. The likelihood that he eventually started missing them on more than a periodic basis is born out by Truman never making it to sergeant, as a man of his abilities and position in the battery certainly would have during his second enlistment. Truman had also discovered a substitute of sorts for his guard activities in the Masons, and spent increasing time on his membership in the lodge in Belton, Missouri, which was much more convenient to the Grandview farm.

Truman missed the brigade training at the new State Rifle Range near Nevada, Missouri, in 1909, writing later that his "wheat cutting time interfered with his chances to go to camp."[15] His last burst of soldiering as an enlisted man came the following year. For the first time since he joined up, no camp of instruction was held by the state's 1st Brigade or other higher headquarters, and Battery B organized its own 105-mile "practice march."[16] This July 17–26 exercise included a week of training outside Lexington, Missouri, but Truman and some of the other artillerymen felt that this was insufficient and made arrangements to take part in that year's maneuvers at Fort Riley in early September as a separate detachment under either the 2nd or 4th Missouri Regiments.

When Truman's second term of service expired on June 13, 1911, he did not reenlist. He did, however, organize a Masonic chapter in Grandview and was made master of the new Lodge No. 618 in May or June, roughly concurrent with his leaving the National Guard. He would remain a Mason all his life and, not surprisingly, would encourage certain of his current and future guard colleagues to join as well.

Truman maintained close ties, both business and personal, with a number of the artillerymen. When, in 1916, Battery B was mustered into federal service on very short notice during the border crisis with Mexico, Truman deeply regretted not being able to rejoin the unit. Unlike, for example, his friend Ted Marks, who could simply padlock his tailor shop and turn over unfinished orders to his father, the death of Truman's father and marriage of his brother had left all the responsibilities of the six hundred–acre farm, a newly acquired lead and zinc mine, plus a variety of debts all on his shoulders—and his alone.

While the frustrated former corporal "stayed at home and pitched hay, threshed wheat, and plowed corn,"[17] some sixteen of the battery's soldiers that he had served with, including nearly all its officers and sergeants, were rushed to the Texas-Mexico border to join Maj. Gen. John "Blackjack" Pershing's gathering army. Captain Collins had resigned the year after Truman left, and Truman's former sergeant, Arthur Elliott, had been elected captain only weeks before the unit was ordered south. Marks, a corporal when Truman left the unit, was now a sergeant, as was Robert Ferguson, while another good friend, Tom McGee, was elected a lieutenant. Truman also knew, or would soon know, virtually all of the officers in the newly raised Battery C from Independence. It wouldn't be long before faraway events gave Truman another chance at soldiering.

"WHEN GERMANY INVADED BELGIUM, my sympathies were all on the side of France and England," Truman later recalled, adding, "I rather felt we owed France something for Lafayette."[18] But the war, for a time, was something far removed from the green farmlands he worked from sunup to sundown at the back of his two-horse Emerson plow. "In 1917 things began to look like war," wrote Truman, and, predictably, it wasn't long before he talked over rejoining the battery with Marks and "renewed his former military acquaintanceship" after he "made arrangements for his sister and a good man we had on the farm to take over its operation."[19]

If Truman spent much time ruminating over the reasons for America going "Over There," he left little evidence in his *Memoirs*, letters, or private writings other than to say that he was greatly moved by President Woodrow Wilson's call to arms. And although he left no writings on grand strategy or the conflict's origins, Truman was indeed a student of war. When expressing his determination to see the fight through to the end—and live to tell about it—he made an astute comment about the massive but ill-used Russian Army that was not at all an echo of the hemorrhage of words pouring from newspapers of the day. Within days of reenlisting, he wrote to his future bride, Bess Wallace:

> We are expected to do absolutely as we are told. Evidently, if we are ordered to go to Berlin, go we must—or be buried on the way. I hope Russia saves us the trip, although I'd like to be present when Berlin falls.[20]

Truman's various accounts of rejoining the guard are direct and almost invariably begin with his dogged efforts to recruit additional citizen soldiers for one of the state's two newly formed artillery regiments, the 2nd Missouri Field Artillery:

> When the United States entered World War I in the spring of 1817, the Missouri National Guard decided to expand Battery B in Kansas City and Battery C in Independence into a regiment. I helped in that expansion, and we raised six batteries as well as a supply and headquarters company . . . and also a battery for the 1st Field Artillery in St. Louis.[21]

Truman turned out to be a particularly effective member of the new regiment's "Flying Squadron" of recruiters. "We had a bunch of fellows," said Sgt. Edward McKim, "who would go down to the Board of Election Commissioners and go through the records there to see fellows who were within the draft age. We had six batteries to form and we'd take the names out of the election records and then the Flying Squadron would go out and try to talk the men into enlisting rather than waiting for the draft."[22] Before the thirty-three-year-old Truman could enlist, however, he needed the cooperation of his own recruiter, who happened to be a boyhood chum in Battery C, 1st Lt. Harry B. "Pete" Allen. The "Report of Physical Examination" filled out by Allen shows that Truman answered the usual run of questions:

Have you ever had any of the following? If so, give appropriate dates:

Spells of unconsciousness: *No.*

Convulsions: *No.*

Gonorrhea: *No.*

Sore on penis: *No.*

Have you ever raised or spat up blood?:   *No.*

When were you last treated by a physician,

and for what ailment?   *Five years ago—broken leg.*

And so on.[23]

Curiously, under "Physical Examination at Place of Acceptance," which included an eye test, there was no data recorded, although Lieutenant Allen signed off on the document. This portion may simply have been waived, however, because Truman and all the others were subsequently passed along to the same Dr. Pittam who had passed him along in 1905. Not surprisingly, Pittam duly recorded the vision in each of Truman's eyes as 20-70, and found him fit for military service. There is no indication on this form as to whether the eye examination (which may have been purely cursory) was conducted with or without his glasses. But since Truman's performance during training activities and in combat would soon demonstrate that his eyesight was perfect when wearing glasses, it seems that he did not have them on. So how did this soldier with "flat eyeballs" score even this well? His brother, Vivian, who liked to say that Truman "couldn't see over a fence without his glasses," later maintained that he had memorized the eye chart.[24]

Truman was sworn in for the third time on Friday, June 22, 1917, assigned to the new Battery F of the 2nd Missouri Field Artillery Regiment, and issued two complete uniforms ("britches, wool" and "shirt, flannel" down to leggings and "drawers, woolen"), belt, service cap, gloves, slicker, field shoes, overcoat, and three pairs of wool socks.[25] For creature comforts he received a "sack bed" (sleeping bag) and shelter half that would allow Truman and another soldier to make a small pup tent. For the time being, though, the shelter halves would be unused, except perhaps as additional padding under their sleeping bags, since Battery F was billeted in Kansas City's Convention Hall with the high-spirited artillerymen—or "cannoneers" as they were officially designated—of the equally new Battery D.

Convention Hall, at the corner of 13th and Central Streets, had been the scene of the 1900 Democratic convention when roughly twenty thousand delegates and observers (plus a wide-eyed, sixteen-year-old page named Harry) packed the cavernous house from the floor to the rafters. Truman and his fellow 2nd Battalion guardsmen were happy to be at their temporary home downtown instead of camping out with the 1st Battalion's A and B Batteries on The Parade, or with C and E Batteries in Independence. His friend Lt. Jay M. Lee, attached to the regimental headquarters, was also billeted there. Said Lee, "Constitution Hall[,] that big concrete and steel assembly building which has housed everything from a national political convention to a horse show, and from a foot-ball game to a grand opera, made an excellent armory." Lee and other officers were particularly pleased that its "floor was large enough for indoor drill when occasion demanded."[26] Most drill was done right out on the street, however, as it allowed the men to show off their new prowess, and helped encourage recruitment.

By the time Truman bedded down that evening, he was as surprised as anyone that he had been voted by the men to be one of the battery's commissioned officers. "I had hoped that I might be a section sergeant, a post for which I was well qualified,"[27] wrote Truman. There were thirteen sergeants' slots in each battery at that time, and competition was tight for the top spots on the then-seven-gun crews and support elements, particularly since there were many veterans in the unit who had returned from service on the Mexican border just months earlier. Truman's recruiting efforts, however, had come to the attention of the officers, including Capt. Harry C. Jobes (yet another banker), who, when manning his desk "in the big empty hall," is remembered as cursing "continually" over the undermanned state of the new batteries.[28]

Even before Truman had himself gotten around to enlisting, he had made himself known as a prolific recruiter for the regiment, much to the satisfaction of Jobes, who would stop cursing long enough to sign up the new men he brought in. Truman had pointedly suggested to some of the officers that he deserved to be made a sergeant over one of the sections, but Capt. John L. Miles, who had personally vetted the thirty-three-year-old farmer and businessman, had other ideas. Truman was flabbergasted to find himself nominated as one of F Battery's five lieutenants, and, in a matter of seconds, he was approved by the acclamation of the assembled guardsmen as a first lieutenant, outranking some of the other battery officers.

The fresh, if not entirely young, lieutenant threw himself whole-heartedly into the routine of drilling in the morning and recruiting in the afternoon, as the Missouri and Kansas units forming for the new 35th Division, of which Truman's was only one, were the center of a patriotic fervor. On the Fourth of July, his platoon led Battery F's parade through Kansas City's Swope Park, and he presented himself at his girlfriend's house in Independence later that evening in "a brand new uniform with a cap, a [riding] crop, and silver spurs."[29] Lee later mentioned that "several farewell entertainments were given by and for the men of the regiment" at Convention Hall,[30] and smaller functions were held in spaces donated by a variety of hotels. After lamenting his tendency toward over-enthusiasm in a letter to Bess, Truman recounted its most recent manifestation when at one of these events his artillery colleagues from Independence backed his good friend Edward Stayton for commander of the regiment, but he supported his own commander, a West Point graduate, for the post.

> Just the other night when Major [Karl D.] Klemm gave his battalion a banquet for making him major, I arose in my zeal and fullness of heart and announced that I was for him for colonel [of the regiment]; for Captain Elliott for lieutenant colonel; and for Captain Miles for the new major. Someone chased right off to Major Stayton and informed him of my brilliant speech and he ceased speaking to me. I didn't care, for I'd have informed [him] how I stood if he'd asked me. But I shouldn't have been so loud in my remarks. Since Stayton got beat all along the line there's no harm done because he can't reach me now, but if he'd

won either high office I sure would have caught the dickens. Maybe a little war experience will tone me down and make a man of me.

Not all gatherings were such raucous events, and Truman described the next meeting, at the nearby Densmore Hotel, in the same letter:

> I have just finished the Regimental Banquet. It was a very solemn affair. Colonel Klemm made us a speech on our duties to God and country, and Lieutenant Colonel Elliott made one on the duties of an artillery officer. They were both from the shoulder and gave us something to think about. I had thought somewhat on both subjects, but not as far as these gentlemen went. According to them, we have placed ourselves in a position of placing the American Government above everything, even our lives.[31]

Battery F reached its full complement of 145 cannoneers sometime in early July, undoubtedly helped by the seductive slogan, "Join the artillery and ride." Everyone was fully aware that artillery units were moved by horse power, and many of Truman's men admitted that they found the idea quite appealing. "This is a lot better than walking in the Infantry with a 90-pound pack on your back," thought future lieutenant Arthur W. Wilson.[32] Prospective recruits Harry Whitney, Vere Leigh, and Emmet LeMaster saw the slogan emblazoned on a large sign at the Kansas City Gas Company building on Grand Avenue and thought its message eminently sensible. "We didn't care too much [for] marching all over France," said Leigh, and all the trio marched— over to the Convention Hall—to sign up.[33]

The regiment's noncommissioned and enlisted veterans drilled, drilled, and drilled the new recruits while initiating them into the mysteries of soldiering. A detachment from Battery B, hauling a complete gun section with horses, limbered caisson, and an ammunition caisson, was also sent over to assist, and the training in Convention Hall "went forward rapidly and eagerly."[34] Truman and other newly minted officers of all ranks were sent to the Manual Training High School building on Fifteenth Street west of The Parade, where the divisional officers' school conducted classes six days a week from 1 to 5 p.m.

One of the Battery F soldiers who had known Truman since his banking days, Pvt. Edward "Eddie" Jacobson, perceived that the drilling might be able to benefit the unit in ways unimagined by headquarters, and succeeded in enlisting Truman in his scheme:

> Our food was all right but it was standard Army fare—beans, hash, and corn willie [corned beef]. We wanted something better, maybe an occasional steak and ice cream—but how to raise the money?
>
> One day I had a bright idea while we were out on maneuvers firing our guns and going through our mock battles, why not record the whole thing in movies? Then, when we returned, we could show the movies at Convention Hall and follow them with a dance. All our boys were from in or around Kansas City, and their friends and relatives would be glad to pay for an evening like that. . . . So I took my idea right to him.
>
> He thought it was great—especially the part about the dance, because in those days he was courting a Miss Bess Wallace of Independence. "You go ahead and make all the arrangements," he said, "I'll back you 100 percent." . . . After the dance was over and all expenses paid, we found that we had cleared $2,600.[35]

The money generated by this first of numerous Truman-Jacobson endeavors greatly enriched Battery F's fund, and a significant amount was apparently still available when the unit shipped out at the end of September. (A fundraising "Military Musicale" for Battery D had earlier been held on the grounds of a mansion still standing near the Kansas City Art Institute.) Yet more money would have been raised but for Jacobson and Sgt. Jim Miller's "thorough job" of wrecking Lieutenant Truman's car while organizing the event. Truman had "turned a stern eye" on the pair and said, "Your show better turn out well and make a lot of money for the boys, or I know two candidates for the guardhouse." In the end, he was "pleased as could be" and told the privates, "All right, you can forget about the guardhouse."[36] Truman, meanwhile, also donated $100 to the 2nd Missouri Field Artillery Regimental Fund, personally depositing the money in the unit's Commerce Trust Company account before the officers' school afternoon session on Thursday, August 9.

If there were any discipline problems within Battery F, they are today unknown. However, it didn't take long for Battery D, with whom they shared their billet along with the Supply and Headquarters Companies, to establish the reputation that it carries to this day. McKinley Wooden, who would serve as the unit's chief mechanic under Truman, related one evening's festivities when as much as half of the battery's personnel went looking for a fight:

> After we were there [at the Convention Hall] for a while, we got into a fight with the Shaw Taxi Cab Company. We had a boy that got out and a couple of those taxi boys beat him up. Some of [our] boys that lived in Kansas City would go home at night, but the rest of us would stay at Convention Hall, you know. Well, when they dismissed us that night, about fifty or sixty of us started down there to clean up on these Shaw Taxi drivers.
>
> Well, they saw us coming around the corner there; they took out, some of them went into the hotel. We knew not to go in there, you know. We just milled around there in the street, and Morris Reilly, a second lieutenant, came along. He blowed his whistle and lined us up in the street, and marched us down on 15th Street in front of a vacant lot and gave us hell.
>
> Well, the next morning old Captain [Charles B.] Allen called us up on the carpet in Convention Hall. There are seats all around up above, and then a floor down the middle, you know. He lined us up there and Colonel Klemm came in, with his swagger stick—hot damn. Of course, they called us to attention; they came in, and he just stood there and he looked at us.
>
> Seemed like a half an hour, you know. Of course, it wasn't five minutes. And directly he said, "All of you men that was in that fracas down at the hotel last night, one step forward, yo-ho." And every sonofabitch stepped forward, every goddamn man. Oh, he

laid us out: "You've disgraced the uniform. You've disgraced the flag. You've disgraced the organization." Oh, he just laid us out. And he said, "I'll tell you what, if this thing ever happens again, I'll court martial every damn one of you." Yeah. Well, of course, he left then."[37]

Battery D, though, was Charlie Allen's problem, not Truman's —yet.

On August 5, 1917, the National Guard was called into federal service. The 2nd Missouri Field Artillery was reflagged as the 129th Field Artillery, United States Army, and Truman exchanged the "Mo." insignias on his collar for "U.S." This also meant that he would be required to take his third physical in as many months. There was no finessing the eye test this time. Dr. J. Reiley, a first lieutenant in the Reserve Medical Corps and assistant state medical examiner, found Truman's right eye to be 20-50, and recorded the vision in his left eye as "20-400 Blind" on the Form No. 378-1-Adjutant General's Office dated August 9, 1917. Nevertheless, his right and left eyes, "corrected" by glasses, were 20-30 and 20-40 respectively, and he was judged fit for duty.[38]

The 129th was assigned as one of the 35th Division's three field artillery regiments under the intermediate command of the 60th Field Artillery Brigade. Within two weeks, its Battery A was marched over to Union Station, where the cannoneers entrained for the division's training area at the Fort Sill Military Reservation in Oklahoma as the 129th's advance element. Under the command of Capt. Roy T. Olney, who had signed up alongside Truman a dozen years earlier at the Coates House, it set up Camp Doniphan immediately west of the main post and adjacent to its Aviation School and polo field. Back in Kansas City and Independence, farewell entertainments were held for the regiment at Convention Hall, local homes, churches, and hotels, and the unit's chaplain, Catholic priest L. Curtis Tiernan, performed a service attended by guardsmen of all denominations from a platform built atop a supply wagon on The Parade. Truman, and likely other officers, also took care of an unfinished bit of business when on Monday,

September 14, he signed the paperwork accepting his commission as a first lieutenant.

The regiment moved its Convention Hall contingent twelve blocks south to the new Sweeney Building during the third week of the month. Dubbed "Camp Sweeney," its location across the street from Union Station's long, low Railway Express Agency annex was perfectly suited as a staging area for the anticipated rail movement to Fort Sill. An added bonus was their ability to drill on the wide plaza fronting the station and its imposing façade, which presented an impressive backdrop to the solemn ceremonies conducted at the flag pole beyond the main doors. The regiment finally began its 450-mile journey on Wednesday, September 26, but Batteries D and F, the headquarters personnel, and Supply Company were denied a festive farewell parade by "a heavy downpour of rain." Said Lee:

> Retreat was had for the last time on the plaza in front of the station, and after a long wait in line, while their friends loyally crowded about to cheer them off, our men filed into the cars provided for them. Meanwhile, C and E Batteries said goodbye in Independence, where they entrained, later picking up B Battery as they passed through Kansas City, with its flat-cars of guns, caissons and artillery materiel added to those of C Battery already on the train.[39]

CHAPTER 3

Camp Doniphan

THE TROOP TRAIN ROLLED OUT OF TOWN just after dark, around 7:30 p.m. by Truman's reckoning. Unlike the rank and file soldiers who rode in regular passenger cars, Colonel Klemm had made arrangements for the officers to be transported in the comparative luxury of a Pullman sleeper containing seats that could be converted into a double layer of berths lining the walls. Sadly, however, the officers found that they still had to rough it. "The steam didn't work and I nearly froze,"[1] complained Truman, but he was pleased to see that the train was making good time in spite of its frequent stops. And while the enlisted men were confined to their cars and only allowed to stretch their legs during a fifteen-minute stop in Chickasha, Oklahoma—when they almost had reached Fort Sill—the officers could apparently leave their Pullman at will, ostensibly to inspect the cars and check with the sergeants. Truman took the opportunity at Caldwell, Kansas, a coaling and watering stop near the state line, to obtain some stationery at the depot and pen a brief note to girlfriend Bess before having to rush back to the train.

Faces filled the car windows as the train slowly chugged through Fort Sill's Old Post and rumbled to a stop at the New Post, where the men would spend the next seven months. It was a fine, Indian summer day when they detrained a scant forty miles from the great state of Texas at 5 p.m. on Thursday, September 27, 1917. Senior officers, including Truman, left immediately with Battery A's Captain Olney to inspect the regiment's slice of the camp, leaving the second lieutenants and sergeants to organize the men as well as supervise the unloading of the baggage and officers' mounts from the boxcars. During Truman's brisk, twenty-minute trek west to the 129th's new home, he was excited by the sights and sounds around him: "Batteries and flying machines, balloons and doughboys are as thick as girls on Petticoat Lane."[2]

The division's three artillery regiments were arranged west to east in numerical order, with Truman's sandwiched between the 128th and 130th Field Artillery Regiments in the area generally centered between today's Northwest Babcock Road and Darby Loop, extending north and south from Miner Road. The camp in 1917 resembled a giant horseshoe nearly two miles deep, as engineer and support units lay in line to the west, with infantry regiments dog-legged to the north and stretched back to the east through the divisional headquarters area and more infantry regiments. Neither of the 129th's sister units had yet arrived, and Battery A's cannoneers were spread about its camp, still making things ready, so the officers found the immediate area nearly deserted when they walked up. This was fine with Truman. Although he exaggerated to his future bride that they had "the choice of the whole post for a camp,"[3] they were able to have their pick of tents to establish "officer country," and Truman shared his with battery commander Harry "Pete" Allen, who had recently been promoted to captain, and Jay Lee. The two second lieutenants, and soon another first lieutenant, were to be quartered next door, with all, officers and men alike, having the same living arrangements.

It was nearly dark when Batteries B, C, and E pulled into the siding, bringing with them the guns, caissons—and Truman's car. Realizing that Battery F, and indeed the regiment, was lacking in motorized support, Truman had put his bright red 1911 Stafford touring car into government service, and it was duly loaded as part of the "artillery material" in Independence. A considerably more high-end vehicle than the Model T Fords owned by his neighbor farmers, Truman had even "had it remodeled into a hot sport roadster"[4] capable of maintaining a blistering sixty miles per hour and able to crest steep hills at a respectable speed. With the only horses then available being Truman's and the other officers' mounts, the vehicle was immediately put to work. "It's a good thing I brought Lizzie," wrote Truman the next day. "The cooks and carpenters and tentmakers have begun to run the wheels off her already. I'm going to have a special tent for her."[5] It would be more than a week before Lieutenant Truman would be able to get into his own car again.

Despite the best efforts of Battery A, the 129th's area was not yet ready. It was hardly their fault, as they couldn't erect tents that they didn't have. Jay M. Lee, who later served as the regiment's historian, wrote:

> Pyramidal tents were provided, but even by crowding them to their capacity there were not enough to cover all the men that night. Many slept on the ground or on the long tables in the mess-halls. . . . The air was chilly, and very light equipment had been issued. With cotton "khaki" [uniforms] and the scant allowance of blankets issuable, the night was not altogether comfortable. But the air was quiet and serene, the sky was clear and filled with the brightest of stars. . . . Alas, it soon developed that our first night was merely a "dud." Wind, wind, and still more wind, always from the north or south, but equally violent and misery-producing from either direction, raising clouds of dust which often obscured objects no more than fifty or one-hundred feet distant, soon proved to be the normal atmospheric condition.[6]

After many newspaper reports of myriad problems at Fort Riley's Camp Funston and a visit to Kansas City by former president Teddy Roosevelt in which he railed at the "unpreparedness" of the army in general and its training camps in particular, the men's loved ones back home were braced for the worst. Rumors abounded, and even a generally upbeat article in the Sunday *Kansas City Star* fed the concerns of Truman's girlfriend, who wrote a worried letter to her beau. Truman, ready to think the worst of anything printed in the staunchly Republican *Star,* fired off a letter to reassure her:

Don't give any thought to what that rotten sheet at 17th & Grand says about us. We have an ideal camping place, good water and plenty of it, will have electric lights in a few days; have to[o] much to eat, good beds to sleep on and our hospitals are going to be palaces when completed which will be very shortly. They are not needed anyway as no one has been seriously sick. . . . Our doctors here have less to do than any of us except the horse doctors.[7]

The men immediately set about making their living quarters as comfortable as possible. One common improvement had the unforeseen benefit of cleaning up the grounds, as soldiers hunted down virtually every piece of scrap wood left by the building contractors to make flooring for their tents. Word also arrived that the division's horses would soon be arriving, and Truman saw this as a very clear signal. "It looks as if we meant business by getting our horses so soon," he wrote, adding, "I understand that guns are on the way."[8] Lee agreed:

Orders came down to go over to the Remount Station, near the Old Post, and draw our supply of horses. This order was received generally with great enthusiasm by the men, as it meant a definite step forward in our development as a regiment and as artillerymen. Each battery was assigned a separate corral in which picket lines were stretched and the horses there lined up by sections. Later in the fall, frame shelters were erected; none too soon to protect the animals from the bitter winds.[9]

Truman already was "suitably mounted at my own expense"[10] at Doniphan and knew a thing or two about the beasts, as he had worked with them most of his life, and his father had intermittently bought and sold them in lots large and small. Truman chose to bring a fine-looking steed that he knew to be steady and dependable even around the loud, wracking noise of farm machinery. These qualities were readily observable, and he was amused to find his property coveted by the other officers. "They all want my horse. He's the best-looking plug on the job so far. If some nut offers me three hundred dollars, he's going to buy something."[11]

Each officer was to receive two mounts, irrespective of whether or not they had already brought a horse to camp. And Truman was surprised to find that his high seniority within the regiment allowed him many animals to choose from:

We had a grand time yesterday selecting our mounts from the issued horses. There were one thousand to pick from and we took turns on precedence. I am the seventh 1st lieutenant from the top and had a grand allotment to pick from. Picked a sorrel with a flax mane and tail. He proceeded to pile three men on the ground one after the other. I am going to get another horse to rest up on when he gets done with me. [We were] like a bunch of six-year-old kids turned loose in a candy shop. The chaplain was given first choice. He picked a beautiful black with one white hind foot. Everyone was offering him advice but I don't think he needed any. We all had lots of fun and I think everyone is happy with the choice he made.[12]

But while the "ride" portion of the recruiter's pitch "Joint the artillery and ride" was uppermost in most of the cannoneers' minds, there was, as Lee describes, a down side to being in an outfit that ran on literal horsepower. And it began fifteen minutes after reveille every day, regardless of weather:

The stable program then instituted, while often varied in detail, was typical of that which became part of the daily life of the soldier, and made him sometimes wonder what was the basis for the cheers with which the original announcement of the issuance of the horses was greeted.

At 6 a.m. each battery marched to the corral in a body, and proceeded to water the animals, rake out the stalls, and place hay in the mangers. This hay was issued in bales, and the disposition of the baling wire so as not to become a source of danger to the horses or of offense to the scrutinizing view of the inspector, was one of the ever-present worries of the enlisted man. During the watering of the horses, the special stable detail put the morning feed of oats in the feed boxes.

At 11:30 a.m, watering and stall cleaning as in the morning.

At 3:30 p.m.* came the call for "Stables." This included not only a procedure similar to that of the early morning, but also the daily grooming. Every officer in the battery not on actual duty elsewhere, was required to be present.

This daily duty, irksome though it often seemed (being in addition to the normal schedule of drill and study), was of immense value in the training of the regiment in the care, management and handling of horses; an experience hitherto unfamiliar to a large majority of the men.[13]

Between sessions taking care of the horses was an evolving progression of activities categorized as "drill" beginning after the half-hour breakfast at 7:30 a.m. and lasting till the men were marched back to the stables. The process was repeated at 1 p.m. after "dinner" and rest, with "supper" dished out at 5:30. Superimposed on this were such things as guard duty and assignment to special details, plus Truman and the other officers combined dinner with an hour of officers' school (principally lectures) beginning at noon. After the evening mess the men attended their units' evening battery conference while "The officers of the regiment were assembled for 'school' in the 1st and 2nd Battalion officers' mess halls, for an hour and a half, where Artillery Drill Regulations, Field Service Regulations, and pamphlets on recent operations in France, were systematically gone over, together with practice in firing-data problems."[14]

"There was little time or inclination," said Lee, "for recreational activities such as baseball, football, song-fests, or the like by our men. By the time taps blew at 10 p.m., they were generally too tired to keep awake if they had wished to."[15] Truman wrote his girlfriend, Bess, that "We have so much to do that we don't have time to get homesick," and added tongue-in-cheek that when the work day was done, "We have nothing to do then until 5:45 a.m."[16] As Bess well knew from previous letters, however, Truman's work day frequently didn't end until an hour

---

* Originally 4:30 p.m.

or more after "lights out" because of his position as lord and master of the 129th Field Artillery's regimental canteen.

THE MYRIAD REQUIREMENTS of the regiment beyond its daily maintenance, resupply, and training were parceled out to the junior officers as extra duties. Lieutenant Spencer Salisbury from E Battery was instructed to oversee the YMCA's operation; Lieutenant Tiernan, the chaplain, was put in charge of the soldiers' mail; and so on. Lieutenant Truman's unenviable task was to immediately set up and manage the regimental canteen. Essentially a post-exchange operation, the canteen was by far the largest and most complex "extra duty" of the regiment, handling thousands of dollars each week and quickly requiring the services of a dozen, and eventually up to eighteen, soldiers during the peak evening hours. The facility incorporated barber and tailor shops and, by default, our hero ended up negotiating the entire division's laundry services after a series of running battles with an association of greedy laundry businesses in Oklahoma City.

Lieutenant Truman had eagerly accepted the challenge, and the first order of business was to acquire goods to sell with money from the regimental fund. He apparently snatched up a variety of choice items—Rut tobacco, Sew apples, and Puritan soft drink—in nearby Lawton ahead of other purchasing agents from Camp Doniphan, thus earning the title "Lieutenant Grab-all" by the 129th's adjutant, Capt. Fielding Carr. Stock was disappearing fast, and local suppliers were not yet equipped to fill the camp's needs, so aggressive action was required. Standing orders at that time from the 35th Division confined the movement of all personnel to no farther than Lawton. Brigade commanders, however, could allow exceptions for urgent government business. Since Truman's regimental commander, Colonel Klemm, was in charge of the brigade during the temporary absence of 60th Field Artillery Brigade's boss, Brig. Gen. Lucian "The Walrus" Berry (so nicknamed because of his robust mustache), Truman found himself on a Sunday night train bound for Oklahoma City. It was not a smooth exit.

Truman had opened the canteen for business in a tent near the mess halls by Friday evening—less than twenty-four hours after stepping off the train—and was promised the roomy building then occupied by the division surgeon, Maj. Raymond Turck, as soon as the nearly completed division hospital was finished. Sales had been considerably more brisk than expected. Writing late Sunday night from the Lee-Huckins Hotel in downtown Oklahoma City, he proudly informed Bess: "I took in $100 before dinner today, which makes about $450 in two days and a half."[17] How much of this was actually profit is unknown, but it was clear that a much larger amount of dollars—far outstripping the regimental fund— would be required to get out ahead of demand. Might the individual batteries' funds be dipped into as well?

> We called a meeting of the Battery commanders today (we means me and the colonel) to make up a fund for the canteen from the Batter[ies'] funds. [Captains] Olney and Sermon and one or two others had so much to tell me that I finally got disgusted and asked Captain Jobes if he would lend me three thousand dollars on my John Henry to start one and he said, "You doggone bettya." I then told the outfit that I didn't want their blooming funds. The colonel wasn't present and when he learned what I'd done he simply reared up on his hind legs and threw a fit. Actually came down to my tent to tell me that he would issue an order making the outfits put up and ordered me not to borrow any money. So I didn't, but I'm going to get what I wanted out of those captains.[18]

And he did. But since neither Lieutenant Truman nor his trusty corporal, Otto Haseman, possessed any retail experience whatsoever, he had two soldiers from his F Battery assigned to him, Private Jacobson as de facto partner in the canteen operation, and Pvt. Morris L. Stearns to manage the barbershop, which had three to four men on duty each evening. Truman had picked wisely and boasted to his girlfriend, "I have a Jew in charge of the canteen by the name of Jacobson and he is a crackerjack. Also the barbershop is run by a Jew, Morris Stearns by name. He formerly owned the [Blue] Ridge Barber Shop—does yet, but the guy he left in charge is stealing the income because Morris says he gets nothing from it."[19] As for Jacobson, Truman had known

him for nearly fifteen years, having met the future sergeant during his
Commerce Bank days when Jacobson waited on him at a downtown
clothing store, and been thoroughly impressed by his ability to generate
money for the Battery F fund earlier that summer. Said Truman:

> We collected two dollars per man from each battery and from
> each headquarters and supply company. This gave us twenty-two
> hundred dollars, whereupon Eddie and I set up a store, a barber-
> shop, and a tailor shop. We went to Oklahoma City and stocked
> up our store with things that would not ordinarily be issued by
> the government—cigarettes, paper, pens, ink, and other items the
> men would want to buy. Each battery and company was ordered to
> furnish a clerk for the store.[20]

Truman had rented a car for seven dollars and spent all day
Monday making contacts and being "run ragged" by salesmen. He had
hoped to purchase an entire boxcar load of Puritan, but returned from
Oklahoma City after midnight with only fifty cases for the soft-drink-
starved troops. Some six hundred bottles were sold in just two hours
the following evening, but while Truman was now awash in cash from
both canteen profits and the mandated "investment" of the regiment's
cannoneers, he knew that it was going to be an uphill struggle to satisfy
the demand, as he'd found that "pop seems to be unobtainable" at any
price.[21] Although the problem would eventually get worked out, he
was still struggling with it several days later and expressed his disgust
that area businesses "have arranged their prices for our benefit." It was
plain to Truman that they had "organized to sell [to] the soldiers at a
fair profit plus all [that] the traffic will bear" with prices as much as
doubled. In frustration, he declared, "I'm not going to sell pop" when
confronted with an apparent runaround:

> I also tried to buy a carload of pop from the Coca Cola bottling
> works in Oklahoma City and Lawton. They refused to let me have
> more than fifty cases. I wired the Seltzer bottling works in K.C. to
> take care of us because we are a Kansas City organization, and they

referred me to the Coca Cola bottling works of Oklahoma City. So
here is another combination in restraint of trade.[22]

Such trials and tribulations were invisible to the men, however, and
they were impressed with the wide array of goods available, so much so
that many of the 35th Division's soldiers frequented the 129th's canteen
instead of the canteens of their own regiments. Lieutenant Marks of
C Battery recalled, "It was considered one of the best-run canteens in
the service. They were very strict. They had quite a large assortment
of things and . . . we'd have men from other regiments coming in." But
the men could not obtain one key staple at the canteen. "We had to go
outside," said Private Vere Leigh, "for the only thing that Battery D was
really interested in . . . alcohol."[23]

The canteen's Hebrew hierarchy, personified by Jacobson and
Stearns, together with Truman's aggressive, strictly business approach
to handling salesmen, prompted an almost immediate modification of
his new nickname, "Lieutenant Grab-all," to ones that the men considered more Jewish-sounding, beginning with "Lieutenant Graballsky."
Truman reported to Bess, "They call me Lieutenant Trumanheimer now
instead of Graballsky," and playfully warned her that she should "just
address my letters as usual because if Father Tiernan, who sorts the
mail, came across a letter from you addressed that way, I'd never hear
the end of it."[24] Truman reveled in the immediate and obvious success of
the regiment's little side enterprise, and prided himself that: "Everyone
says ours is the best canteen on the job. Jacobson is some manager.
That's a grand combination—Jacobson & Trumanheimer."[25]

IN BETWEEN THE DUST STORMS, the New Post was an impressive sight
when viewed from the surrounding hills.

At night anyone who dropped suddenly into our midst would
have thought he was in the suburbs of a great city. Newly installed
electric lights lined the macadam roads, and in the distance the
lights across the Horse-shoe or at the Aviation Field, a mile distant
to the eastward, gave a semblance of city streets or illuminated

viaducts. The hum of the ever present aeroplane overhead added to the impression of city life. Automobiles, as always, were ubiquitous, skirting the outer edges of the Horse-shoe. Only by riding out for miles on the prairie or among the Wichita Hills in any direction would one realize our distance from settled civilization.[26]

The letters and oral histories left by the men, however, dwell less on such sights than the daily grind centered around horses, cannons, horses, the nearly impossible job of keeping things clean, and horses. Although Lieutenant Truman had early entertained the laughable idea that "the colonel seems inclined to relieve me of some of the duties in favor of the work in the canteen,"[27] he was neither removed from the officer of the day rotation, nor did he escape other basic matters that had to be attended to:

> I have been branding horses today. We take a red-hot iron and put 129 F.A. on the right front hoof and the number of the horse, beginning with 1 and F, on the left foot. Then I had to make a complete description with his age and weight and his government number, brand marks, etc. It took me about two hours to do thirty head. One hundred forty-eight had already been done.[28]

Teaching cannoneers the proper care and training of their horses was of critical importance, as the artillery could not accomplish its mission without the mobility they provided. As luck would have it, two of the most dangerous beasts in the 129th were assigned to Truman's F Battery, "Dynamite," who was even noted in the regimental history, and "El Diablo" (The Devil), of whom Truman wrote, "If anyone gets near him he lets fly with both feet. He kicked a corporal square in the face today but fortunately didn't seriously injure him."[29] According to Lee:

> Several men went to the hospital with more or less serious injuries from kicks. But soon both men and horses grew accustomed to each other; and a keen rivalry for the best appearing outfit produced the natural result of well-cared-for, well-trained, and well-handled horses. . . . The instruction in handling of the horses

was systematic and gradual. Besides the training of both men and horses in the processes of care and grooming, the horses were given daily exercise by being led out in pairs. Then some twenty-five or thirty at a time were saddled and ridden out, occasionally with a companion horse being led. Later followed harnessing and driving in harness, then with limbers, until regular mounted drill with full artillery equipment became the regular order.[30]

Truman, by temperament and experience, was well suited to this task and respected by the men. And much to the surprise of his soldiers, who certainly wouldn't suspect that *an officer* knew how to operate such a piece of equipment, Truman even demonstrated the proper use of a grader to level the area around the battery's picket line. The drill schedule was arranged so that all six firing elements could use the limbers, caissons, and 3-inch guns of the pre-mobilization B and C Batteries every other day, and the neighboring 130th Field Artillery's redesignation as a 6-inch howitzer unit allowed their now-excess 3-inchers to be split between the 128th and 129th. The men greeted this with satisfaction, and Truman was particularly pleased that "they have begun to teach us the English and French methods of artillery fire" in mid-October.[31]

WINTER CLOTHING WAS ALSO ISSUED at this time, a great relief to the men, as even the few Indian summer days always ended in a frigid night. Virtually nothing, however, could combat the winds and dust. Even the unfailingly optimistic Lieutenant Lee recorded, "The wind and dust storms were more than a discomfort. They seriously interfered with the effective training of the army. They did not even have the theoretical value (dear to the heart of some commanders) of 'making the men used to it'; for the weather conditions at Doniphan were not like anything in . . . any part of France." And while Truman's letters during this period touch on many things—his pride at initiating one of his Battery F soldiers as a third-degree Mason in the Lawton lodge, the death of a Battery A sergeant when a caisson rolled over on him during an "artillery contest"[32] to see which battery could set up the fastest from a galloping start—his girlfriend in Independence was most thoroughly briefed on the living conditions:

October 9 . . . There was such a terrific dust storm blowing that it was impossible to see your hand before you hardly. Our tent and all our trunks were full of dust. The table that I am writing on was covered to the thickness of a sheet of this paper. The wind blew a gale from the north all day and until about seven o'clock this morning. All of our horse pens are directly north of camp and you can imagine the grand amount of dust 14 or 15 [hundred] horses can stir up. It rained about five o'clock this morning just about enough to settle the dust. It was sure enough cold, and is still. . . . Some of the boys are sure sick of army life. I think most of them expected to go on one long picnic at the government's expense. When they find that it's work from 5:45 a.m. until 6 p.m., it's not so funny. . . .

October 18 . . . When we came back at midnight the weather was as fine as could be wished for. About the time I got in bed it began all of a sudden to blow from the northwest at about sixty miles an hour. Mr. Lee jumped up and tied up the tent and began to yell, "Captain Allen, Captain Allen." . . . It very nearly blew our tent over and has been getting fresher and fresher ever since. I went to the picket line this morning and it was almost impossible to see a horse from one end of the line to the other. The dust storms we have had before have been mild breezes compared to this one. . . . I'm going to stay right here in the canteen and keep books. The dust isn't quite so bad in here. A tent fifty yards away is invisible. Dust is in my teeth, eyes, hair, nose, and down my neck. The cook next door brought me a piece of apple dumpling and it was sure fine, but when I ate it there was a grinding sound as if a butcher knife were being drawn across a piece of crockery. I ate it anyway, sand and all. I have sold a whole case of goggles and could sell two more. . . .

October 19 . . . The Colonel was just in and paid me a visit. He wanted to stay in the tailor shop. It's the most comfortable place on the job. We are all happy though. Everyone has a cuss for the Weather and a joke on his neighbor. The Colonel had the dirtiest face I've seen on a white man lately. . . .[33]

In addition to being lord and master over the least dusty spot in the regiment's cantonment, Truman's popularity with the officers was further enhanced by the possession of his four-passenger touring car. This nearly didn't come to pass. First there had been the "unpleasant incident" before the men left for training when Jacobson and Sergeant Miller, ostensibly on battery business, found "time to drive around with the top down and impress our girls," and "crept back to the barracks to confess our sins" after doing a "thorough job" of wrecking the car.[34] Once at camp, Lizzie essentially disappeared into the supply section. Then one day, when "loaded to the guards [rails] with ice and potatoes," the strain "busted the universal joint and some other contraption, whose name I never heard, all to pieces."[35]

An embarrassed Captain Allen moved quickly to rectify the situation. "Pete brought back the parts to make her go," said Truman. "She runs like a top . . . and I am using her exclusively for Lt. Harry S. Truman from now on."[36] Well, not exactly. Although Truman still made business trips to Oklahoma City by train, he used the Stafford on runs closer to camp, and his colleagues were often anxious to hitch a ride to Lawton rather than take the crowded five-mile trolley ride to town—an expensive forty cents each way. Truman would also play chauffeur for favored officers when parents and wives came to Doniphan's "Hostess House" near the rail station, and all were delighted by his generosity (and the door-to-door service). Over time, Lizzie became somewhat worse for wear and broke down at least once in December, but that mattered little to his grateful riders. Months later, before shipping off to France, Truman "sold Lizzie to a poor sucker for two hundred dollars, which I consider as a find in the road, because I'd already charged her off to profit and loss, less the profit end." Jacobson was amazed. Said Truman, "My former Jew clerk in the canteen watched me make the sale and then told me that he still had something to learn in salesmanship."[37]

Chapter 4

"No Trifling Test of Patriotism"

B Y MID-NOVEMBER, six weeks into the War Department's standard sixteen-week training program, the 35th Division began to get down to the serious business of drills and maneuvers in conditions that approximated, if only vaguely, what the army believed they would experience on the Western Front. Before that could be accomplished, however, the area had to replicate the trench system that arced from Switzerland to the English Channel—no mean feat. "Much of the excavation was in rock;" said Lee, "and even the soil, from long lack of moisture, was almost equally hard."[1] He described hacking down into this earth as "no trifling test of patriotism," and no soldier was exempt from the task. Truman, with perhaps a degree of amusement, wrote:

> I told the whole canteen force they had to go dig yesterday and they went. It nearly killed the barber and the tailor. The tailor said there was some difference between a number 10 needle and a number 2 shovel.[2]

The 129th's cannoneers found themselves positioned at the center of the artillery brigade's zone between Signal Mountain and McKenzie Hill, a slightly roundabout five-mile march west from their cantonment that felt much longer on the return trip. By the time they were done, Battery F and its sister batteries had constructed "four gun-pits, each with a shell-proof shelter, a Battery Commander's and telephone dugout, and an ammunition dugout, nearly all connected by trenches."[3] An old stone blockhouse atop Signal Mountain, dating back to the Indian wars, quickly became the most useful aiming point for the triangulation of targets during gunnery drills, but the army-wide scarcity of ammunition resulted in few rounds being made available for training. "I don't suppose we fired more than ten rounds per gun," recalled Cpl. Eugene Donnelly of D Battery, and this would not change until the regiment arrived in France.[4] All batteries were oriented to the northwest, thus allowing them to fire over, or "support," the infantry trench system being built two miles away. Unfortunately, on any given day nearly two-thirds of the gun pits had no weapons.

THE B AND C BATTERIES' 3-INCHERS that the regiment had brought with it, supplemented by as many as four from the 130th Field Artillery, were the only cannons that the men would have at Doniphan. The 129th would remain far short of its table-of-organization strength until June of the following year, when it finally received twenty-four 75mm rapid-firing guns from the French. Naturally, this impeded training, and the division as a whole was not receiving high marks from army inspectors reviewing its progress. Colonel Frank M. Caldwell, a West Point graduate, was "most favorably impressed" with the men individually, rating them of "excellent" physique and "high" intelligence whose conduct "was as a rule excellent." Yet he was "less satisfied with the manner in which this good material was being handled," and judged that in comparison to the division's other elements, "The artillery, having little material to work with, had done more with the individual instruction of the soldier."[5]

Truman found the war games held "under the direction of a French officer [Captain Masson-Forrestier]" to be "very interesting but very hard work." More often, though, the references in Truman's letters home are to lengthy road marches and rides (as part of the equestrian training) that appear to have been taking place a little more frequently than might otherwise have been the case if the men's time could have been used more profitably. In addition to having roughly half the number of needed guns and almost no ammunition, the unavoidable inefficiencies in the training regime were also due to the ongoing lack of communications and topographical and observation equipment— all basic tools of the cannoneer's trade. But most fundamentally, a lack of leadership exaggerated all these problems. On top of the inspector general's (IG) report by Caldwell was an equally pessimistic assessment by IG Col. Alfred A. Starbird that directly addressed this. The 60th Field Artillery Brigade was found "not to be making satisfactory progress on account of lack of competent instructors and equipment," and at least part of the problem was that "the brigade commander was temporarily commanding the division," instead of seeing to the proper training of his regiments.[6]

In spite of its shortcomings, the artillery as well as the engineers were acknowledged to be receiving consistently better training than the 35th Division's other elements, particularly the infantry who made up the bulk of the formation's manpower. That this appears to have been invisible to Lieutenant Truman should not be surprising, as he was well down the chain of command and had little interaction with infantrymen of similar rank (the officers' school he attended was a strictly regimental affair). Thankfully, there were hopeful signs that, if communications were properly maintained, the artillery could provide the direct support that the men at the front would surely need. Truman's Battery F supplied the example cited in the regimental history:

> The division was given a try-out in the field. The Infantry occupied three lines of trenches they had dug just below the northwest slope of Signal Mountain, [and] Batteries of the 128th, 129th, and 130th Field Artillery regiments took position in the respective emplacements and trenches they had constructed on the southern side. For twenty-four hours actual battle conditions were simulated,

close telephone communication being maintained with the infantry P.C.,* and with gun crews constantly at their posts. All calls for a barrage were started at the infantry front line, came through the infantry [communications] wire to the Infantry P.C., and thence through the artillery liaison officer on his own wire to the artillery Battery Commander's P.C., whence the command was given direct to the guns. A careful check made at the Infantry P.C. on one of the calls (when Battery F happened to be on duty) showed that from the time it originated in the infantry front line until the sound of the artillery fire (blank shells being used) came back over Signal Mountain, there elapsed but thirty seconds.[7]

THE NOVELTY OF MILITARY LIFE for the citizen soldiers was long gone by November. They were looking for something—anything—to do. The few hundred men per day who received town passes thronged the downtown of little Lawton, but with few amusements available, soldiers milled around the streets and hung out on corners. Locals, excluding the shop keepers, were "completely upset by the large number of troops"[8] who apparently made little real nuisance of themselves. The few restaurants did a very brisk business, and the soda fountain that formerly employed two clerks now had a dozen or more working the counter. Oklahoma, by law a dry state long before the passage of Prohibition, nevertheless had enough whiskey available "under the counter" that humorist Will Rogers would quip, "Oklahoma will be a dry state as long as voters can stagger to the polls."[9] At this point, however, the soldiers had little or no luck obtaining liquor, as, just like with the merchants selling legal wares, area bootleggers were caught short by the sudden influx at Fort Sill.

Whatever were the 35th Division's YMCA activities organized by Lt. Spencer Salisbury (he and his Battery E mates were known as "Carranza and his forty thieves"),[10] they seem to have left no great impression, as they received nary a mention in the voluminous oral histories and letters left by the men. Despite this, the determined efforts of Truman

---

* From the French term *poste de commande* (forward command post).

and the other officers to keep the men busy—and out of trouble—paid off, even if the quality of the training was less than desired. Incidents like the occasional fights picked by men in Battery D were uncommon. Letter writing and card games after the day's grind were at worst accompanied by pranks, as when Salisbury, quite the role model, "put a good one over on the officers." According to Truman, Salisbury caught the 139th Infantry's mascot, an old billy goat, then "cut his throat and took out a good piece of him and [had it] fed it to the officers telling them it was beef."[11] On another occasion, a significant number of the 130th Field Artillery's E Battery troops, driven by boredom, conducted raids on nearby units, including Truman's, with the objective of scooping up every dog they could find. Private Edward P. Wilson explains:

> [Major Roy Waring's] airedale was as unpopular as his master. He snarled at enlisted men and seldom left the officer's area. There came a night when he paid an unscheduled visit to the entire regiment with a tin can tied to his tail. The regiment came boiling out of the tents. The howls of laughter and the ribald shouts about the dog's owner drowned the yelps of the dog. We suspected another major and a captain of the job, as only an officer could have done it.
>
> A few days later, one of the geniuses in our squad came up with the query, "If one pooch can cause that much pandemonium, what would half a dozen do?" The idea caught fire. That evening after mess, a few of us scoured the division. Cpl. (later sergeant) Algot Hedstrom brought along cookies as "come-along" bait. By eight o'clock we had ten dogs in our two tents. To keep them quiet we fed them cookies and candy. At five minutes before taps we tied on the tin cans and opened the tent doors.

Not surprisingly, the pranksters' steady supply of goodies convinced the animals that this was the place to be.

> Two dogs were pushed out, but they acted as though they had been blackballed from the club and lay down in the street whimpering.

The echoes of taps died but still no pandemonium. Most of the dogs had their heads on our knees. As we removed the cans they licked our hands, crawled under our cots and went to sleep.[12]

Such "harmless fun" had a potential for unintended violent results. In one of his relatively few bursts of anger in the letters to his girlfriend, Truman wrote:

Some lowdown infantrymen or good for nothing regular artillery man stole our dog Casey. He wore about $11.00 worth of harness and was a brindle, full as ugly as any picture of one you ever saw. The ninth section (our roughnecks) are going to clean up on some one if they can find who took him.[13]

Nothing more seems to have come of this, which was just as well for Truman, since, on top of his training and regular duties, plus the canteen and laundry operations, Major Gates assigned him in November to oversee Battery F's mess hall because the chief cook, Mess Sgt. James Miller, "succeeded in getting the kitchen everlastingly fowled up and Pete expects me to untangle it."[14] Unlike the laundry situation, which settled down after he beat various businessmen into submission, the mess hall remained a continuing irritation and drain on Truman's limited time. Even after Lieutenant Truman had "fixed" it, there were difficulties maintaining efficient service, and frequent inspections were imposed to ensure that the unit's five cooks—and especially the mess sergeant—were on their toes. Still, this paled before the needs of the regimental canteen, and letter after letter mentions Truman working long after lights-out, "invoicing this devilish place."[15]

The amount of business being handled was impressive, and it ballooned every payday. "I counted money until my head ached," said Truman, who bragged that he had "changed five thousand dollars in ten-dollar bills in about a day and never lost a penny."[16] Other canteens, most of them in fact, were having substantially more trouble keeping their accounts and inventory in order. Complaints to the division canteen officer inevitably brought trouble down on everyone in mid-December.

Even though Truman had shared a whopping $3,000 of the first $5,600 profit with the regiment's roughly 1,100 original "investors" from the first two month's business, he quipped that division inspectors "have been auditing the canteen to see if they can send me to jail."[17] The results of the audit were made known within days. "They say I have the best canteen on the reservation," said Truman. "I came out with flying colors. Even the colonel couldn't find anything wrong. The sanitary inspector came around and told me I had the cleanest place on the job too."[18]

The one time his clerks did come up short, Lieutenant Truman took quite a personal hit, as he had to make things right with "about ninety dollars of my own money."[19] There is no indication that he believed that foul play was involved in this costly mishap, and early on, Truman had wisely followed Jacobson's advice:

> I saw right away that our canteen was headed for bankruptcy. We had 18 men working in it but not a single cash register, just cigar boxes in which the change was kept. I've always believed that most people are honest and I know that Harry Truman always goes on that assumption too—but there's such a thing as offering too much temptation. Our first move was to persuade the commanding officer, Colonel Klemm, to let us spend $700 for cash registers. He granted his approval reluctantly, but the investment paid off.[20]

It is also likely that the stern justice meted out to a thief shortly after the canteen opened for business also served to encourage honesty among the soldiers assigned to Truman.

> I caught one of my men stealing money out of the cash drawer night before last and had him put in the guardhouse. It took me all afternoon yesterday to draw up the charges. I guess he'll get about two years. I backed him into a corner and made him admit that he took the money. He had ten dollars in one pocket and three dollars in another, and two in another, and three in another. Did it all in about an hour. I was at school when the canteen steward

called me out and told me about it. They say the poor fellow is a good soldier but so much money in sight all at once was too much for him. There has been someone stealing constantly from the till for the last two days. I suppose he was the guy.[21]

Several weeks later, the private was brought before a general court martial. "[They] convicted him," said Truman, "but I don't know how hard, for the court won't tell until the judge advocate general of the division reviews the findings of the court. I guess the poor kid will get about three months hard labor. Pretty expensive eighteen dollars."[22]

It would have been wiser for the young soldier simply to have asked the lieutenant for money. A thin (2 1/2 x 4 1/2–inch), six-ringed notebook that Truman maintained contains a list of loans he made while at Camp Doniphan, and a few of those he made later in France. Sixteen soldiers, half of them from Battery F, including his aide, Corporal Haseman, received twenty-five loans amounting to $1,004.50—nearly six months' base pay for Truman—before he shipped out. One fellow, Pvt. Francis X. Berry, practically used Truman as a bank, borrowing sums ranging from $10 to $85 on five occasions and dutifully paying all $200 back. Remarkably, almost everyone made good, with only three—all from his own battery—skipping out on their obligations totaling $41.50; 2nd Lt. Herbert J. Hale, Stable Sgt. Paul M. Springer, and Pvt. William Harding, whose loan of $15 was made as Truman was preparing to leave for France (and was money he probably never really expected to see again).

With the 35th Division's thousands of privates earning $30 per month (and having ostensibly few ways to spend it, since Lawton was just about the driest of dry towns, and Oklahoma City's brothels all but out of reach), much of the men's money was either sent home, disappeared into carefully hidden dice and card games, or otherwise squandered. If circumstances had been different in Lawton, "women and song," to put it delicately, would have harvested a significant number of the ten- and twenty-dollar bills counted out by paymasters. Maybe it was just "soldier talk," but even Private Jacobson implied that he longed for the saloons and prostitutes back home, and he swore to Truman that "he'd go into the guardhouse thirty days for one night on

Twelfth Street." Truman, one-upping Jacobson while still displaying his "proper" intentions to Bess, wrote, "I'd go in for forty days if I could see you thirty minutes."[23]

Harry S. Truman and Bess Wallace had known each other ever since their school days in Independence, had been a couple since 1910, and had been engaged for the last several years as Truman worked to get his financial house in order. Efforts to obtain leave and visit her had run into a brick wall in the form of brigade commander Berry, and then by the division commander, Maj. Gen. William M. Wright, after his return from France. At one point, Truman believed that he had succeeded in manipulating a way around the uncooperative officers by arranging a meeting with Kansas City merchants—regimental business, of course— but was again thwarted at the last minute. The chagrined lieutenant wrote a letter to Bess explaining what happened and expressed his astonishment: "I was willing to bet a month's salary Tuesday morning that I'd be in K.C. Wednesday and there were no takers. The boys all thought I had a cinch, [and] so did I."[24]

Plans for Bess to accompany his mother and sister Mary down to Fort Sill in mid-December fell apart when Bess became ill at the last minute, immediately prompting her beau to send a wire inquiring about her health. Although Truman was happy to see family members, her absence was particularly disappointing, because many of the other officers' wives (such as Colonel Klemm's), girlfriends, and families made the long trip from Kansas City with some frequency. Dances and other social events were held in Battery F's and other mess halls as well as the hospital, sponsored either by the individual units or local patriotic groups. Indeed many officers obtained lodging for their wives. Captain Sermon's son later chronicled the Independence wives in residence:

When they entrained . . . for Camp Doniphan at Fort Sill, Oklahoma, many married men were accompanied by their wives. Among those were Mary Bostain who went with her husband, [William, first lieutenant, Battery C]; Laura and Spencer Salisbury [captain, Battery E]; Anna Hinde accompanied Edgar [first lieutenant, Battery C]; Pete Allen's wife was there also and my mother

accompanied my father [the captain of Battery C]. The married
women found limited quarters in Lawton, Oklahoma, and when
leave was available, socializing and visiting was done in Lawton.
There also was horseback riding and dinners at the fort.[25]

A decision had obviously been made to keep the men close at hand
by maintaining a restrictive leave policy combined with an attempt to
soften the sting by granting ready access to the camp for friends and
family willing to make the trip. This did not play out as expected. Lonely
or bored soldiers apparently took advantage of day passes to Lawton,
using them to get off post before heading to Oklahoma City and points
north. Moreover, Colonel Caldwell duly reported to his superiors that
instances of "absence without leave [AWOL] were numerous." He was
also extremely critical of the visitation policy and advised that "the
division be sent abroad . . . to complete its training there; the reason for
this being that . . . the division could not take its work seriously so near
home, with constant visits and distractions."[26]

Truman came away from a December 13 meeting with the division
commander certain that "General Wright is not in any mood for
Christmas holidays for anyone," and the men settled in for a relatively
sumptuous Christmas on the Oklahoma prairie. The details of what
transpired at headquarters around this time are today unknown, but
Truman's letters began to chronicle fewer comings and goings of civilians
at Doniphan. Had Colonel Caldwell's report prompted some words of
advice from above? The tight-fisted leave policy suddenly loosened up
as well, and several days after Christmas Truman received a full two
weeks' leave back to "God's country."[27] It would be more than sixteen
months before he would see his family and sweetheart Bess again.

ON A COLD THURSDAY AFTERNOON in mid-December, Lieutenant
Truman got his first look at the type of cannon he would take to war, the
French 75mm gun. Although word had only recently filtered down to
Truman's level, the army staff had known for some time that American
industry would be unable to produce its standard 3-inch field piece at
a pace matching the establishment of new artillery units. It was just as

well. The American cannon had a slightly larger bore and more rugged construction, yet could not *accurately* fire near as many rounds per minute as its French counterpart even with the best trained and most disciplined gun crew. The French 75's reputation among artillerymen as a fearsome "miracle weapon" had long preceded it, and even before the gun's arrival at Doniphan, the officers and gun sergeants received a booklet produced by the Army War College that described its technical specifications, operation, and well-known combat capabilities. Its authors were clearly enamored with the cannon, and their gushing introductory paragraphs read like an auto club magazine article extolling the fine points of a new Stutz Bearcat:

> With the exception of the German "42," [42-centimeter mortar] no gun in the war has created more interest than the famous French 75mm field gun, popularly known as the soixante-quinze. That it did magnificent work in the early stages of the war can not be doubted, and if its influence is at present not so great as it was, the reason is to be found in the siege conditions that prevail and to the momentary need of heavier pieces. We do not doubt, however, that the "75" will come by its own again soon, when this interminable trench war reaches an end and more rapid movements begin.
>
> It will surprise many of our readers to learn that the "soixante-quinze" is not a new gun. It was invented as far back as 1897, and two such famous artillerists as Deport and Sainte-Claire Deville had a hand in its design. Studying it in detail, as we are now able to do, through an admirable article recently written by M. Dumas for *Le Genie Civil*, we are struck by the excellence of the design. In all respects it is far ahead of any gun not only of its time but of later years. It represents the first real attempt to produce a field piece that could quite correctly be called a quick firer, and it was probably the earliest in which independent recoil was combined with independent training, a quick-action breech mechanism, and fixed loading—that is to say, loading in which the projectile and the charge are united in a single cartridge, just as they are in the charge of a rifle.[28]

Truman did not share the authors' enthusiasm, and his skeptical Missouri "show me" attitude was front and center after the weapon's initial demonstration. "I went out and observed fire yesterday by the French 75," he wrote. "It is some gun but I think ours has some good points that it hasn't."[29] The lieutenant believed that the cannon he had trained with all these years as a National Guardsman was up to the job ahead. His future chief mechanic, Sgt. McKinley Wooden, who was responsible for the maintenance and efficient operation of D Battery's field pieces, held a different opinion of the now-obsolescent 3-inch gun: "They weren't worth a damn. They were no good. We would have lost the war if we had gone over there with them. The biggest problem was the recoil [mechanism] on them; they had three springs in there, you know. They'd bounce around" after firing and have to be relaid on the target. "You couldn't do anything with them," but the smooth, pneumatic system of the 75mm—"the best there ever was," he maintained—allowed a fast-paced, accurate fire despite the drawback that the "recoil systems had to be adjusted frequently [during] long battles."[30]

With only one of the French guns available, training continued with the existing equipment as winter grew more nasty. The vertical sides of the pyramidal tents had been boxed with wood since late October, and sheds erected by the score to protect the horses came next: forty-two two-horse stalls in each so that a pair of such structures protected the animals of an entire battery. Though unheated, the sheds provided adequate protection from the northern winds. Each three-man tent, said Lee, "was equipped with a Sibley stove in the center [with a] chimney running straight up through the ventilating aperture in the peak."[31] At first, the men were unhappy with the stoves, and Truman complained, "The cussed thing smokes like Vesuvius. It smells like a refinery, and tastes like quinine in here now."[32] Originally designed for much larger twenty-man tents and fed by a seemingly inexhaustible supply of firewood hauled in by civilian contractors, the Sibley threw off a prodigious amount of heat. An obstruction of any kind in the slender stove pipe, however, could send the temperature plummeting, as Truman was distressed to find out firsthand: "Our tent is usually as warm as a house, but for some reason our stove refuses to draw this morning and we have a cold tent."[33]

Field exercises were periodically canceled due to blizzard conditions or deep snow, yet it was during the first months of 1918 that the 129th's officers and men felt that they received their most effective stateside training. This was accomplished under the leadership of Col. Robert M. Danford. Klemm, who along with Elliott (now a lieutenant colonel) was sent to Fort Sam Houston for special instruction at the Brigade and Field Officers' School, took credit for Danford's temporary appointment to the 129th, and the regiment couldn't have been more pleased.

A rising star in the army's artillery branch, Danford would eventually become chief of field artillery from 1939 to 1942 and oversee the advances in artillery doctrine and technology that the army used in World War II. Even in 1917 he was well known as the soldier who had co-authored the lyrics to the artillery's pounding anthem, "The Caissons Go Rolling Along," when stationed in the Philippines, and as the author of *Notes on Training Field Artillery Details*. Danford's book explained the mysteries of this complex, arcane subject with such thoroughness, yet simplicity, that it was immediately adopted as the basic manual for field artillery training; the army soaked up four printings of the Yale University Press release between May and September of 1917.

The regimental history goes into considerable detail on Danford's tenure, which saw a revamping of the training methods and schedule, a greatly increased emphasis on the officers being directly involved in all aspects of training (which pleased the army inspectors), and even an internal shuffling by color of the unit's horses for both morale purposes and so that they could be more easily identified in the field (A Battery, black; B Battery, dark brown; C Battery, light brown; D Battery, bay; E Battery, sorrel; and F Battery, black, white, and gray). Truman was delighted "to get the use of a man like him" and told Bess that his new commander's book "is considered a regular Bible by most artillerymen."[34] Colonel Danford's brief time at Doniphan truly left its mark on the regiment. It was also to have a major impact on Lieutenant Truman's military career.

CHAPTER 5

Jacobson & Trumanheimer

T RUMAN WAS BECOMING INCREASINGLY ill at ease as 1918 approached, and he nervously wrote Bess, "Some of the officers of this division have gone home on account of inefficiency and one or two on account of physical disqualifications."[1] The army was of the opinion that two to three months of training to Regular Army standards gave ample time to judge if a National Guard officer, or any newly minted officer, was unsuited to command. And it was bad enough that a review board could send a long-serving guardsman packing at the drop of a hat, but these decisions were handed down even as the guardsmen saw seemingly unfit, even incompetent, regulars remain at their posts. Commonly referred to as a "benzine board" after the noxious-smelling cleaning fluid, they appeared to be arbitrarily scrubbing the service of men not unlike those who passed muster. Being "benzined" didn't at all mean that a fellow was drummed out of the service; some took stateside training or administrative jobs, but most guardsmen chose to leave the army entirely if such an embarrassing calamity befell them. Truman's succinct statement: "I would rather be shot," reflected what was on everyone's mind. Ted Marks of Battery B later said:

I was tense and wanted to make sure that everything was just so. . . . We went to school and the regular Army would have an officer there and quiz us to see what we knew about our jobs as battery commanders. We had to be on our toes, because they were sending officers home all the time; and the last thing I'd want to do, and I'm sure anyone else would want to do, was to go home and say you weren't qualified.

We didn't have much time there to waste. . . . At night the commanding general [Berry] would walk around and see if you were on the job studying. One night he came into my tent—I couldn't hear him walking around, he had slippers on—and sat on the bed. He sat on the corner where the pillow was and the pillow slipped and he fell over. We'd always have a drill book out, reading it when he came around. He would ask where some other officer was and I'd say, "Well, he's down at the canteen; he was here a few minutes ago."[2]

Irregularities in a ridiculously large number of unit funds—many quite profound—also led to the early termination of some officers, including D Battery commander Charlie Allen, who, according to one of his sergeants, Edward McKim, "got himself involved with a red-headed woman and our mess fund seemed to disappear."[3] Incredibly, *every* canteen in the 35th Division went bust except for that of "Jacobson & Trumanheimer." With obvious pride, Jacobson later wrote, "At the end of the year our canteen was the only one out of 17 that hadn't gone broke."[4] Early on, it had become clear to the regiment, as well as the division's officers, that the canteen operation was going to easily repay the original $2,200 that the men had invested by decree. But it is unlikely that any of the 129th's cannoneers expected the windfall that blew into their pockets. "In six months we paid $15,000 in dividends to the battery fund," said Truman, "and still had our stock on hand to do business. That Jewish boy and I really thought we were businessmen."[5]

This also came as a pleasant surprise to the lieutenant's new boss. At a commanders' conference almost immediately after his arrival (and while Truman was still on leave), the pitiful state of the 35th's canteens was outlined in detail by the division judge advocate, Maj. Victor E. Ruehl. Apparently to save some of the officers present from undue embarrassment, a highly unusual procedure was carried out. No specifics were given as to which unit's canteen was attached to any in the litany of horror stories, although it could be assumed that the details had already flowed through the officers' grapevine. One canteen, and one canteen only, was singled out for high praise, and the regimental history of the 129th tactfully ignored the utter shambles of the other concerns:

> Shortly after his arrival, Colonel Danford attended a meeting at Division Headquarters at which the condition of the various canteens in the Division was discussed. An especially commendatory report on the business-like and efficient management and condition of one canteen, without naming it, was made; and Colonel Danford was later much gratified to learn, and to pass the information on at his next [regimental] officers' meeting, that the canteen in question, so highly commended, was that of the 129th Field Artillery.[6]

Truman returned from leave without the slightest idea that the whole canteen system had come crashing down during his brief absence.

> They sent me a general order closing all canteens until they had paid their debts and shown that they are solvent. I passed out the word that last night would see the finish of the canteen and they almost mobbed the place. Sold six hundred dollars' worth in three hours. I have been working like a nigger ever since getting invoiced and billed out. It seems like you're never up with the hounds in the army.[7]

The troubled circumstances of the other operations resulted in Truman's canteen having a virtual monopoly on the trade during its last month in business. Since the dividend paid out to "investors" from October through early December had totaled $3,000, it is apparent that the huge influx of cash came during this period when the 129th's canteen was the only game in town. "Jacobson & Trumanheimer" closed down for good on Friday, February 1, 1918, and Fort Sill would eventually establish a post exchange unaffiliated with individual units. In the meantime, Corporal Jacobson's performance had ensured that he was well on his way to a third stripe. As for Lieutenant Truman, he soon learned that Danford had put him, plus Marks and a D Battery friend, Lt. Newell T. Paterson, all up for promotion to captain.

TRUMAN WAS EXCITED AT THE PROSPECT and felt honored, telling Bess that even if he didn't pass, "it is a compliment anyway to get ordered up."[8] But to earn his second bar, he would first have to get past "the Walrus," General Berry. Truman's letters are peppered with comments like, "General Berry was in a bad humor yesterday afternoon,"[9] and he wrote that during gunnery practice, "General Berry always eats 'em alive after they fire. He's very expert at making a person shake in his boots."[10] An example of Berry's training method was expertly provided by Lt. (later Maj.) William P. MacLean of the 130th Field Artillery:

> Berry followed his usual tactics of shooting questions at me in a lightning-like fashion[,] but having just been over this work at the School of Fire, I was able to answer them. Then he called upon me to do something which was impossible to do. He had Lieut. Spotts sit on the gun seat and handle the elevating and traversing gear which moves the gun, and I was to give the commands which would cause Lieut. Spotts to so move the gun as to place the fine, crossed horsehairs at the muzzle of the piece in a direct line with the fine, black marks on the testing boards some one hundred yards away.
>
> This is a delicate operation and usually takes a little time and is all done by one man. Of course when I would tell Spotts to move to the right he would go too far to the right and when I would tell him to move a little to the left he would move a little too far to the left again. He could not see how far to move and I was trying to devise some method of command that would get him to move the

gun ever so slightly in order to adjust it properly, but I could not get it with enough speed to suit General Berry.

He told me to get up and give the place to somebody who could think faster. He made a great speech about wearing out the eye instead of the brain, and bellowed for another victim. Of course, the only impression this made on me was to give me the unalterable feeling that the General was unfair[,] and although I afterward followed him over a good many miles and through a great many difficulties[,] I never did have the confidence in him which a young captain would like to have in his commanding General.[11]

In early March, Truman had a potentially promotion-threatening run-in with Berry that was sidetracked in the nick of time by the unintended intervention of another officer from the 130th, 2nd Lt. (later Maj. Gen.) Harry H. Vaughan, who years later recalled that "Berry was a 24 karat s.o.b."[12]

He would have a brigade officer's call to which some 150 to 175 officers would report. . . . If the officer's call was for 3:00 and he got there at ten minutes to 3:00, he would start the meeting. If you got there at five minutes to 3:00, you were late and you caught the devil.

On this particular day, there were three or four of us walking over to the Brigade Headquarters, young second lieutenants from the 130th, one of whom was Jim Pendergast of Kansas City. We were talking and laughing and as we went through the door, we were clear inside before we realized that the meeting had begun and that General Berry had a young first lieutenant out in front of him, giving him unshirted hell [about something] . . . . Berry was distracted from what he was doing, and he turned and looked us over. We, of course, snapped up to attention and acted like there was nothing the matter at all, and Berry looked right at me. I was the first one in and the biggest and probably making the most noise, and he said, "What is your name, Mister?"

In those days you had to be a first lieutenant before you had any rank; second lieutenants were called "Mister."

So, I was standing like a ramrod and I said, "Vaughan, sir."

He said, "How long have you been an officer in the United States Army?"

I said, "Three days, sir," with which he proceeded to go into detail as to how he doubted very much if I would ever be an officer in the United States Army if I lived to be a hundred. And while he was giving me the business, much to the amusement of everybody who was behind him, whom he couldn't see, why, this first lieutenant stepped back in the ranks with all the rest of the officers who were standing there, and when Berry got through with me, which took two or three minutes because he really covered the subject, he forgot who he had been talking to and he went on with the meeting. Well, the meeting lasted twenty to thirty minutes and on the way out, this officer grabbed me by the arm and said, "Much obliged Mister, you got me off the hook nicely."

After we got outside I said, "Who was that?" Jim Pendergast, of course, knew him, because Jim had been in the 129th Regiment before he was commissioned. Jim said, "Why, that's Lieutenant Harry Truman. He lives in Independence; he's a friend of mine."[13]

News that Truman would fall into Berry's "kill zone" came while he was preparing, albeit with numerous false starts, to leave Doniphan for specialized artillery officer's training in France as part of the 35th Division Overseas Detail with other picked commissioned and non-commissioned personnel:

The overseas detachment is again having spasms of preparation to leave. I am still on it: thank heaven, and so of course I am having spasms too. I had a regular one yesterday when Colonel Danford ordered me up before an examining board—not for efficiency, but for promotion. I think I failed miserably because General Berry was so gruff and discourteous in his questions that I forgot all I ever knew and couldn't answer him. . . . We [Truman, Marks, and

Lt. Newell T. Paterson] had no opportunity for preparation and I suppose that it would have been no better if we had.[14]

Years later, in the 1930s, Truman recalled further particulars of General Berry at the examining board:

His object was not to find how much we knew, but how much we did not know. When we could answer, it displeased him but when we couldn't he'd rattle his false teeth, pull his handle bar mustache and stalk up and down the room yelling at us. "Ah, you don't know do you? I thought you were just ignorant rookies. Now you aspire to be officers and gentlemen sure enough by becoming Captains in the United States Army. It will be a disaster to the country to let you command men etc. etc."[15]

On the heels of what he, Marks, and Paterson believed had been an utter fiasco, Truman had to finesse his way through another eye test before he would be allowed to continue on to France.

They almost sent me home on a physical, too, yesterday but I talked past the M.D. He turned my eyes down twice and threatened to send me to division headquarters for a special examination and then didn't. I guess I can put a real good conversation when circumstances demand it.[16]

He was right. No hint of this eye exam exists in Truman's voluminous army personnel records which extend from 1917 to 1953. It is also important to note that, in the army of the day (and despite Teddy Roosevelt), soldiers of Truman's general age and younger were frequently perceived to be in some way deficient and lacking in military bearing if they wore spectacles. Illustrations in official and semi-official military publications frequently contrasted the erect purposeful demeanor of an ideal officer (sans glasses, of course) with that of a bespectacled, ever-so-slightly hunched businessman wearing a bowler hat, and sometimes packing an umbrella as part of the civilian uniform.

Paradoxically, Lieutenant Truman had developed a reputation within the regiment as being something of a hotshot when it came to gunnery. This was no small feat. For artilleryman in the field, glasses presented additional subtle problems beyond such obvious things as impaired ability to see distant targets in the rain. The eyepieces on standard-issue Bausch & Lomb six-power field glasses (binoculars) during this period allowed the focus to be adjusted separately for each eye, as did the standard battery commander's (BC) telescope, both of which Truman could effectively use with his glasses removed from his face after he had gotten a fix on a target's location.* Standard practice, however, entailed that a second member of an observation post (OP) double check the data gathered from use of the BC scope. If either of these men wore glasses, the necessary readjustments could slow the process significantly every time observation was switched over.

Despite these disadvantages, Truman excelled at observing and adjusting the fall of shot. On one occasion, he wrote that he "was unlucky enough to observe more shots correctly than anyone else"[17]—including his battery commander—in front of General Berry, whose likely response was to berate the lieutenant for not doing better. In little more than six months, he would prove his worth, and the general would use Truman's deadly efficiency as a shield to help ward off criticism that he and the division artillery had let its men down.

---

* Although later publications such as *Field Artillery Material* (1920), *Field Artillery Manual*, vol 1. (1925), and *Elements of Field Artillery* (1925) would provide varying amounts of detail on the separate adjustment of the BC scope's eyepieces, it was Danford, sensitive to the problem because he himself wore spectacles, who provided in his trusty *Notes on Training Field Artillery Details*, 85–86, a series of practical tips on allowing the eyes to focus properly when using the scope. Rain, of course, was an added complication for an officer wearing glasses, and the BC scope had to be kept perfectly dry, requiring that a makeshift hood be created from shelter halves if there was a need to direct fires in the rain.

NO LONGER CHAINED TO THE CANTEEN, Truman was able to put his own stamp on Battery F's education instead of strictly following the established training routine. A fine horseman, he had eagerly taken part in the officers' equestrian instruction the previous fall; reveled in a hard, fifteen-mile ride led by Colonel Klemm; and taken every opportunity to ride alone or with colleagues and friends, as when he escorted Captain Sermon's wife—hastening to add in his letter to Bess that Pete Allen and his niece were also along, "so I guess it was perfectly proper."[18] Now unleashed, he worked on his own men's horsemanship:

> I took some sergeants out riding today to show them how to figure
> a deflection and also how to sit on a horse. We rode up Signal Mtn
> and down again and one or two were very glad to get back to camp.
> One of them informed me that he would [have to] stand up to rest
> for a couple of days. I must be getting to be a tough guy because I
> don't get tired and I can ride all day without unpleasantness. [19]

Truman was more frequently called in to judge the cases of soldiers brought up for courts-martial, where he "hear[d] evidence against some poor son of a gun who has used government funds for his own use or done something against the 4 million regulations you're supposed to know and don't." He also increased his efforts on behalf of the Masons, laying out his recruiting successes to Bess like a gunslinger carves notches in a six-shooter. "I have made Masons out of both Colonel Klemm and Colonel Danford since we've been here, so I guess maybe that helps my drag [influence] somewhat, although it's not supposed to," said the calculating lieutenant, adding, "General Berry is one and I am going to help make General Wright one next Wednesday if he shows up as expected."

When his 60th Artillery Brigade was called out on review before General Berry and the IG colonel, Starbird, it was the first time that Truman (indeed, all the division officers up to and including Berry) had ever seen such a mass of firepower concentrated in one formation. Despite dust kicked up "so thick you could hardly breathe," it was an impressive display, and an awed Truman wrote, "I never saw so much

Artillery all together in my life."[20] Although Starbird and the other inspectors found little to applaud, Truman, whose overseas detail had been delayed several times, expressed his satisfaction with the training:

> I don't much care whether we leave so soon or not because we are getting some very good schooling. Had an examination yesterday in which we had a problem like this: a scout measured the angle found by two trees on the opposite bank of a river, it was 150 mils, he walked back fifty yards and the angle between the same two trees was 120 mils. How wide is the river? I got the right answer, what do you think of that. It is two hundred yards wide. A mil is the 1/6400 of a circle which is the measurement we use instead of degrees. That was one of five we had to work besides several on drill regulations. We'll sure be wise birds when the war's over if we don't get shot first.[21]

All good things must come to an end. On March 10, Truman sadly reported:

> This is Sunday morning and a magnificent one but we all have the blues. They have taken Colonel Danford away from us, sent him to Washington to report to the artillery commander-in-chief. I don't know what for, unless it is to be a general or something because he knows more artillery than Napoleon Bonaparte himself. The whole regiment is feeling badly over it. Captain McGee told his first sergeant about it as they were walking to the stable. The sergeant stopped and said, "The H-l?"[22]

Danford did not know how long he would be in Washington, but rightly believed that maintaining a horse would be "too great a burden."[23] Much to the consternation of Colonel Klemm and Major Miles, who each wanted the animal for himself, Danford gave his horse to Lieutenant Truman—or, at least tried to. Truman described the valuable, Kentucky-bred male as "pretty as a picture and gentle as a dog. He's a very dark sorrel with a dark sorrel mane and tail and a pretty, little[,] intelligent head like Rosa Bonheur puts on her horses."[24] Truman told the colonel that he couldn't just *take* the animal, so Danford named a token figure of $100, which was gladly accepted. Truman promised that if they both survived the war, he would happily return the handsome stallion, explaining that "it would have been stealing to buy him for $100."[25]

Truman continued with his training and started taking long horseback rides on his Sundays off, roaming as far as twenty miles with his orderly, Corporal Haseman, or making a solitary journey to little Medicine Park at the edge of the Wichita Mountains "because I don't ever expect to come back to this place again if I live to be a thousand" (he took Haseman with him on another visit to the town).[26] He still shunned social functions, however, such as the banquet thrown by "the Irish of Btry. D," who were still "having a big time" the following day.[27]

Coming down with what a division doctor diagnosed as acute autointoxication, a potentially very serious intestinal ailment, briefly put him in a small panic, as the doctor confined him to quarters for three days and "almost sent me to the base hospital when my fever went up to 102 degrees." Truman told Bess that it had just been a bad cold, and recovered sufficiently to get back with his men on March 10, but had been "afraid that if I went to the hospital the overseas detail would leave without me"—a fate that would befall his tentmate Lee at the last moment. He needn't have worried. The soldiers were still in camp, and some wag among them said, "People going through here twenty years hence will see some soldiers sitting on a pile of baggage expecting to leave suddenly, and that will be the overseas detail of the 35th Division still awaiting orders to entrain."[28]

Division headquarters was issuing instructions almost daily by now that no man assigned to the detail be allowed a twenty-four-hour pass, with the result that Truman and the chosen few were, in effect, confined to post. Bess had written him of a dream she had that the soldiers would come through Kansas City, and Truman, intimately familiar with the rail routes east (and with a helpful friend in headquarters), let her know that there was a good chance that "your dream comes true"[29] if they took the Rock Island line toward Chicago instead of the more direct, yet slower, St. Louis & Santa Fe Railway. Finally, on the afternoon of Tuesday, March 19, the soldiers were ordered to pick up their bags, draw travel rations, and gather in the mess halls that evening to await further instructions. Truman had already sold Lizzie two weeks earlier to "a poor sucker" for $200 and made arrangements to have his two horses sent home to Grandview (Danford's was "too fine to go to war"), along with those of Klemm and Elliott for safekeeping.[30]

The men cooled their heels until they were able to board well after midnight, and the train began to slowly chug north at 1:30 a.m. The late start meant that it would be nearly the next midnight before the scheduled coal and water stop in the rail yards across the state line from downtown Kansas City gave Truman a chance to call Bess. Ten officers from the 129th under Major Gates and perhaps a half-dozen from the 130th occupied the Pullman with him, while one hundred more of the regiment's soldiers—principally sergeants, corporals, plus privates judged capable of earning more stripes—filled the seats in one and a half coaches. In all, 144 officers and 456 men of the 35th Division were headed for Camp Merritt, New Jersey.

Truman penned a letter to Bess as the train slowly ground its way north, pouring out his anger that Lieutenant Lee had been yanked from the detail at the last second, even after his baggage had been loaded. He wrote down his temporary address at Camp Merritt and told her that Lieutenant Boxley, who had signed him up eleven long years ago at the Coates House, would send her a telegram when his ship arrived safely in France. Although his plan was to phone her and his mother while his train took on coal and water in the Kansas City area, there was no sure bet that he could find, let alone gain access to, an outside line while his train was serviced. In those days, mail with special-delivery handling was as close to a guaranteed overnight delivery as one could get and cost a whopping ten cents on a standard letter, more than triple the normal rate. In an effort to make sure that she received at least some word from him soon, but unsure of the cost charged by the U.S. Post Office, he plastered an envelope with a line of three- and one-cent stamps, scrawled "Special Delivery" across the front, and mailed it at the El Reno stop near Oklahoma

City. Processed at 7:20 p.m., it was likely delivered by early afternoon of the next day, but his girl wouldn't have to wait that long to hear from him.

It was nearly dawn when the train squealed to a stop in the massive Armourdale Yard. There was already going to be precious little time to talk to Bess and his mother, and Truman almost immediately found that, as was common in many rail facilities of the period, it used its own internal telephone system. One can imagine our lieutenant scurrying up and down the tracks between the dim street lights of the Argentine rising close to the north, and those of little Rosedale, Kansas, dotting the bluffs to the south. Kansas City, Missouri, lay directly in front of the hissing steam engine but might as well have been on Mars.

"We only stayed in K.C. about twenty minutes and I spent fifteen of that hunting a phone," said Truman, who complained that none could be found within a mile of the train. Finally, he located an outside line in the yardmaster's office. "I am terribly thankful it was there and that it was a Bell."[31] He later recalled, "The switchman was a patriot too," who told him, "Son, call hell and heaven if you want to and charge it to the Company." Truman explained that he was trying to reach his fiancee, and the switchman declared, "If she doesn't break the engagement at four o'clock in the morning she really loves you."[32] Gates undoubtedly noticed that he was a soldier short as the Rock Island men were finishing up their chores, but Truman made it back through the blackened obstacle course of railroad ties and steel rails—without breaking his neck—just before the train pulled out.

They have been kidding me pretty strong today because I called you out of bed to the phone. Major Gates said he expected to see in the society column where you were engaged to someone else because of it. I told him not to worry his head about that. It was not a very pleasant thing from your point of view, I don't suppose, to be called out at that unearthly hour, but it gave me lots of pleasure to hear your voice once more even if it was only over the phone. Besides it may be a whole year or more before I'm in Kansas City again and if it had been two o'clock instead of five I'd have done it. I am sorry to have disturbed your mother but I hope she'll forgive me this time. [33]

Truman sent postcards home from Fort Wayne and Cleveland as the train worked its way east, but it never did make up the lost time in Oklahoma, and Bess was surprised to receive a telegram, not from Lieutenant Boxley, but from her Harry at a hotel in New York: "MISSED BOAT. . . . WILL BE AT HOTEL McALPIN TILL 2 PM MONDAY. CAMP MERRITT FOR SEVERAL DAYS." And in a reference to news of a massive German offensive that had erupted in France while the men were on the train, he added, "THE HUNS HEARD WE WERE COMING AND ARE TRYING TO WIN BEFORE WE ARRIVE"—a comment more true than he may have suspected at the time.[34]

CHAPTER 6

"Wondering if We'd Be Heroes or Corpses"

IT WAS ALMOST MIDNIGHT on Saturday, March 23, when the overseas detachment pulled into Camp Merritt, which sprawled across the rolling countryside between Dumont and Tenafly. They received quite a welcome after Major Gates was called away on detachment business:

> [We] were carefully inspected by a colonel of cavalry at what they call the "showdown inspection," where you lay down all of your equipment, when we got through this doggy colonel, you know, with his whip and his spurs, [who] said, "Who's in command of this outfit?" I thought, "Oh, here's where we get hell." "Lieutenant Paterson, sir." "I'll say one thing, this is the finest unit that I've seen go through this camp."[1]

This was hardly an idle statement, since the colonel's observations were genuine, and his praise was imparted to the post's commander. This precipitated a message that both surprised and gratified the headquarters back in Oklahoma, where a "report came back that the '35th Division Detachment' was the best equipped detachment that had gone through" Camp Merritt.[2]

ALTHOUGH TRUMAN WAS PLEASED to find that there was "steam heat, hot baths, and private rooms for officers," neither he nor his colleagues were interested in hanging around. Passes were granted to New York and eagerly snatched up by Truman and "four other Missouri guys"[3] (whom he never named). The would-be doughboys crammed into a taxi for the fifteen-mile ride south to the Edgewater Ferry dock, crossed the Hudson River, and went in together on a room at the posh McAlpin Hotel on Thirty-fourth Street, where they gawked out the windows up busy Broadway. Ultimately, though, Truman was not impressed, and writing from the officers' club on West Fifty-seventh Street several days later, he told his cousins Nellie and Ethel Noland that:

> I am in the most touted town on earth and it is a vast disappointment. I have stopped at the McAlpin Hotel, been to the Winter Garden, walked down Broadway & 42nd Street at night, up 5th Ave in the daytime, been on top of the Woolworth Bldg, crossed Brooklyn Bridge, been to a Chinese Chop Suey joint, rode the subway from the Battery to 130th St. . . . and done everything I can think of . . . . New Yorkers expect you to fall dead every time they pull one of their best press agent stunts on you and if you don't, they are dead sure you are lacking somewhere.
>
> The Waldorf and the McAlpin are no better than the Muelbach or Baltimore. . . . and Wall Street is an alley. The view from the Woolworth Bldg is grand and *magnifique*, though. You can see old Lady Liberty holding up her torch. Some of Jersey City burned up today while we were on top of the Bldg. It was a fine sight even if some Hun ought to be shot for doing it. This town they say has 8,000,000 people, 7,500,000 of 'em are of Israelish extraction. Kansas City can produce more good looking girls than two New Yorks.[4]

Not all of his time in New York (with the exception of his visit to the Woolworth Building) was a waste, as Truman was able to up the number of eyeglasses he was taking with him to France by acquiring two pairs during a second trip that "was strictly business."

I accidentally ran into an honest optician who happened to belong to my goat tribe (i.e., Scottish Rite) and he sent me to the best or one of the best oculists in the city. He gave me a complete and thorough examination, a prescription I can use in Paris or Vienna, and lots of good conversation all for the whole sum of $5.00, and then he asked me if I thought I could stand that. How is that for the crookedest town in the universe? Then the optician, who also gave me lots of good advice, only charged me $17.50 less 10 percent for two complete pairs of regulation aluminum frames and glasses, throwing in an extra lens that he happened to chip on the edge in the grinding. I can't understand it. [Harry] Watts stung me for $22.00 for two pairs, and Dr. [Ward H.] Leonard charged me $10.00 the last time I bought any, and they were supposed to be friends of mine too. This place is on Madison Avenue just off 42nd Street [6 East Forty-second] and I know he pays more rent for a week than Watts does for a month. Evidently these are patriotic men. . . . one of them is named [Albert] Haustetter. That's the optician's name and he says it loses him business, although his son has made some wonderful inventions in observing instruments for the U.S. Navy since we went to war.[5]

Truman had been forewarned to expect another eye test before he could board ship for France, but the dreaded exam appears not to have happened. He spent all day Thursday preparing his gear and "reading orders and instructions as to how we must act, what we must say and not say when we arrive in General Pershing's jurisdiction,"[6] and at 3 a.m. on Good Friday, March 29, 1918, he was rousted awake. Along with the rest of the detachment, he performed the last checks to make sure everything was in order before boarding one of the troop trains shuttling between Camp Merritt and Hoboken on the Port of New York's Jersey side of the Hudson. From the station, the Missouri boys marched to River Street then past ship after ship berthed at the "German docks" facing lower Manhattan. Finally they were directed onto a massive pier and called to a halt beside the towering, rust-streaked hull of the converted passenger liner that seemed to fill the entire slip.

Keeping to their ranks, the men stood "at ease" next to the giant hulk of the USS *George Washington* and waited amid the organized chaos along the pier for their turn to board, eventually marching up a long gangway ending at a yawning hatch that opened into the bowels of the ship. When she had sailed on her maiden voyage nearly nine years earlier, the *George Washington* was the third-largest passenger liner in the world and the biggest ever built in Germany up to that time (its Bremen owners gauged that its name would boost ticket sales among Americans, and they were proved right). She plied the northern Atlantic as the pride of the Norddeutscher Lloyd (NL) passenger fleet until interned at New York upon the outbreak of general war in Europe when Germany invaded little Belgium. It was finally seized along with fifteen other ships of the NL and Hamburg-American Lines by the 1st Battalion, 22nd Infantry, when America entered the fray in April 1917.

The *George Washington*'s once crisply painted black hull, topped by an elegant white superstructure, was covered with a fresh coat of "Standard Navy Gray" when readied to serve as a troop ship at the nearby New York Navy Yard. Now, after seven months of hard sailing, she looked weathered and beaten, but hints of her recent glory days could be glimpsed all over the ship, including flashes of bright yellow-orange glistening through the spots where the dull gray paint had chipped away from the funnels.* Tug boats churned the waters below as the *George Washington* backed slowly into the Hudson at midnight and glided past the lighted clock tower on Hoboken's ferry building. She anchored briefly in the estuary below the Statue of Liberty as a convoy of ships formed up behind her before proceeding south through the Narrows, then east and out to sea.

Truman could clearly see the Woolworth Building speckled with lights and silhouetted against the slight glow of clouds reflecting the street lamps below. With Lieutenant Paterson, he "stood on the deck that

---

*After this round trip, the USS *George Washington* would be repainted in a gaudy "dazzle" camouflage pattern intended to confuse the aim of enemy submariners.

night and watched the skyline of the great city disappear"[7] as the ships moved carefully away from the tip of Manhattan. The giant monoliths that he had walked among just days before were slowly obscured behind the dark jumble of buildings and trees that made up Brooklyn, as singly, but more often in small, hushed groups, the two thousand soldiers began to drift away from the railings, "wondering," like Truman, "if we'd be heroes or corpses."[8]

By the time dawn broke on the morning of March 30, the *George Washington* had picked up speed and was racing toward the battlefields of France, although "racing" is, perhaps, the wrong word. The liner could move no faster than the slowest ship in the group, and additional plodding convoys were folded into the mass by mid-ocean. It was further slowed by the irregular zig-zag course—"sailing around the Atlantic,"[9] as Truman called it—in an effort to make the oblong formation of ships a tougher target for the German submariners. Rather than the customary six, it took fully thirteen days to reach its destination. The U-boat threat was taken seriously even though the institution of protected convoys almost exactly a year before had greatly reduced sinkings. No one had to be reminded that the *Lusitania*, one of only two liners that were larger than the *George Washington* when it was launched, had gone down, taking 1,198 people with it when torpedoed off the coast of Ireland.

The cheeky American and German mariners who crewed the liner delighted in teasing the landlubbers by reminding them that the smooth seas and clear skies being experienced during the voyage spelled danger, but Truman apparently was a little skeptical and wrote Bess, "The weather has been fine all the way across, ideal submarine weather so they say."[10] He did admit to getting sick during a patch of rough seas, but he was one of the lucky ones:

> Some of the officers have been sick all the way, and I'm sure from my one day's experience, have spent a very unpleasant time. Everyone has a remedy and none of them work but Christian Science and sometimes it fails in a rough sea. We have had a very pleasant time except for the monotony of it. There are six lieutenants in our cabin, all congenial spirits. We play cards awhile then go on

deck and hunt for submarines awhile and sleep the rest of the time except when we're on guard.[11]

The first-class state room Truman and five other officers occupied was intended to accommodate two passengers, but the pair of narrow, three-man navy bunks allowed them enough room to move about without continually jostling each other. Meals prepared by the *George Washington*'s own cooks and chefs were eagerly anticipated events, and the officers' mess was situated in the dining saloon, where long, military-issue tables replaced the six- and intimate two-person dining tables that once graced the floor under a high, gilded dome. If Truman pulled up the heavy protective canvas that now hung down the walls, he would have found them "decorated in white and gold [that] trimmed floral designs executed against a blue background."[12] Of more interest to Truman and the other artillerymen, both personally and professionally, were the four big 5-inch, 51-caliber naval guns strategically positioned from bow to stern so that no fewer than two of them could be brought to bear on any approaching enemy. Truman was also put in charge of one of the five provisional companies of enlisted men and noncommissioned officers that made up the overseas detail. Sadly, while copies of the ship's single-sheet daily newspaper, *The Hatchet*, exist from the voyage that brought President Wilson back from the Versailles Conference in 1919, the editions Truman sent to Bess have not survived, and he wrote little of his two weeks at sea.

The most dangerous part of the transit was the last three hundred miles as the *George Washington* approached the French coast through the dreaded Western Approaches—a graveyard of Allied shipping sunk by U-boats. Portions of the convoy peeled off north toward the Irish Sea and English Channel, then on the Saturday morning of April 13, 1918, an uncharacteristically bright day for this time of year, the *George Washington* and remaining ships glided past Pointe des Espagnols and into the Brest roadstead. The slow process of transferring the convoy's seven thousand soldiers to the large personnel lighters *Rin-Tin-Tin* and *Nenette* and paddle-wheel ferry *Tudno* for the trip to the dock was not a speedy affair, but Truman was ashore looking for a place where he could wire home by late afternoon and was comfortably ensconced in his billet—a sumptuous, if overdone, room at the Hotel des Voyageurs—by evening. The enlisted men and sergeants of the detachment were quartered at the artillery barracks of nearby Camp Pontanezen while the officers were sprinkled about the hotels and villas. Having private quarters was something of a treat for Truman. The room was icy cold but the bed warm. His only real problem getting some sleep came from the severely out-of-sync church bells in the neighborhood and even on his hotel, which he sarcastically wrote "was one continual round of pleasure all night long."[13]

The detachment ahead of them at the 2nd Corps Field Artillery School in Montigny had not finished its training, so the Missourians spent the better part of a pleasant week sightseeing, watching French and American silent movies (Truman and Gates also went to the opera), and sampling whatever the French had to offer. Many soldiers, after their long "dry" spell in Oklahoma, "are trying to drink all there is here," wrote Truman, adding, "They can't[,] as the supply seems to be inexhaustible." The ample supply of spirits was a happy surprise and did not appear to be dampened when it was discovered that, as at Lawton, "prices are marked strictly on the American plan in French money and they skin us alive."[14] Truman, and almost certainly the other officers as well, also explored the countryside, taking careful note of the type of terrain that in 1944 would bedevil both the American forces attempting to seize Brest from the Germans and the sons of their own division's soldiers attempting to break out of the Normandy beachhead to the northeast. Unlike in the United States, where the plotting of farm land is based on an easily defined grid pattern broken only by major features such as steep hills and rivers, the confused jumble of tree- and hedge-lined farm land left him scratching his head:

> The fields make an irregular patchwork of the landscape. . . . Their boundary lines run in every which direction and I don't see how they describe a piece of property when they want to transfer it. The cities seem to be just as bad. [15]

The men were moved briefly to one of Napoleon's old training camps, Coetquidan, located between Saint-Nazaire and Rennes, which was now serving as one of the principal artillery schools of the American Expeditionary Force (AEF). Despite the obvious connection to the detachment's mission, they did nothing of consequence there beyond observing some training, and it is likely that the men were simply pushed out of Brest to make way for the arrival of more troops from the States. After just a few days they were loaded aboard another one of those French troop trains that Truman found so amusing because some French steam engines seemed small and toy-like, and even those that were large and powerful could only let loose with pitiful, high-pitched chirps from their "peanut roaster whistle[s]"[16]—similar to those atop street vendors' pushcarts in Kansas City—instead of the full-throated blasts of their American cousins.

The train seemingly meandered all across France before depositing the advance detail far to the east and forty-five miles from Troyes at the 2nd Corps Field Artillery School, often referred to as the Montigny School. It was about time. Some two weeks had passed since the men landed at Brest and nearly six since leaving Camp Doniphan. Truman had enjoyed his time as a tourist, expressing in many letters to Bess his admiration for the French and the beauty of the country, but was frustrated that, in the midst of the desperate fighting that still raged, he'd "been touring France quite extensively at the expense of the American Government and hadn't gone to work yet," and complained, "I'm getting fat and lazy from lack of work."[17]

The detachment arrived at Montigny-sur-Aube on Sunday, April 27, and Truman settled into a comfortable room "with four of the most congenial first lieutenants in the regiment at an old chateau with a beautiful garden, a moat, a fine park, and a church with a chime clock with the most beautifully toned bell I ever heard." Truman remarked that "the hardships of this war are sure easy to bear so far," but this promptly ended with the onset of school the next day. What followed was the most intensive six weeks of study he had ever experienced, and he told Bess all about it from "Somewhere in France," as a soldier's location was a military secret:

May 5 . . . The confounded church bell next door woke me at 5:30 a.m. and I found I was 4,000 miles from where I wished I was. When I come home I'll be a surveyor, a mathematician, a mechanical draftsman, a horse doctor, a crack shot, and a tough citizen if they keep me here long. We have periods of lectures and exams and everything just like West Point. The day begins at 7 a.m. and ends at 9:30 p.m. with an hour and a half of study. There is hardly time to get from one class to another and they even give us thunder if we are late.

May 12 . . . I passed this week's exams with flying colors. Even worked out my probabilities [of where individual fired rounds would strike] right, and that's some job. I'm getting a college education in geometry, trig and astronomy. I can be County Surveyor when I get back.

May 19 . . . I am still Somewhere in France going to school like a darned kid. . . . We have been working harder than ever. I had an examination Saturday that would make the president of Yale University bald-headed scratching his head trying to think of answers. I think we'll all be nuttier than an Arkansas squirrel if we study this hard much longer. I am now an orienting officer (whatever that may be). From what I can gather in a casual survey of the situation, I am supposed to go out on the earth somewhere and find out where I am and then tell everybody else. It's a nice job as far as I can discover if I can get a little surveying, geometry, astronomy, and a few other things into my noodle inside the next three or four weeks. If it doesn't bust, I guess I can do it.[18]

Truman's class notes show that the course of study was divided into five parts: "I Elements of Firing, II Calculation of Data, III Ranging & Observation, IV Keeping of Records, [and] V Actual Firing." A glimpse of what our lieutenant labored over in the days before calculators replaced slide rules can be obtained from this small taste of the cryptic notes he kept in one of several pocket notebooks and pads used during his schooling, in this case, a French ledger book he labeled "Fire & Orientation":

> Battery in position at an altitude of 121 meters. Registration point has Y az of 918 map range 4210 altitude 111 meters. Target A is a Telegraph Central Y az 786. 1002 Map Rn5600 Altitude 110. At 14 o'clock you are ordered to fire on Target A and you decide to use a Trans out of fire from registration Pt. Use HE shell I fuse +++ Pvrd Temp +10
>
> > Soundage at 14 o'clock
> > wind 31-5 Pressure sea level 761
> > 200 32-4 Temp +17
> > 500 32-5
>
> You decide to fire enough rounds on registration point to get lot Ks or Dvo. Adjusted data on registration is Y az 900 & elevation (including site 8 57'). What is your Ko or DVo and what is initial elevation for Target A using K method of Tr[illegible]
>
> You are called on during night for harassing fire on Target B. Use same ammunition with IAL fuse. [19]

The army wisely made an effort to "take out the cobwebs that the studies put into our brains"[20] by instituting a team-oriented exercise program that also involved listening closely to instructions. It likely helped Truman get rid of some of the fat that he was worried about as well.

> We have a private park all enclosed within a high stone wall where we have O'Grady exercise every day from 11:30 to 12. These exercises almost kill some of us old men. The muscles of one of my arms and one of my legs are so sore I can hardly move them. [21]

Truman further explained:

> They make us run and walk and play leap frog and carry men on our backs and run relay races while we carry them. Then they line us up and give us exercises by separate command in which "O'Grady says"

has to precede each command[.] If a man moves at a command that isn't preceded by "O'Grady says," he has to run a hundred yards and back. Then they make a big ring and make everyone face in and one man runs around and hands out a couple of shellacking[s,] and the man on the right of the one who gets the whip has to run around the ring. If the one with the whip can catch him he wales the mischief out of him. It's sure funny to see a little short man like Major Gates or [Lt. Walter] Slagle try to get away from some long-legged guy much to the delight of the rest. I ran so fast the other day that I got a Charlie Horse and was not able to run for two days.[22]

TRUMAN REGULARLY ASSURED Bess in his letters that "French girls are pretty and chic, but they cannot hold a candle to American girls," adding, "Every man in the room agrees with me too." Still, he had to produce additional reassurance from time to time: "No, I haven't seen any girls that I'd care to look at twice, and when I'm happiest I am dreaming of you, so that ought to be the right and proper condition of mind, oughtn't it not?"[23] Hardly a letter went by where he didn't encourage her, directly or indirectly, to write: "It would surprise you to see what a grand glorious feeling it puts into a man over here to get a letter," said Truman. "Some of our dignified Majors & Captains simply go wild when they get one."[24] He also described a rare treat that he enjoyed during a brief Sunday trip away from camp:

I played the piano at the officer's YMCA at the town I visited today. It was the best piano I've seen since leaving USA. It was a dandy, evidently belonging to some rich Frenchman who had given his house for YMCA purposes. There were whole volumes of music by Mozart, Beethoven, Schliemann, Mendelshon [sic], Listz (can't spell 'em) and everyone else you ever heard of. It was sure a rest after the week's work.[25]

Although Truman was unfailingly modest about his performance at the artillery school—comments such as "I just barely sneaked through"[26] pepper his letters—he was singled out to command a mostly notional battalion during maneuvers conducted during an inspection by the AEF commander, whose headquarters was nearby at Chaumont.

> We had a maneuver yesterday and General Pershing himself was there. I was in command of a battalion of artillery and he didn't even come around to see if I could fire that many guns. I'm very happy that he didn't because we had more figures and things than would fill an old Ray's arithmetic. My part was mostly play-like except the figures. I was supposed to have three batteries which were represented by their second lieutenants. Had a second lieut. for adjutant and a major for regimental commander. We had a good time and walked about six miles besides. . . . We are going to have a critique on the problem today and I suppose will get a lot of useful and useless information. I'll sure be glad when we get back to the battery and don't have to figure $x-y = pdq$ or something else equally as enlightening.[27]

He and the other junior offers also took particular delight at another aspect of the maneuvers.

> There were Major Generals, Brigadiers, Colonels, Majors, and more limousines than a Tammany [Hall] funeral. It was a great pleasure to see a Major General click his heels together and nearly break his arm coming to a salute when the General came along. You don't often get to see Major Generals do that.[28]

After six weeks of close tutelage by Lt. Col. Richard C. Burleson (a cantankerous yet witty master of artillery who prefaced both praise and scorn with the words "By God!"), the detachment reached a high level proficiency in direct and indirect fire of the French 75mm field gun. Truman came to know him fairly well at Montigny, well enough to call him Dick Burleson in letters, and would meet him again during fighting to the north when circumstances on the 35th Division's flank dictated that Truman call for fire into the sector covered by Burleson's own guns.

This technical "proficiency" however, only involved the most basic elements of the employment of the guns, and the lack of time available to the AEF necessitated that training on other important aspects of fire support be dangerously abbreviated.

Colonel Burleson, like Danford, advocated pushing at least one battery of light artillery from each regiment out with a corresponding infantry regiment in order to supply direct and immediate support. The use of these "accompanying batteries" (or "infantry batteries") was a precursor to what in later years would be called combined-arms operations. The AEF's artillery commanders looked upon the idea favorably, and their infantry brethren always responded with an enthusiastic "yes" when the batteries were offered, but there was simply no time to train units up to the standards that such complex maneuvers required. Seasoned field artillery officers were painfully aware of the situation. Burleson's worries concerning the lack of preparation for mobile warfare, maintaining proper liaison between the disparate elements, and how this would affect their ability to seize and maintain the initiative, would soon be confirmed. In a postwar assessment of the situation he wrote:

> A very brief study of the problem of conducting the fire of a battery of field artillery discloses the fact that while the mechanism of the conduct of fire is relatively simple, the application of the same on the manœuvre field . . . is very much more difficult. In fact, I think that I am safe in saying that it is one of the most difficult problems that confronts the field artillery officer.
>
> It must also be realized that the problem that confronted the field artillery at the time of its reorganization for the World War was that of attacking and defending lines which had been fixed in position for more than two years, and on ground about which everything was known. [Thus,] the instruction of the battery commanders and lieutenants . . . followed the natural line that relat[ed] to map and precision firing. The amount of instruction in the open field methods of conduct of fire with its rapid changes of position and quick, but only approximate, adjustment of fire was, unfortunately, very limited.

To expect the young and inexperienced officers to quickly adapt themselves to an old but, unfortunately to them, strange method of the conduct of fire about which they knew very little, was expecting too much.[29]

While the training of "fire and maneuver" was very limited, Truman apparently absorbed much of what Danford and Burleson expounded—especially the need to operate with initiative and daring. In a few short months, he would become one of the relatively few American battery commanders who, while operating well forward, were lucky enough spot German batteries in reach of their guns. When these opportunities presented themselves to Truman, he displayed both initiative and a high level of craft by successfully setting down indirect fire on German artillery batteries "out of sector" on his division's exposed flank in spite of being ordered not to (and was later publicly applauded for doing so). But, right now, Truman was simply relieved to have "passed all the exams" and that the army wouldn't "send me home for inefficiency yet."[30]

Unbeknownst to Lieutenant Truman, General Berry had recommended him for promotion effective April 23, 1918. Five other officers, including Ted Marks, had also been approved for various ranks, and the War Department duly rubber-stamped Berry's decision on May 2. As was custom, the list of promotions was released to the press. However, if any official notification was sent back to headquarters at Camp Doniphan, it was lost as the division scrambled to ship out, and was not forwarded to either Truman or his commander in France, Major Gates. Truman, and even Bess, had heard the most recent rumors—all of which could be traced back to Captain Allen—that he would soon wear twin bars on his shoulders, but that was all. Truman would find out about his promotion the following month when, at his next duty station, another officer showed him an old copy of the *New York Times* that had his new status listed in tiny type among the promotions and transfers of a thousand or more other officers.

CHAPTER 7

"Dizzy D"

T HE DETACHMENT FINISHED its schooling on Saturday, June 8, and it was none too soon for Truman who wrote, "I've worked $x-y = bvd$ until I'm plum dizzy." By now, the 35th Division's 60th Field Artillery Brigade was gathering at Angers, some 250 miles west, as its elements arrived in stages from the United States, and Truman felt, "It will almost be like home to get with the regiment again." The detachment entrained the next day on "another grand trip across France,"[1] and Lt. Arthur W. Wilson found Truman a good traveling companion:

> I was amazed at his knowledge of French history. For example, on this troop train the officers rode in the first class compartments, (the men were back in the box cars, the 40 and 8 cars—40 men or 8 horses). He had maps and he knew where we were going. It didn't mean anything to me that we were going across eastern France. And he said, "Art, we've got an hour here in Orleans and down two, three blocks from the station is the statue of Joan of Arc. Let's go down and look at it."[2]

Upon reaching Angers on June 11, the men marched to Brain-sur-l'Authion, five miles east of the city, and billeted throughout the area. Gates was assigned two comfortable rooms at a local inn and chose Truman to share his quarters. Truman found that his Battery F had not yet arrived, but this was of little matter, since Gates was having him transferred out of the unit so that he could work as the 2nd Battalion adjutant, today called an executive officer or "XO." The officers from Montigny immediately set about establishing brigade- and regimental-level schools, with some teaching assignments being parceled out randomly, such as Wilson coordinating the instruction of noncommissioned officers, while others were assigned on the basis of what the officer appeared to be strongest in. With Paterson's promotion to captain and ascension to the 129th's regimental adjutant, Truman found himself taking the lead to "organize a regimental school and teach the balance of the officers what I learned (which won't be a whole lot)."[3] For Truman, this aspect of his double-duty job was a little troubling:

> I just barely sneaked through at the school and now they've got me teaching trig & logarithms and surveying and engineering and a lot of other high-brow stuff that nearly cracks my head open to learn just before class. . . . If some inquisitive nut asks me a question, I'm up the creek and usually answer him by telling him he's ahead of the schedule and I'll tell him tomorrow. Then I'm safe to look it up and still have my prestige. Some system.[4]

One can't feel too sorry for Truman, since he'd known all along that this was coming, and he eventually came to enjoy the irony of "an old rube to be handing knowledge (of a sort) to the Harvard and Yale boys."[5] Truman was more secure in his work with the battalion. "A right hefty job," he said, "and one that gives me precedence over all the Battery captains, even if they do outrank me."[6] In the beginning, the regiment had no telephone equipment on hand except for a pitifully small amount reserved for training, and he told Bess, "I nearly walked my legs off paying visits to various places where the batteries are quartered."[7] But even had there been equipment, the phone and messengers (often called "runners") would not provide the "eyes on" that the new exec wanted, so Truman had to take to the roads at least twice daily. His major combat and support units were spread from headquarters in Brain to a crossroads a mile to the north and then east another mile to Andard and its environs, where all of the 1st Battalion's batteries were billeted.

It was here that both the 129th and 128th received their first issue of French 75mm guns, caissons, and horses. Lieutenant Lee wrote, "The daily program was consequently a busy one. In the morning, drill of the battery; in the afternoon more drills, schools for officers and non-commissioned officers and special details; and in the evening more schools, and study."[8] Very little firing of live rounds was done at this time, and wouldn't until the brigade's field artillery regiments moved to the wide spaces of nearby Coetquidan. The men were immediately impressed with the gun and its superb recoil system, but were appalled at the condition of the horses. It was bad enough that the strange French harnesses used for hitching up the beasts gave the Missouri wagon and caisson drivers fits, but most of the horses were weak castaways of the French Army's earlier battles, and 1st Section Sgt. Edward "Squatty" Meisburger was certain that "some had already been subject to gas" that greatly damaged their lungs and observed that the animals turned over to the battery included farm horses unused either to operating in teams or being harnessed to a limber, the long pole that anchors the rearmost horses to a caisson. Worse yet, their allotment contained stallions, which, it would soon become apparent, were unused to heavy work of any kind. But the soldiers could hardly refuse them. "The war had been going on since 1914," said 2nd Section gunner Cpl. Eugene Donnelly, and they "were pretty picked over."[9]

This was an army-wide problem for which there was no good solution. The need to get massive numbers of soldiers to France as quickly as possible, together with the limited amount of shipping to haul them across the Atlantic, necessitated that through August 1918 only officers' mounts be allowed to take up space on the troop transports. These few animals represented only a tiny percentage of the AEF's requirements in spite of table-of-organization cuts,* and the hundreds of thousands of American horses and mules left behind had to be replaced by U.S. Army purchasing agents in France, Britain, and Spain. The result at Truman's level was the sad collection of French beasts turned over to the 129th. The regiment was informed that the situation was unlikely to improve.

It was while Truman was at Angers that he received the news of Rufus F. Montgall's death in letters from both Bess and his sister Mary, hastily penned after the War Department's June 8 casualty list was released to the newspapers. Truman's second cousin on his father's side, Montgall was a captain in the Quartermaster Corps and a member of the 1st Division, which was preparing to assault Cantigny at the tip of the German penetration north of Paris. No one knew it at the time, but he was not with his unit when killed, but at Chaumont during an air raid on the AEF headquarters area shortly before Pershing had inspected Truman's detachment. With American troops finally beginning to pour into France, the German high command had evidently chosen that moment to try to disorganize and dispirit the Americans by harassing—and if they were extraordinarily lucky, killing—the AEF commander.

Today, the event doesn't even rate a footnote. Montgall's death coincided with no epic battles, occurring between the German's Lys and Aisne offensives, was two weeks before his division attacked Cantigny, and fifty miles from the nearest frontline trenches at Saint-Mihiel. Because of Montgall's rank (he was also the second officer from Kansas City to be killed in the war), his name topped the list of 108 American killed and wounded during this lull in the fighting. The British term for

---

* Because of the shortage, the number of animals allowed to the 35th and other combat divisions was reduced in January 1918 from 7,701 to 7,578, and in June to 6,663, but slow deliveries plus losses due principally to fatigue among already substandard animals resulted in few divisions being able to attain even this number. In August, when the shortage was greatest, it was proposed to motorize artillery brigades and other units and cut the number of animals per division to 3,803.

such losses was "normal wastage," and Truman took the opportunity to indirectly prepare Bess and his family in case the worst happened:

> You can never tell what will happen to you in this war. . . . I was mighty sorry to hear of Rufe Montgall's death. Hadn't heard until I got your, and Mary's, letters. He was a fine boy and his mother's only child. The French say, *"C'est la guerre."* One old lady over here had eight sons killed. She asked that the ninth one be sent to the reserves. Her request was granted but before the order got there he was also killed. They are stoics though and are satisfied to give all for the principle they are fighting for. I'm for the French more and more. They are the bravest of the brave. If there were only millions more. [10]

THE ARTILLERYMEN HAD another two months of training ahead of them, but the rest of the 35th Division, which had been stationed close behind the lines near Epinal for their own training, was already preparing to move into a "quiet" sector along the front where they would be supported by a French artillery brigade. The 60th Field Artillery Brigade began shifting its units from the Angers area to Camp Coetquidan on Sunday, July 7. Napoleon Bonaparte, himself an artilleryman, had established Coetquidan as an artillery training center more than a century before the first doughboy pulled a lanyard at the site. The ensuing decades had seen little change, as cannons continued to be smoothbore weapons with little more than incremental modifications. The advent of rifled barrels, better propellants, and other improvements allowed shells to be fired at greater and greater distances and prompted a profound expansion of the camp. By the time that Truman's and the other regiments arrived, "The military reservation was a large one, and even included some abandoned villages, and wind-mills and farms, woods and quarries; all of which furnished a great variety of targets for practice firing under conditions closely resembling those at the front."[11]

Coetquidan, today the home of the École Spéciale Militaire de Saint-Cyr, the French national military academy, had grown to the point that it could and did handle two artillery brigades simultaneously, even boasting three YMCAs for the men and one for the officers. Its atmosphere was much like that at Camp Doniphan, and the heady news of victories won by the first American units in combat provided an added edge and urgency to the training. Although Coetquidan appeared much like the more developed training camps in the United States, dirt floors were the rule in the enlisted billets (the officers' quarters had flooring), and the roofs were not completely rainproof, which resulted in a constant dampness that encouraged illness during the wet summer that year. For the men eager to get into the fight, though, the important difference between Angers and Coetquidan was the ability to shoot, shoot, and shoot now that French equipment and ordnance was flowing to them.

Sadly for Truman, his work took him away from the guns. Battalion adjutant was an important job, with wide-ranging authority to operate in Major Gates's name, yet was outside of the formal chain of command running down to the batteries and logistical elements. He had made no secret of his desire to lead men in combat, but in his current position he commanded everyone and no one, with trouble of infinite variety lurking around every corner. No sooner had the 129th marched into Coetquidan, and barely a month in the job, than Truman was ordered to report to Gates's boss, regimental commander Klemm, with no explanation of what was up.

> On the 10th of July the Colonel sent for me. I went over everything I'd done for the last ten days to see if I could find out what I was to be balled [bawled] out for, but could think of nothing. I waited around in his office until he'd dressed down a second lieutenant or two and then my time came. He suddenly said to me, "Harry, how would you like to command a battery?"
>
> "Well sir," I said, "I hope to be able to do that some day."
>
> "All right, you'll take command of D Battery in the morning."[12]

So, he wasn't being court-marshaled, being sent home to train new recruits, or receiving a tongue lashing for some ghastly infraction, but the news was ominous in other ways.

I saluted about faced and walked out. Then I told the Major that my tour of duty in France would be short because Klemm had given me D Battery. They were the wild Irish and German Catholics from Rockhurst Academy [High School] in Kansas City. They had had four commanders before me. I wasn't a Catholic. I was a 3rd Degree Mason. I could just see my hide on the fence when I tried to run that outfit.[13]

While occasionally touching on the roughneck tendencies of the battery in oral histories conducted after Truman's presidency, with few exceptions its members steadfastly maintained that any problems that earlier Capts. Charles B. Allen and Rollin Ritter may have had were completely of their own making. (The members appear to have had a certain affection for the man Truman replaced, John H. Thacher, who was moved into the adjutant slot at 1st Battalion.) Whatever is the truth of that, Battery D did in fact have a "reputation" and a nickname, "Dizzy D," and was a physically imposing bunch that filled much of the 129th's sports teams (wrestling, boxing, tug of war, basketball, and football) in competitions with other regiments. This was so much the case that Instrument Sergeant Fred Bowman quipped that when a team "came out of the 129th Field Artillery, it wasn't a 129th Field Artillery, it was a Battery D team." Bowman may have also offered the best analysis— certainly the best spin—on the why his battery was looked upon warily by the regiment: "Until we started filling up with some draftees . . . we were all high school graduates and many were college men; and were just the type that . . . could be led, but they couldn't be driven."[14]

It also appears that one of the reasons that the men were so fond of Captain Thacher was because keeping them in line was not high on his priority list. In one letter home, Thacher matter-of-factly mentioned that he got the men to France "without having any of them get into very serious trouble."[15] How "very serious" the trouble had to get before he intervened is unknown, but much of the battery— including six sergeants—was under arrest in quarters when Truman got the assignment, principally for various infractions falling under the general heading of "disorderly conduct," such as drunkenness, refusal to obey orders, and failing to report for reveille. Truman knew all about this and more, since he had mess at the same table as Thacher and Father Tiernan, and his good friend Pete Allen had been involved in a disturbing incident with the battery just before Truman took command. Allen went over to quiet some soldiers who were "raising a little devil down there" and the men "formed a big circle around him chanting, 'Hurray for Pistol Pete!'"[16]

Colonel Klemm and Lieutenant Colonel Elliott had decided that if Truman couldn't get Dizzy D turned around quickly, they were going to "break up" the battery by dispersing the troublemakers throughout the regiment, refilling its ranks through a draft of the other batteries and supply echelon. At 6:30 a.m. on Thursday, July 11, 1st Sgt. Glen Woolridge called the men to attention before their new commander. Writing in the third person some years later, Truman confessed that he "was so badly scared he couldn't say a word and he could feel the battery sizing him up and wondering how much they could put over him."[17] He was right.

D's blacksmith, Sgt. Edward L. Sandifer, had served with Truman when he was a driver in Battery B. Sergeant McKim recalled that Sandifer "gave us the tip off on the new captain," and McKim had seen enough of Truman in Kansas City to form the opinion that he was a "sissy."[18] The men were curious, but did not care much one way or the other who was in command. Private Vere "Pup" Leigh's comment likely echoed the thinking of most of them: "We'd have officers go through our outfit and this was just one more as far as the Battery was concerned.... I knew that there was somebody named Truman down there in F Battery, but that was the end of it. It didn't mean anything anymore than Joe Jones, you know."[19] According to bugler Albert A. Ridge, however, there was a sizable contingent that took Thacher's ouster personally:

> Thacher had been well loved by all the men in the battery. . . .
> When it was learned that Captain Truman had been assigned
> to Battery D, there was a good deal of talk about mutiny, about
> causing trouble. . . . There was a stirring among the fellows in the

rank. Although they were standing at attention, you could feel the Irish blood boiling—as much as to say, if this guy thinks he's going to take us over, he's mistaken. I think perhaps Captain Truman could feel it too.[20]

"[Thacher] was an emotional type guy," said Leigh. "But Truman wasn't, and he stood there and he was kind of a rather short fellow, compact, serious face, wearing glasses; and we'd had all kinds of officers and this was just another one you know. And he announced to the Battery that he was going to be in charge, and when he gave orders he wanted them carried out. He made it pretty plain." Ridge describes what happened after Truman's jarringly brief address:

He looked the battery over, up and down the entire line, about three times, and the men were all waiting for the castigation that they really knew they were entitled to from a new commander because of their previous conduct. But Harry Truman, he just continued to look at them, and then his only command to the battery was—"Dismissed!"

Well, of course the dismissed battery went toward their barracks. But I think that that command to the Irish group was a sort of benediction. He had not castigated them. He had dismissed them as much as to say—like the Good Lord said to Mary Magdalene—"Go and sin no more." From that time on I knew that Harry Truman had captured the hearts of those Irishmen.

This impression was far from universal. "He turned the Battery over to the First Sergeant," said Leigh, "and the First Sergeant told us to fall out, and then we gave Captain Truman the Bronx cheer, that's a fact." Truman ignored it—for now—and walked on while, according to Cpl. Harry Murphy, "remarks were heard such as, 'Well, I wonder how long he will last.'" Murphy added, "To squelch any doubt that he intended to last a long time, his first move was to call a meeting of us noncommissioned officers, saying, 'I am sure you men know the rules and regulations. *I* will issue the orders and *you* are responsible for them being carried out.'"[21] Further, according to Murphy, Truman told the noncoms, "I didn't come over here to get along with you. You've got to get along with me. And if there are any of you who can't, speak up right now and I'll bust you right back now."[22]

The first test was not long in coming. More horses and equipment had been made available to the Americans upon their arrival at Coetquidan and, before a mounted drill, some of the men precipitated an equine riot by allowing some large number of beasts to "accidentally" get free. A wild scene ensued as cannoneers tried to corral the stampede among the guns and caissons. More soldiers joined in on the fun by making an ostentatious, shouting show of rounding up the careening animals. The instigators had likely hoped to send their new captain into a frenzy trying to control the chaos and, if the Gods of War were on their side, the prissy fellow might even be catapulted into the dirt by his own spooked horse. Truman, however, was a practiced horseman and kept his mount well under control. He also understood exactly what was going on and was apparently amused that the men would go to such trouble just for him. After briefly surveying the performance from atop his horse, he smiled and instructed the sergeants to put things in order.

The next ruckus occurred that night. A long line of local drinking establishments dotted a road called "the Pike" from the camp all the way to the Guer railhead and, as usual, a goodly portion of Dizzy D had visited them after duty hours and was drunk again. Later in the barracks, Corporal Murphy called out to a large gathering of crap shooters and onlookers that it would be "lights out" soon, and was knocked out cold for his trouble. A rumble ensued, and daylight found four soldiers reporting to the infirmary with a variety of injuries. Someone also spotted a new battery order prominently posted, and saw that it included a long list of names. "The next morning, on the bulletin board," said Leigh, "about half of the noncoms and most of the first class privates were busted. And then we knew that we had a different 'cat' to do business with than we had up to that time. He didn't hesitate at all."[23]

Truman had been keeping close tabs on who had taken him seriously and who hadn't. Battery clerk Cpl. Leo P. Keenan (soon to be Truman's own "Radar O'Reilly") typed up the orders, and the men found out that "This cookie meant business."[24] Not only was it a public punishment of some of the most visible characters in the unit, but a costly one as well for the twenty or so men involved, since all were now relegated to a common private's pay of $30 per month. The first-class privates had lost $2, and the sergeants, a whopping $8. Four promotions to sergeant would follow in a few days—and Captain Truman was keeping a close eye on First Sergeant Woolridge—but for now, he wanted to make things perfectly clear to the somewhat smaller group of NCOs before him. According to Eddy Meisburger, Truman warned them, "I can't be monkeying with these people down the line that want to cut up some. That's up to the sergeants and corporals to take care of that."[25]

TRUMAN "PRACTICALLY TURNED THE BATTERY OVER to the noncommissioned officers," and Corporal Murphy believed "that was the key to his success." His move immediately instilled confidence, and "it gave us to understand that he was going to back us up to the hilt for anything that we did. All we had to do was do our duty and he was going to back us up, and he did."[26] Some men still "tried him out," said Private Leigh. "That's the nature of a soldier. [But] every time they tried him out, they got the worst of it." The new captain couldn't just fire a man to get rid of him, as was done on the rough railroad work gangs of his youth. Consequently, Battery D's extra duty roster, Truman's personal roster and reference book, and the battery's official correspondence book display a steep uptick in punishments and rewards after Truman's arrival. One week after taking command, he tried, and failed, to have a recent arrival at Battery D, Pvt. John V. Sands, court-martialed on July 18, but ultimately had to be content with simply having radioman Sands and five other soldiers transferred out on the last day of the month. Major Gates denied the proposed transfer of a seventh soldier. Leigh guessed that "it took him about a week or ten days to convince everybody he was boss."[27] And it also didn't hurt, recalled Pvt. Floyd Rickets, a gunner, that the mess food noticeably improved and that the soldiers "found also that he was much interested personally in each individual."[28]

Even before all the men had come around, it was clear to Sergeant McKim (who had originally thought him a "sissy") that Truman "not only commanded the outfit, he owned it."[29] Truman's appearance coincided with an extensive period of daily gunnery drills and related training that soon showed some surprising results. In spite of Battery D's well-earned reputation as a "problem unit" and steadily deteriorating discipline since its departure from Camp Doniphan, the men had generally performed adequately in their duties. Almost overnight, however, the battery seemed to have caught fire. Truman wrote Bess: "They were so anxious to please me and fire good that one of my gunners got the buck ague* and simply blew up. I had to take him out. When I talked to him about it he almost wept and I felt so sorry for him I didn't even call him down."[30] Within a week, D was outscoring the other batteries, and at least one officer teased their proud captain by Irishing his name—"O'Truman." He wrote:

> I have the Irish Catholic Battery but they seem to like me pretty well and I am satisfied that . . . . The men are as fine a bunch as were ever gotten together but they have been lax in discipline. Can you imagine me being a hard-boiled captain of a tough Irish Battery? . . . I've been most everything and done most everything in this man's army since August 5 and now I have attained my one ambition, to be a Battery commander. If I can only make good at it, I can hold my head up anyway the rest of my days.[31]
>
> If I am a success as the commanding officer of a Battery of field artillery I shall have accomplished the best thing I could do in this war. I have my doubts about my bravery when heavy-explosive shells and gas attacks begin. I am like a fellow Uncle Harry used tell about. I have the bravest kind of head and body but my legs won't stand.[32]

---

*"Buck ague" is a game hunter's term which, in this case, indicates that the soldier reached such a state of nervous agitation in anticipation of the day's drill that he was unable to perform his role within the gun squad properly, possibly freezing up completely at the opening of the session.

The French kept the ammunition coming, and the battery continued to do well during increasingly complex gunnery exercises. At one point Major Gates called his other battery captains, Pete Allen and Spencer Salisbury, over to Truman's unit so that D Battery could demonstrate some aspect of battery fire. This greatly satisfied some of the battery's men, as a rivalry existed between them and Salisbury's E Battery:

> My Irish Battery went out on the range the other day and outfired the others in the battalion, on account of which I am rather swelled up. The major remarked that "D Battery is all right" and then he proceeded to tell the others why they weren't. I was awful lucky. [33]

Truman was luckier than he realized at the time. It was on Monday, July 29, as the time neared for the 60th Field Artillery Brigade to rejoin the 35th Division, that a new lieutenant reported for duty at his unit; a burly, black-mustached fellow named Victor H. Housholder. As with the appointment of Eddie Jacobson the year before as canteen steward, this was fortuitous. The Arizona man proved to be an extremely effective XO—a virtual alter ego to his captain—and just how effective became almost immediately apparent. With Housholder's arrival, Truman now had a full complement of officers: a senior first lieutenant (Housholder) in charge of the firing battery and serving as adjutant; a junior first lieutenant (Gordon B. Jordan) in charge of the ammunition train; a senior second lieutenant in charge of the back-echelon personnel and the firing battery's horses, which would be kept as nearly out of danger as possible; and a junior second lieutenant in charge of the "supply train" of *fourgons*, small French wagons.

More horses were turned over to the battery shortly before its move to the front, and with the arrival of another experienced horseman and artillerist in the outfit, Housholder, Truman immediately delegated the job of honing the battery's technical proficiencies in the little time it had left. While leading a detail on mounted, cross-country training, Housholder noticed that the 130th Field Artillery, which moved out before the 129th, was loading up their big 155mm howitzers at the Guer railhead—change of plans. The lieutenant led the men over and ordered them to observe the proceedings closely because they would soon be performing the exact same tasks.

Within days, the expected orders came down for the 129th to depart Camp Coetquidan on Sunday, August 18. Unlike Truman's seven pages of technical notes on this subject in one of his pocket notebooks (all legibly hand-printed in small letters so that it could be passed to subordinates as needed), Housholder's account of the train-up and rail loading provides such a clear description of the command relationships and interaction between Truman, his officers, and his men that extended portions of it are worth reproducing in full:

> Much detailed instructions came down to us thru channels, and much time was given over to putting these instructions into action. On the day preceding our departure, Capt. Truman assembled his complete light field artillery battery; and I mean complete down to the last item, for the first time. This involved much last minute checking & many last minute requisitions to fill out shortages. . . .
>
> With all details attended to and cared for, we made a practice march down to the loading ramp or dock at the Guer station. There we went through a complete (but simulated) action of entraining our outfit. We ironed out many difficulties and snarls & worked out an organizational procedure that really paid off the next day when we took on the "real McCoy."
>
> It would be in order, I think, to interject here a bit of detail concerning the physical layout at the railroad station, so the reader can better follow the procedure. In the railroad yards at a rail head such as this one at Guer, there are long wooden platforms with a ramp at each end, standing alongside a railroad track. These platforms are strong enough and long enough to accommodate the type of mobile unit that they are to be used for. Accordingly, when you come in to entrain, you move your equipment up the proper ramp, depending upon which direction you are heading out and string it out full length on the platform. When your train

is spotted—and it must be made up in proper sequence, with flats [flat cars] for material & wagon equipment; box cars for horses (animals); box cars for men, etcetera, etcetera—you receive the "green light" to proceed entraining.

As we came into the yards—Aug. 18, 1918, to entrain, Capt. Truman had turned the battery over to my command, as he had ridden on ahead to ascertain which track ramp and platform we would load on. I was met by one of the captain's orderlies just at the edge of town and escorted to the yards over the proper route that would lead to our platform. As we approached the proper spot, the "halt" and "at ease" orders were given & I proceeded to report to Capt. Truman at the station that the outfit was there and ready to entrain. The regimental commander, Colonel Klemm, a couple of Lieut. Colonels; three Majors; several Captains, including Capt. Truman were in a confab with the French Station Master & several attached United States Army officers when I approached the group. As I reported to Capt. Truman, I was told to hold the unit "at ease" until our train was spotted & at that time I would be advised to proceed. Very fortunately we did not have to wait too long.

As I reached the ramp, at the head of the column, I was met by Capt. Truman & the station master & was advised that the loading operations would be done, under a stopwatch—the reason for such procedure being very obvious because there were several outfits entraining here each week, and time was important & valuable. With my assurance that all was in readiness, the station master gave us the "green light," & with the stopwatch moving & Capt. Truman now in command, the unit moved up the ramp, onto the platform & strung out alongside the train. When the unit was in proper position on the platform, Captain Truman halted it, & turned to me with the command, "Lieutenant, take charge & proceed to entrain the battery. Report to me at the station when ready to move out."

I'm not going to burden you any further with details. I had that battery really organized & instructed for this particular

occasion. Each sergeant (section chief) had his particular duties
to perform & when completed, he was to get to his respective
lieutenant on the dead run & so report. When a lieutenant's
command had reported completely to him, he was to do likewise
in getting such information to me, & when I received the report
from the last lieutenant, I dashed to Capt. Truman at the station
& so reported to him & the station master. I was met by a couple
of stares, but the stopwatch was stopped.[34]

The regimental history reports that all of the rail loadings were
"accomplished by each battery in turn in about an hour" except one:
"The R.T.O. [rail transportation officer] at Guer officially advised
D Battery that its time of loading, 48 minutes, was the best record
time up to that date."[35] Thus, the unit that was "always in trouble"
and on the verge of being broken up just five weeks earlier had left
the artillery school having established both a firing record and a
logistical record.

THE LONG, SLOW, "LEISURELY GAIT across France"[36] was old hat to
Truman by now, but for most of the men in Battery D and the 129th, the
three-day journey in boxcars labeled *"chevaux 8 hommes 40"* ("8 horses
or 40 men") seemed strange and foreboding after the excitement of their
departure wore off. The men were ordered to keep legs and arms inside
the boxcars, but doors were open wide, and all craned to get a distant
look at the Eiffel Tower as they skirted past the southern environs of
magical Paris. Pulled by one of those "toy" engines that Truman always
found so amusing, the battery occupied one of eight trains traveling an
hour apart and consisting of seventeen flatcars, thirty boxcars, a first-
class passenger coach for Truman and his lieutenants, and a caboose at
each end, the car in front of the engine for the convenience of the engine
crew. Beyond the guns, men, and horses on the six trains carrying the
firing batteries were "caissons, *fourgons, chariots-du-pare,* and rolling
kitchens, extra rations, barracks-bags, battery records, fire-control
instruments, etc., and horses, harness, hay and feed, horseshoeing
and saddlers' outfits, mechanics' tools, extra supplies of various sorts,

and all that goes to make up the equipment of an artillery regiment, for a trip of indefinite length in time and distance."[37]

Neither enlisted men nor horses were allowed off of the train: only the officers, noncommissioned officers, and the mess detail responsible for distributing rations could detrain. The sergeants performed regular inspections of such things as bedding and the rudimentary toilet facilities in each boxcar. Horses were given rubdowns, and manure was shoveled out the doors even as the train was underway. At each of the frequent water and coal stops, one horse would be carefully walked back and forth within the confines of its boxcar so that at least some of the stiffness could be worked out of its legs. The trains ran essentially nonstop.

The men were never officially told where they were or where they were going, and the town names on the little stations they passed told them nothing. They could tell, however, that shortly after rolling past Paris, their train began to travel in a generally southeast direction instead of east. After one of the afternoon coal and water stops on the second day out, the sergeants told the men to check all their gear while they still had some daylight because they were nearing their destination. That night, they noticed that the towns they passed were thoroughly darkened, and if there were farms and chateaus along the way—surely there must be some—no light was allowed to escape from their rooms. By now, all knew how many stops there were till the battery detrained, and for the soldiers who couldn't sleep, a nervous countdown began, ending only when the train began to slow before the black, angular roofline of Saulxures after midnight on Tuesday, August 20, 1918.

CHAPTER 8

"Un Secteur Tranquil"

THE LITTLE ENGINE SLOWLY PUFFED and rumbled to a halt amid the sounds of squealing brakes and a final cough of steam. Like every other town they had passed that night, Saulxures was blacked out for fear of air attack, with only a few railroad workers carrying easily extinguished lanterns. Truman, followed by Jordan, Housholder, and the second lieutenants, hopped off and exchanged introductions with the liaison party of American and French junior officers who would see to it that Battery D's sections were secreted in the right locations. Then the lieutenants, flashlights in hand, moved off to make a quick inspection of the wooden station platform and ramps. The battery's sergeants were already organizing—and quieting—the men as they disgorged from their boxcars, and more lanterns came dimly to life up and down the line while the men awaited orders to move their equipment and horses.

As Truman discussed his soldiers' billeting with the liaison officers, the gun-section sergeants reported to Housholder and supply section sergeants to Jordan. With all present and accounted for, Housholder gave the order to detrain. Stable Sgt. Joseph Wimmers carefully released the long-suffering animals one boxcar at a time, and they were immediately led to a watering spot by a bridge that joined the station and town. Meanwhile, chief mechanic Wooden supervised the frenzy of activity along the flatcars as guns and rolling stock were unlashed and manhandled across to the platform and down the ramps to await the horses' return.

This was the first—but far from the last—time that Truman and his men would haul themselves and all their implements of war from a train in the black of night. Battery D had engaged in a night gunnery exercise at Coetquidan, but there had certainly been no preparation for this, and all were relieved that the maneuver went off smoothly, and excited about what was to come. As the activity slid into a temporary lull, they experienced another first when it was noticed that a low, almost imperceptible rumble, rumble, rumble drifted through the air. Was it thunder? They didn't know it at the time, but it was the big French guns near Saint-Die; a sound that would remain, in some fashion, a constant companion for the next three months.

The horses were unused to watering at night and likely drank little, but it was important to have them walk out some of the stiffness before being hitched to the wagons and limbers. Leaving the process to the section sergeants, the lieutenants reformed around Truman, who told them that the liaison officers would direct elements of the battery to their assigned destinations and that all carriages were to be parked "under trees or close alongside buildings to prevent, as far as possible, their being seen from the air."[1] Suddenly the men were startled by a series of deep booms and rolling reverberations more near at hand that were unmistakably the sound of large-caliber cannons at the front. Said Housholder, "It was indeed a strange and indescribable feeling and realization."[2]

Every piece of equipment had been loaded and unloaded from the train in proper march echelon, so Captain Truman's unit, still called the "bay horse battery" in spite of the mangy assortment of French animals they now possessed, was ready to move the moment it received a final check. Surveying the scene as best he could from his own mount in the darkness, he heard 1st Sgt. Glen Woolridge call out, "Drivers to the front," followed by "Harness and hitch" from the section sergeants. The sound of shuffling feet and hooves drifted through the station; there were more orders, clanks, bangs, and the dull rubbing and slapping of leather gear worked by a hundred hands as harnesses were fastened and carriages hitched. Soon the sergeants began to call out to Housholder and Jordan, "Section 2 ready!" "Section 5 ready!" "Section 1 ready!" The final reports in, Housholder notified Truman, and with a "Prepare to mount! Cannoneers and drivers mount! Right by section! March!" Battery D clattered across the bridge and toward the dark shapes of Saulxures.

Morning reveille on Wednesday, August 20, came too soon and saw the artillerymen emerging from a scattering of pup tents erected close under the trees, makeshift frame barracks, and hay lofts above Alsatian stables. The officers were quartered in the comparative elegance of private houses, and Truman stepped outside to behold an almost picture-postcard scene that, despite the dull pounding of guns in the far distance and the comings and goings of uniformed Frenchmen and Americans, looked absolutely untouched by war. Housholder found Saulxures a "beautiful little French village," and Truman's good friend Lieutenant Lee later wrote:

> It nestled among the mountains, or the beginnings of the mountains, on the banks of the Moselotte, and was clean, prosperous and attractive. Near the eastern end of the long main street was a large public fountain, with a big trough, rectangular and divided into compartments, in which, respectively, horses were watered, laundry done, and water drawn. Farther down was the substantial, spired church, with its adjoining cemetery, and across from it the Mairie or City Hall, where our regiment had its headquarters. Pretty good stores, not large, but with a fair supply of necessities and reasonable luxuries, were to be found; and a hotel where a most creditable and appetizing meal could be had.[3]

Ominously, however, the view from town also offered a glimpse of what the regiment would soon be facing farther to the east. Said Lee, "Across the river, as well as above the village on this side, were the heavily wooded and increasingly abrupt ridges of the Vosges Mountains, here beginning to assume a size suggestive of their character as foot-hills of the Alps."

With the exception of the work details taking care of the horses and cleaning harness, Mess Sgt. John Carney's section, the officers, and Truman's ever-attentive battery clerk, Corporal Keenan, Battery D— indeed the whole regiment—settled in for what one private referred to as "three days of rest."[4] The completion of morning drill freed most men for the rest of the day, and they contented themselves with wandering about the town, taking in the sights. All, that is, except the head of the machine-gun squad, Sgt. Theodore Murphy, who missed the drill and got slapped with extra duty. There was even some entertainment provided for the men in the form of a German air attack about a half-dozen miles to the east in the general vicinity of where elements of their brigades' 130th Field Artillery were forming.

"We saw first a puff of white smoke high in air," said Lee, "then another, and another, till twenty-five or thirty were floating at once lightly and gracefully. Then we saw that an aeroplane was the cause of it all; and these were the smoke of anti-air-craft shrapnel fired at it as it passed over the Allied lines."[5] Such displays would become almost as regular a feature as the constant drum of artillery and the fascinated men on the ground *never* lost interest in them. The 130th, which had arrived with its 155mm howitzers a few days before the 129th, was settling into its battle positions when the attack came, and thus had a ringside seat. Said one of its battery commanders, Capt. William MacLean, "It was hard to keep men at work with this free show going on right over their heads and the putt-putt-putt of machine guns and crack of the archies [anti-aircraft guns] quite close."[6] If Truman noticed the activity, he didn't consider it worth mentioning.

There was no "three days rest" for the captain and his lieutenants. Although Truman apparently sampled the local beer, which met with his approval, he spent his time with paperwork; meetings with battalion commander Gates and the other battery captains; an inspection of the horses with Lieutenant Jordan; attempts to acquire more animals; and skinning Sergeant Murphy. (The disciplining of Pvts. Harry Dabner, Chester Smith, and Earl Van Buskirk, who had been caught "hanging [their] feet out of the boxcar door,"[7] a dangerous practice and severe breach of regulations, was handled further down the command chain.) With, as yet, no maps of where his unit was going, he likely pored over whatever Lieutenant Colonel Elliott at headquarters could scare up. The inveterate letter-writer didn't even have time to pen a quick note to Bess.

Major Gates informed Truman that he was to inspect his assigned position at the front, and that a truck would pick up him and his reconnaissance party at 5 a.m. the next morning, August 21. At the appointed time, Truman turned over his roster to Jordan and climbed up next to the driver as Housholder, Sgts. Fred Bowman and George Brice (respectively the instrument and telephone sergeants) squeezed into the back of the diminutive army truck with the rest of the detail. Not knowing that the captain had left, an old high school buddy of Truman's serving with Battery E, Lt. Bill Bostain, later took the occasion of returning a pair of Dizzy D drunks as a perfectly good reason to pay Truman a visit, and he personally marched the miscreants home only to find his friend gone.

Other reconnaissance parties would follow the next day, but apparently Truman's group was the only one from the 2nd Battalion being sent forward, and for good reason. Half of the 129th's guns, Batteries B, E, and F, were to replace French artillery units in existing positions while A and C went into abandoned sites that required some rehabilitation. Battery D, however, was being sent high up on Mount Herrenberg more than 2,200 feet above the valley floor at Kruth, to a site Housholder found "as bare of any human activity as any primeval forest that ever existed."[8] Batteries D, A, and C, in fact, were aligned almost perfectly with a spot in the front line that the regiment planned to pummel the following week, Le Kiosque, just east of the wrecked and deserted town of Metzeral held by a battalion of the 35th Division's 139th Infantry. Battery C would lie closest to the target, at 2,952 feet above sea level. A kilometer to the southwest and nearly 1,000 feet higher was Battery A's destination, and Truman's guns were in line just over a kilometer back at an impressive height of 3,870 feet.

Truman knew he was in for quite a climb, but was eager for combat and contented himself with enjoying the scenery. "We rode about 15 kilometers," he said, "through some of the prettiest and hilliest country I ever saw to a town called Kruth which was full of German sympathizers and French soldiers."[9] Along the route, his truck rumbled past the Franco-German frontier that French troops had surged across during the early days of the war. Germany had seized Alsace and the neighboring province of Lorraine from France in 1870, and the border was marked by large stones every one hundred meters with an *F* painted on one side for France and *D* on the other for Deutschland. After some forty-eight years as an integral part of Germany, the population was by now thoroughly mixed, and the newly arrived Americans, officers and enlisted alike, were repeatedly warned that it was "necessary to be cautious of speech" even among civilians who appeared friendly.[10]

Truman's truck wound its way higher and higher and then swung around a final, gentle curve, and Kruth suddenly appeared below. The big 155mm howitzers of the 130th's 2nd Battalion were nowhere to be seen in his Folker's eye-view of the valley town and surrounding countryside, but he knew that the batteries would be tucked along the relatively few convenient tree lines that offered a clear field of fire to the east. Further, he knew that the batteries were not too far from the principal valley road, and close to the wagon trails of local farmers so that telltale tracks would not be left for the sharp eyes of Boche aviators. Soon he was passing assorted supply wagons parked in groups beside a thin grove of trees and along the town's buildings. He and his party were deposited at regimental headquarters located in the town hall, or *mairie,* where he received orders, maps, the coordinates of Battery D's position, and horses from his battery that had been sent forward the night before. He was also "assigned a French Lieutenant who understood not a word of English."[11] It was still early in the day, but there was no time for sightseeing, and the artillerymen immediately set off for "the real climb" up into the Vosges.[12]

Food, ammunition, and other supplies took a direct route to Truman's first destination via an overhead cable tramway that belonged to a German lumber company before it was commandeered by the French Army. Stretching four kilometers from Kruth to Boussat, its large, square gondolas moved in a steady, never-ending stream to the cable head and then back to the valley. The captain's little band covered the distance the hard way, as their route zigzagged up the slopes and wound 'round hillsides, often taking them in the opposite direction of the upward-moving supplies. "It took us until noon to reach the head-quarters of the French group commanders," said Truman, "and it was a steady climb all the way."[13]

Reaching the final summit just short of Boussat, Truman came upon an area that would have made a German artilleryman smile with delight. As the gondolas moved inexorably along a lengthy, earthen platform held in place by a rock retaining wall, a soldier or two would leap into its bay, or onto the cargo itself, and quickly heave its contents, item by item, to waiting soldiers on the platform. Anything that didn't make it out by the time that the end of the platform was reached—including, one imagined, the soldier stevedores—was destined to take a long, round trip to the valley and back before the men had another chance at it. From here, the fresh supplies were quickly moved off to a nearby wood, sorted, and dispatched in all directions through an adjoining crossroads.

Other targets abounded. A battery from the 130th Field Artillery's 1st Battalion had taken the convoluted, eleven-mile road march from Kruth to site its howitzers near the spot, and the enemy could not be ignorant of the abundant activity from the many supply and head-quarters units. In spite of all this, the only thing being shelled was the crossroads itself. Even here, though, the shelling was desultory but occasionally picked up in spasms at irregular intervals that, neverthe-less, according to the 129th's official history, "did little damage."[14]

Captain Thacher, now 1st Battalion adjutant, and other officers found that the French commonly referred to the area as *"un secteur tranquil."*[15] The Germans here initially had little fear of the newly arrived Americans, whom they greeted with a large banner reading "Welcome 35th Division"[16] erected from a front-line trench. The local Boche had to learn to forego such thing as sharing lakes with the French *polius* on alternating days lest they be peppered by American Lewis guns, and the 35th Division's regiments had conducted a series of small raids that would later loom large in the division's history, but the appearance of American infantry in early June had ultimately led to few changes. With little or no aggressive behavior by French artillery or air elements—most of the admittedly limited action was taking place at the wide passes to the north and south leading to the Rhine valley— there seemed no reason for undue concern, and the Germans' lackadaisical attitude toward shelling the crossroads was indicative of that.

There was an expectation—some might call it a fear in the case of some French soldiers—that arrival of aggressively handled American artillery could well upset the status quo. It was not that the French had ever failed to lay down accurate fire for the 35th when requested, but all one had to do was look at the map of the division's 60th Artillery Brigade's proposed dispositions to see that it meant business. The three batteries of Truman's 2nd Battalion were spaced across an expanse of seven kilometers, but the northernmost battery, Truman's D, was actually part of a cluster of four made up of principally 1st Battalion guns, all positioned to lay effective fire on the unsuspecting Germans occupying the Kiosque area and any "Prussians" unfortunate enough to be ordered to their relief. Moreover, not only had some of the 130th's big howitzers been pushed well forward, but an almost mirror image of the 129th's dispositions was being established to the north by the 128th, again with Le Kiosque in the crosshairs.

The Germans were already beginning to sense the buildup to the west and within days their guns would start searching out the most forward 129th batteries, but the French could already see quite well what was coming as American cannons rolled eastward. Major William Thurston, who would soon be promoted and command the 130th in the Meuse-Argonne, noticed that some French officers were hastily evacuating a charming stone house at a crossroads between a pair of his 1st Battalion batteries. Curious, he asked why they were moving.

Why? You Americans have moved in here with your guns and you will be shooting all over the German lines and they will fire back and as this house is at a crossroads and they will shoot at it first. We are going.[17]

But for now, the Germans were content to drop rounds only at the high Boussat crossroads, and the regimental history noted that at least it "gave those present their first impressions of what it was like to be under fire."[18]

Truman found the shelling "not a very pleasant sensation" and thought that it made "Camp Doniphan seem very pleasant and now far away."[19] He and his men moved through the target zone "without getting any shells on or near me" but not before running into Major Stayton of the 110th Engineers, whose command post was hidden nearby. Stayton, a longtime Missouri Guardsman soon to play a key role in the fighting near Exermont, had not seen Truman since they last had dinner together at Doniphan and "treated me like a long lost brother," said Truman. "I was just as glad to see him too."[20]

Truman reported in at the French headquarters farther up the mountain, and hoped to be on his way after seeing to it that the men and horses were fed. Major Gates was already there, having made the climb earlier to take over a command post at Larchey on a ridge nearly two kilometers farther east. Invited to dine with Gates and the French commandant, Truman was caught as surely as if he had been bore-sighted by a German "77." Truman had sat through these things before, and while he had no complaints about the many toasts to President Wilson, to Marshall Foch, to King George, to General Pershing, and to the success of American arms, time was in short supply. He had hoped to get Battery D's position thoroughly reconnoitered before the early mountain nightfall, but there was nothing he could do but graciously accept, even though the day was half gone and there were still many miles of twisting trails to cover.

The captain's party was fed in a nearby mess, although the French guide and Housholder, being *officiers* and, thus, a thing apart, would have likely been called to the commandant's table. Truman later poured out his frustration in a letter to Bess:

> It was noon by this time and Major Gates and I ate dinner with the French commandant. They served it in usual French style, a course at a time and a clean plate for every course. French officers

always eat that way. It takes them so long to serve a meal that I'm always hungrier when I get done than I ever was before. We finally got done and the French lieutenant and myself and my instrument and telephone sergeants started around to my position.[21]

And things got worse. Housholder later wrote that "we were shown our coordinates on the battle map," and a quick examination alerted Truman that his "battery position . . . was to be an entirely new one in the Foret de Herrenburg some seven kilos further yet."[22] The route was fairly direct on a good road, running north, then northwest, from the Boussat crossroads to the cluster of structures called Huf, where the trail curved into a generally northeast trace until it passed just to the west of Battery D's coordinates. The entire route ran along a high ridge but along its reverse slope, hidden from German observation. There still should have been plenty of daylight left in which to plot the position.

Unfortunately, this was *not* the route that his guide led them. Although armed with a detailed map, they were completely unfamiliar with the area, and no one noticed when they passed the turnoff to Huf. Instead of taking the reverse slope, they were brought far north along the forward slope of the ridge line past the future sites of A and C Batteries, which ultimately required the party to make several lengthy backtracks as they zigzagged up over the heights and finally traveled south to their destination.

They had essentially ridden, as the captain said, "around a mountain to get to it," wasting valuable time in the process—and the mountain they laboriously worked their way around was the very same one where D was to locate. Even more time was lost when they had to "cross a ridge in plain view of the *Boche.* The Frenchman made us go over the ridge a hundred meters apart so the Hun would not suspect that we were going to put a battery in that place."[23] Truman's guns and carriages would never retrace the French lieutenant's path, but he would find himself on it again and again because, when utilizing certain cutoffs, it was the most direct route to Major Gates's command post at Larchey. Such precautions against German observation, however, did not have to be repeated. They were "never necessary afterwards because I don't ever remember a clear day after that one," said Truman.[24]

After coming around to the reverse slope, they doubled back to the north on a steep trail and continued along the top of the ridge. Housholder found that the battery coordinates were "a spot just in under the edge of a forest, with an open meadow land lying before us and the enemy's position across a valley"[25] and with the front lines running irregularly along the floor of the valley. "It was on a bare knob about two kilometers long," said Truman. "One end of which is called Schniepfenreith and the other Foret de Herrenburg because the roads comes up to the edge of it at that end."[26]

The site clearly was going to need considerable preparation before the guns could be installed. With the 2nd Battalion scheduled to move up to Kurth in just two days, Thursday the 23rd, and the guns conceivably being sent up as early as that same night, work had to begin immediately. The map was examined closely, whereupon Truman "found that there was a road about half as long as the one I first came up running directly to my position from Kruth."[27] The sun was sinking fast as Housholder, map in hand, galloped off with telephone sergeant Brice for the long ride back to Saulxures to collect supplies and carve out as large a work detail as practical from the battery sections.

Instrument Sergeant Bowman, as well as Pvts. Milton R. "Bob" Evans and Albert Ridge, stayed behind with Captain Truman, and the exhausted soldiers sat down to a supper of "cold beans, and this corned beef (or monkey meat as we called it), and hardtack," said Bowman, "and some canned Pet milk." Ridge and Evans had also spotted some wild red raspberries, filling "a whole mess kit" with their find, and "the Frenchman had brought along a bottle of champagne."[28] Afterwards, Truman made an attempt to survey the ground as best he could. But even though the last rays of light were strongest on the reverse slope facing the west, it was a hopeless task. The day's reconnaissance was over, and the men settled in to a soft serenade of distant cannons for their chilly night in the mountains.

CHAPTER 9

Code Name "Chicago"

Dawn gave Truman his first good look at the site and its approaches, but the mountaintop view to the east was less than encouraging. He and Instrument Sergeant Bowman were frustrated by the weather, which reduced what should have been a breathtaking vista of the German-held ridgeline, broken by the Fecht River valley stretching all the way to Münster, to a hazy, gray mass, with the valley features dissolving into a formless white. If this weather held—and, in fact, it was usually worse—all firing would be plotted by grid coordinates on their exquisitely produced French terrain maps, and the Americans would consider themselves extremely lucky on the rare occasions they could discern the fall of shot.

Still, if they couldn't make out the German positions, the German observation posts likely couldn't see them either. The same was generally true for the "Hun" aircraft flying seemingly routine missions beyond Truman's southern flank to Kruth and northern flank to Gerardmer—unless, of course, a hole suddenly opened up in the soup, sending the sun's ray like a spotlight on their position. Even though their patch of the front would be obscured by clouds, rain, and haze for the duration of Battery D's stay, Truman couldn't know this, so what he could not arrange back from the tree line at the top of the ridge, he positioned along the reverse slope:

I chose a place in the edge of the woods for the battery and a place further down in the woods for the kitchen. There is a rock road running down the side of the hill, and it was about 200 meters straight up from this road to my kitchen. All the supplies, water, etc. had to be carried up by hand as well as all the material for construction.[1]

Housholder returned not long after first light with men and fourgons piled high with food, tools, and huge, green bundles of camouflage netting requisitioned in Kruth, for it had been immediately clear when eyeing the terrain the previous evening that the limited space along the ridgetop would force them to site the guns in front of the tree line. Thus, the tree line had to be moved forward visually. The bare top was comparatively flat, with steep, thirty-degree drop-offs east and west, but there was no truly level ground. Overnight, a sleeping Private Evans "kept rolling down on top of me," said tentmate Bowman. "I'd kick him in the hind end and I'd say, "Get up the hill you little so-and-so." Truman informed the pair that they "kept him awake all night" (and probably that if they weren't going to carve out a step into the hillside, that they should at least face their tent uphill). Decades later, when they visited their former captain at the White House, he looked up from his Oval Office desk and greeted them with "Get up the hill you little . . ."[2]

Truman showed Housholder where he wanted the guns, field kitchen, and latrines as well as "a place to keep my saddle horses."[3] Mounts belonging to the officers, buglers (who doubled as dispatch riders), and sergeants required a concealed location near one of the Vosges's fast-flowing streams, where they could secure their horses until duty called, but there was simply no place for the large number of draft animals. They and their wagons traveled the long journey back to the railhead after bringing up supplies, and after the 2nd Battalion moved to Kruth, they would use the regimental horse line hidden under the trees spreading down one of the hillsides reaching almost to the town. Once satisfied that the lieutenant understood what was expected, Truman mounted up and escorted his wagons to Saulxures.

The supply wagons, diminutive French fourgons noticeably smaller than the wagons the men had used on their Jackson County farms, could not be conveniently driven along the ridge-top trail to the battery because of the danger that they could be spotted by the Germans across the valley. Only the guns and ammunition would take this route after the gun pits and camouflage had been constructed—and then, only at night—because it was neither practical nor desirable to disassemble them and drag the components up the hill. Consequently, a supply dump was hastily established along the rock road far below, near where the saddle horses were kept, and all deliveries made through the back door up a tortuous, wooded track from the dump that ran through a gap in the rusting German barbed wire strung seemingly at random among trees.

The first order of business was to make the forest appear deeper than it was by extending the camouflage netting out from the trees along a roughly two hundred–foot strip of the meadow. Once erected, work could begin in earnest on the gun pits. Said Housholder:

> Keeping yourself from being seen, or your activity from being observed by the enemy is the prime prerequisite for remaining alive or uninjured. . . . At our new position, where there was no sign of any human activity or habitation when we took over, it became doubly necessary that every precaution be taken to keep all our activity sufficiently hidden, so that it would not show up on the aerial photographic plates that were being made almost continually all along, and well behind, the front lines.
>
> The waste, or diggings from our gun emplacements was piled under the cover of the tree branches around us. Also there was the problem of pathways being developed within our small area, especially leading from our pup tent shelters to the "mess hall," to the four gun positions, and to the latrine, that would show up in an aerial photograph like a white pencil mark. . . . Wires which we salvaged from a nearby fence, [were strung] from tree to tree marking just where the men should always walk in going back and forth. Great care was taken in locating these

wire guides to make sure that they were always under dense tree growth above.[4]

Back in Saulxures, Truman found a full plate of personnel problems to deal with. Jordan, who doubled as Major Gates's intelligence officer, was a competent enough soldier in matters relating to the supply echelon and horses, but Battery D's rowdies apparently felt free to take liberties when the cat was away and only the lieutenant in charge. Truman's personal roster and the unit's extra-duty roster tell the tale. As Truman likely expected, some members of Dizzy D took more interest in the local spirits than sightseeing and wound up drunk. In addition to Pvts. John Grady and Earl Van Buskirk, "handed" to Jordan by Lieutenant Bostain (Van Buskirk being one of the miscreants caught "hanging his feet out of a boxcar door"), Pvt. Harry McConnell also "got drunk and committed a nuisance in the street." Private 1st Class Harold Baker and Cpl. George Hardy were both reduced to private for missing reveille, although a notation next to Hardy's black mark reads, "Made him a corporal again. Made good."[5]

The captain was still being tested, and another note for the 22nd reads: "Gordon, John, Private 1st Class reduced to private because he lied to me and then missed reveille." An ominous portent for events the following week was scribbled in a note behind First Sergeant Woolridge's name: "Sent him out with horses. Was not with them when I met them." Yet there were also some bright spots as Pfc. Fred Cunningham was promoted to corporal, and Cpl. Curtis Smith was verbally commended: "Told him he was making good."[6]

Awaiting Truman's return was also Field Order No. 1, Headquarters 129th Field Artillery, A.P.O. #743, 22 August 1918, with his name scrawled diagonally across the cover sheet's bottom left. Distributed to all the regiment's battalion and battery commanders and certain headquarters in the chain of command, it was essentially the 129th's warning to prepare for battle and how they were to arrive at the spot where they would engage the enemy. The order gave the regiment's order of march, locations where command posts were to be located, and the manner in which the guns were to be secretly moved into the hills. Field Order No. 1 also instructed all battery and battalion commanders to be ready to leave on a truck convoy at 5 a.m. the next morning for a reconnaissance of their positions.

Of course, Major Gates had already pushed Truman up to the top of Mount Herrenberg because D's position was going to need a very considerable amount of work before it was ready to receive the guns. Orders were orders, though, and this second trip was one that the bespectacled captain would have made anyway. But this time he would get a ride all the way to Boussat to meet again the French group commander, by retracing the long road march of the 130th battery to the high crossroads. There he would be assigned yet another guide who would accompany them on the drive along the reverse-slope road to where Housholder's detachment was already busily at work. Each battery commander's party was instructed to bring two days' food, since they were to stay at their new positions, leaving the subordinate officers to bring the batteries to Kruth that night.

There was great anxiety by officers and men alike over the condition of the French draft horses allotted to the regiment. Jordan had been unsuccessful at finding additional horses—a hopeless task to begin with—and the battery was just going to have to make do with what they had, being extremely careful not to overtax the animals. The regiment had been lucky enough while at Coetquidan to have obtained its full complement, or close to it's full complement, of spare horses, and Colonel Klemm and his staff decided upon a wise course of action, instructing that the extra animals be used when pulling the carriages. Each 75mm gun section—cannon, caisson, and limber (as the lead caisson was called)—was to have an eight-horse team instead of six. Likewise, the fourgons were to have four-horse teams instead of two whenever possible, gunners were to walk instead of ride on the carriages and horses, and ammunition chests were to remain empty until they reached a supply dump at Kruth.*

---

*The 130th Field Artillery's 155mm howitzers leaving the valley were pulled by twelve-horse teams using only the better mountain roads, yet still had many animals "play out" along the way.

With close care paid to the harness and frequent rest stops, the sad lot would get the battery up Mount Herrenberg, and Truman expressed his confidence to Jordan and Stable Sergeant Wimmers, the second lieutenants, and noncommissioned officers that they would take good care of the battery. He would meet them in Kruth, and lead the first platoon of two guns up on Saturday night, August 24. Truman left for the front with a picked selection of platoon sergeants early Friday morning. Telephone Sergeant Brice and his section left Saulxures about the same time as their captain, likely bringing forward his and the sergeants' mounts as well as his own equipment (principally reels and reels of telephone wire) packed in a fourgon.

Truman's trip back certainly took longer than if he had traveled directly from Kruth, but at least there was no painful, multi-course meal, only a briefing and some stirring words by the French group commander. Dropped off at Battery D's supply dump, he and the sergeants worked their way up through the trees, reviewing the progress on the reverse slope as they went. Up top, camouflage nets were in place, and the under-manned work detail had started on the gun pits. Housholder was also dealing with a "bothersome problem" that was possible to fix now that more men were coming available:

> Directly in front of the No. 1 gun emplacement, at a distance of some fifty yards, stood a large lone tree that partially blocked the field of fire. Off hand, that was no problem—cut it down and it would be out of the way. Yes, sure it would, but on more somber thought, how about those damned aerial photographs? Consequently, we cut it down all right, but about 16 feet above the ground and with much effort and many guys—and here I mean both men and guy wires and ropes, we lowered the top portion of that tree, in a vertical position, until the butt rested on the ground and there we lashed it to the 16 foot tall stump. All this at night too. Our obstructing tree was not an obstruction any more, but as far as any aerial photograph could detect, nothing had happened.[7]

Soldiers were detailed to dig a niche into the hill for Battery D's command post just down from the gun pits, and Brice's men immediately set to work. Although they would take over the French communications net, there obviously were no lines running to Truman's remote location, and the time-consuming task was begun of laying wire across hill and valley to connect with not only the other batteries, but also the battalion and regimental headquarters far to the southeast, and the observation post (OP) near Pourchet. An addendum to the 35th Division's memorandum on telephone codes directed that the names of Kansas towns be used for certain border locations, such as "Leavenworth" for Le Collet and "Salina" for Calvaire. Battery D was code named "Chicago" and its observation post, "Canary."[8]

Tents were sprouting in clusters at convenient locations along the reverse slope as the first wave of artillerymen sought out prime locations under the tall pines. The most coveted spots were those that required the least shoveling into the hill to create a level shelf for their pup tents. Housholder related that the men found that they could lessen their digging by "being careful to hold onto the spoil, or waste, and form it into a bench just in front of the niche."[9] No kitchen facilities had yet arrived, but the meager rations that had reached the site were stored at the "mess hall" Truman had picked out, "an old abandoned rock shack, with no roof, about a hundred yards down the slope."[10]

Although the horse teams would pull the 75s, limbers, and caissons to their camouflaged position in the dead of night along a steep but relatively easy trail that generally leveled off along the crest of the ridge all the way to the gun pits, all other deliveries were made through the back door up a tortuous track from the supply dump. An idea of just how long and steep is the west side of Mount Herrenberg can be gained from one of the favorite stories of Battery D veterans which occurred shortly after the position was fully established. Truman recalled the incident which involved a five-gallon tin of rendered hog fat—a rather precious commodity at the time:

> One of the men dropped a can of lard when they were bringing up
> the kitchen supplies from the lower road and it rolled all the way

to the valley before scattering lard on every tree it hit and finally landing a battered piece of tin at the bottom. One of the kitchen police went down the next day and gathered in the lard, getting a chunk from a tree and a chunk from a bush, and maybe some on the ground. Anyway, the cooks rendered out the sticks and saved a half a can.[11]

Truman added, "It was surely some steep hill and the trees were all full of wire entanglements. If a man had started to roll down, he'd have been in shreds when he got to the bottom."[12] Occasional ruined villages dotted the successive valleys on the other side of Herrenberg, and barbed wire marking the long-stagnant no man's land was as thick as anywhere along the Western Front. Other evidence abounded of the confused fighting that swept through the area nearly four years earlier including, said Lieutenant Lee, "the ever present gray crosses, in groups large or small."[13] The entanglements behind Battery D had, in fact, been part of the German's main line of defense overlooking the much lower foothills retained by France after the Franco-Prussian War of 1870. It is likely that this same mass of rusting wire was still present when the German 16th Volksgrenadier Division defended Mount Herrenberg against the new French 10th Division during the Colmar Pocket battle of January 1945.

On the night of August 23–24, Battery D said goodbye to Saulxures—and their blue denim duffle bags stuffed with personal items that they had been told ever since they left Camp Doniphan they would eventually have to discard. The regiment started its road march at 9 p.m. beginning with Battery A, and with ten minutes between batteries and twenty-five yards between sections. Battery D started on its way after roughly an hour, with Lieutenant Jordan, one of the buglers, and Truman's orderly, guidon bearer "Smack" Evans, in the lead. The long, horse-drawn column clanked, creaked, bumped, and snorted through the dark at a soldier's walking pace that took them over the summit near Ventron before midnight. There, at the international border, the town names on the map abruptly changed from French to German, and the rest of march was largely downhill to Kruth. Well before dawn, the battery was greeted by an eminently pleased Captain Truman and directed to its camp site. The fragile horses had held up well during "a long, hard pull,"[14] but a much more demanding climb awaited them the coming night.

Except for those still on duty, most of the soldiers were fast asleep before the first hint of gray appeared in the sky. During the day, battalion ammunition carts made the rounds of the batteries with cases of 75mm shells; enough for the caissons, but not the ammunition chests in the limbers, since they would be returning to Kruth after the guns were deposited on the mountain. Plans called for each battery to bring a single two-gun platoon to its assigned position after dark that night, and its second platoon the following night, August 25. The French batteries being replaced by the 129th would match the movement as they pulled their own guns out by platoon to store them at nearby, tree-canopied artillery parks. Battery D's guns, caissons, rolling kitchen, and most of its supply fourgons were brought up on schedule, without incident, and with no horses falling out.

One of the machine-gun crews (attached to the BC, or battery commander's, detail) accompanied each two-gun platoon, and, with the 75s in position, Housholder stationed "a Hotchkiss machine gun on both our flanks for protection against air attack." Throughout most of the activity setting up the battery, Housholder "was in command, with the battery mechanic [First Sergeant Wooden] as my right hand man."[15] By Sunday morning dawn of August 25, Truman had nearly all his men on Herrenberg, with only the limber drivers and Sergeant Wimmers's fifth section maintaining the horses in the valley.

Unlike the other 2nd Battalion positions, D had to build its own command post and defensive bunkers. Truman was supposed to be able to requisition lumber and additional tools directly from saw mills run by Major Stayton's engineers at Mittlach and Holtzplatz, but a conflict of some sort developed (likely involving infantry officers with somewhat more rank than Truman demanding priority), and Colonel Klemm was forced to intervene with a formal request over his signature for 171 feet of lumber at assorted thicknesses; six rolls of tar paper and other roofing materials; thirty pounds of nails;

hammers, picks, shovels, and even a cross-cut saw for Housholder's tree-pruning project.

Food, however, quickly became scarce, and Truman wrote in his notebook, "Nothing to eat. Not likely to get anything." This statement must have made the postwar regimental account of the problem ironic reading: "At first the ration supply was not over abundant, especially at the more advanced positions, but not absolutely lacking; and shortly this situation was met adequately and satisfactorily."[16] There were also communication problems throughout the battalion and certainly elsewhere as the regiment sorted things out:

2nd. Battalion Headquarters, 129 F.A.

26 August 1918

Memorandum:

To commanding officer of "D" Battery:

Explanation will be made in writing why written ammunition report was not at these headquarters by 8:30 A.M. this date.

By order of Major Gates.

W. H. Younger Jr.

1st. Lt. 129 F.A.

Acting Adjt. 2nd. Bn

Truman didn't have Corporal Keenan type up a formal response. Instead, his "in writing" reply was scrawled in pencil across the bottom of the memorandum on the spot and sent back:

The order had not been received and I didn't know at the time when you wanted it.

Capt. Truman[17]

A similar exchange took place the following day between Gates and F Battery's Captain Harry Allen.

With no idle hands, personnel problems dropped to almost zero, but Pvt. Alonzo F. Fowler, whom Truman considered "absolutely worthless," was "sent down off the hill and court-martialed at Kruth for disobedience of Sergeant [Verne] Chaney's order,"[18] forfeiting two-thirds of four month's pay. While his officers and NCOs developed the battery position, Truman turned his sights to plotting his guns' fires to potential trouble spots, like Hilsenfirst, where opposing trenches were only thirty yards apart, and cover various contingencies, all neatly outlined in a 35th Division translation of a month-old French field order. Particular attention was paid to the the planned savaging of enemy positions around Le Kiosque. Major Gates's pushing Truman's battery out early provided Truman with the time he needed to develop the remote location, but, ironically, this was not where the Dizzy D would trade salvos with the enemy across the valley. "Well, I worked on that position and followed all the rules in all the books to the letter," said Truman, "and never did fire a shot from it."[19]

The Germans couldn't help but notice that something was afoot, particularly when Battery C of the 1st Battalion and elements of the 130th were ordered to conduct limited firing for registration on August 26, followed that night by the 35th Division's infantry regiments sending up an awe-inspiring fireworks display. A message arrived late in the day warning that the doughboys all along the front were going to try out their rocket and flare signals and that what the artillerymen were about to see were *not* calls for fire. From his forward observation post, Captain MacLean watched the brief, but highly entertaining, show:

> It was beautiful; rockets, flares and parachutes of every color and description. We also tried to remember what each rocket called for. One with two white stars was for a barrage, one with three green stars meant shoot a little farther, your barrage is falling short etc. About ten o'clock the fireworks ceased.
>
> The Germans got quite nervous during this display and they would open up with machine gun at the points where they thought the rocket was going up from. They also sent up starshells which lighted the whole country within a radius of a mile.[20]

The following day, German shelling, which had previously been at best desultory along the principal roads, killing only a single member of the regiment (a soldier blown off his mount which, badly wounded, galloped riderless down the trail past Captain Marks), now picked up substantially. Batteries B and E, located at long-established French positions, became subject to steady harassing fire, while C, which fired the registration shots, received a mix of gas, shrapnel, and high-explosive rounds. Although C Battery, like D, occupied a previously unused site and visibility was poor, its gun flashes had marked its general location for the German observers, with the result that the enemy gunners walked fires left and right, back and forth, through the area, hoping to land some rounds among Marks's guns.

The shelling came from two batteries across the valley and behind the peak Petit Bailon-Kahler Wasen and another pair in the woods just to their north. Captain Truman, who had by now plotted fires for just about every target that could be reached from Mount Herrenberg, was at battalion headquarters far to the south in Larchey when orders came in from Colonel Klemm to move A, C, and D Batteries to "fleeting" positions for a poison gas bombardment of the troublesome German guns. Suspicion that the Germans had somehow tapped the new telephone wires prompted all messages to be dispatched by riders, and a 2nd Battalion orderly galloped off to Herrenberg with Truman's orders that Lieutenant Housholder "proceed at once to our rear echelon and bring up the horses for the firing battery, and to hold same in concealment along the mountain road below our mess shack for further orders."[21] Housholder later wrote:

> This indeed was full of interest, and particularly so because of the vagueness. How clearly do I recall my trip down that steep mountainside. I seldom followed the twisting, curving road, but rather took the many cutoffs and made very good time. A similar order had gone down to the echelon at the time mine was sent to me. The result was that all was in order awaiting my arrival. The trip back up over that mountainous road was with just the limbers (the front carriages of the field pieces and caissons) because the battery was, of course already up in position.[22]

Truman's orders were "to be ready to go to the front and make a reconnaissance for the purpose of going into position at 4 a.m. the next morning."[23] In late August, dawn comes at 4 a.m. in the high Vosges, and though the mountains were still wrapped in a gloom of rain and clouds, this could not be depended on to hold, and his battery risked detection if it were not secreted in the woods near the "fleeting position" before daylight. Truman and his small party rode off to reconnoiter the area as soon as he was dismissed. "Every battery commander got the same order and there was great hubbub and excitement about going into position before the enemy for the first time." He later wrote that "a real creepy feeling" came over him and, although his battery would be sent into firing positions again and again, he "never felt about them exactly as I did that first one."[24]

Truman's destination was the Auf Rain area near Captain Salisbury's Battery E, where he was to find a spot for his guns and horse line (and he may well have run into C Battery commander Marks and Capt. Keith Dancy of A Battery, who were both sent down from 1st Battalion Headquarters at Gibrat to scout the same area for their own units). Great care had to be taken, because the Germans were periodically shelling Salisbury's well-known position and a main north-south road roughly 150 meters east of it. A parallel road on the opposite side of the ridge was more protected from shelling, and it is likely that this is where Truman decided to establish his horse line. Ominously, it was at this point that the inquisitive Germans moved five observation balloons to Munster, then spread them north and south before sending all aloft at once to get as good a look as they could through the rainy gloom at the commotion to their front. Satisfied that he had found adequate places to hide and then site his guns, Truman rode south to Boussat, then as fast as his horse could carry him back along the muddy road north to Herrenberg.

The spot where Truman was to go into action the following night was "two kilometers closer to the Dutch lines,"[25] and although it was only three kilometers to the southeast of his mountaintop, a night march up and down eleven kilometers of twisting mountain roads was required to get there. "J-Day," as the 60th Field Artillery Brigade's shoot was designated, apparently was originally scheduled for the evening of Friday, August 30, but was moved forward to Thursday because the 35th Division had been ordered to displace to the north in support the first great American offensive at Saint-Mihiel. If the shoot wasn't done then, it wouldn't be done at all. "I was supposed to have 24 hours to get ready but only had about six," complained Truman. Making matters worse, "My horses were seven kilos away" because there was "no place for them" at Herrenberg.[26]

CHAPTER 10

First Blood

Beginning about 9:30 p.m. the positions of Batteries D and E were subjected to a combined high explosive and gas shell fire; of limited intensity, but continuing during the most of the night, and which fortunately resulted in no casualties. While withdrawing from its temporary firing position after the barrage, D Battery had four horses killed, and on account of the mud it was not possible to move two of the pieces with the horses remaining. Officers and men joined in running one gun back under cover, and the other was camouflaged with branches, and both were left until they could be returned for with sufficient horses the following evening, and safely removed back to the old position.

For their cool courage on this occasion Privates John Gordon, William O'Hare and Glenn Woods of "D" Battery were later cited in General Orders.

—Citation Orders No. 9, GHQ, AEF, August 1, 1920

THIS IS THE 129TH FIELD ARTILLERY REGIMENT'S bare-bones description of Battery D's trouble-plagued withdrawal from the meadow north of Salisbury's position. That no one was killed was largely due to the muddy soil absorbing most of the blast from the falling German shells and the raw luck that few were thrown D's way before the Germans adjusted their shot, which had fallen wide of their actual target, Battery E at Auf Rain. An added bonus was that enemy fire did not pick up until after Truman's men had exited the area. Nevertheless, that D had sat immobile and in the open near a site whose coordinates the Germans had long known was due to the negligence of the battery's ranking NCO, Woolridge, and, ultimately, Capt. Harry S. Truman, who had retained him as the first sergeant on each of three previous occasions that warranted his replacement: First, when Truman took over D Battery, he left Woolridge in command, even though Woolridge clearly had not maintained control over his own sergeants, fully a half dozen of whom were under arrest in quarters that very morning. A month later, on August 14, Truman discovered that Woolridge had failed to report Cpl. James T. "Skinny" McNamara and two privates for being out after taps. And most seriously, on August 22, Truman had "sent him out with the horses," but when Truman reached the detachment, Woolridge "was not with them."[1]

How is it that time and time again Woolridge was allowed to retain his stripes? The battery's chief mechanic, Sgt. McKinley Wooden, described his first sergeant as "a little bitty old squawky, hard boiled fellow—yeah, a hard boiled boy."[2] Woolridge was also considered one of the regiment's old-timers, having served with Battery B during the Mexican campaign. Maybe it was simply a matter of misplaced deference to an old soldier, but within days of Woolridge's lack of diligence in carrying out Truman's orders, his actions would put the battery in mortal jeopardy.

THE HORSES AND LIMBERED CAISSONS were brought up from Kruth and, amid considerable "hurrying and scurrying,"[3] the battery was readied. Because of the risk that sounds of its movement could well carry to the Germans across the valley, every precaution was taken to dampen preventable noises—extra grease on the axles, burlap bags or freshly chopped wedges of wood packed or tapped against items that might rattle—with special attention to the metal-rimmed wheels. Although taken deadly seriously at the time, Sergeant Bowman looked upon it years later as "all a big joke." Said Bowman: "It was after dark and they had wrapped burlap around the wheels of the guns so they wouldn't make too much noise and all that kind of stuff.... [Lieutenant Colonel] Elliott came storming out of there a couple of times bellowing out a few orders and so on. Nobody paid much attention to him."[4]

The march down Herrenberg and around to Auf Rain, begun during a driving rain, was uneventful but nerve wracking nonetheless, as the men half-expected German star shells to light the night sky above them at any moment.

The final leg of the journey was northwest along a well-used ridge-top track high above the protective blanket of fog in the valleys. The column marched past Salisbury's position to the highest point, Hörnles Kopf, then a short distance down a gentle grade until they were directed off the road during a light rain to a meadow on their right. There, the horses were unharnessed, then the guns were detached and manhandled into a tree line where the angle of the slope began to increase markedly along a north-facing point of the ridge. Meanwhile, the horses and limbered caissons were led down the road to a point where they doubled back at least six hundred yards along a narrow logging road to a sheltered spot in the north-south valley below Hörnles Kopf—a path resembling a sort of backward, inverted J that placed the horse detail somewhat south of D's gun line. The road and meadow were essentially free of activity by 4 a.m.

The weather had been cold and rainy all the previous day. And although the threatening clouds shed no more rain until well into the afternoon, it was still a thoroughly miserable Thursday, August 29, that the artillerymen spent secreted among the trees at the upper edge of the slope. For most of them it had been three days since they had warm food, and the evening before, Truman had scribbled in his calendar book, "Nothing to eat, not likely to get any."[5] Whatever the men carried with them, probably small quantities of hardtack (large, stiff crackers) and cans of beans or corned beef, was all that they were going to see until they got back to the mountain. Although the Germans' ability to observe the area was very low due to the weather, Truman and his BC detail generally kept out of the meadow until 2 p.m., when they staked out the gun line and aiming circles used to measure azimuth and elevation angles for the coming night's shoot. They also had to plan both the wheeling of the cannons from the tree line and exit from the position to the road with unusual care in order to avoid old shell holes and areas that were so thoroughly sodden that there was a very real risk that the guns could become mired.

The men were excited to be going into action and went about their duties with a will, but Truman later learned that his use of an abandoned, shot-up brewery as an aiming point almost instantly led to a rumor that the brewery was itself a target. This prompted "much lamentation over the fact that there might be some good beer spoiled."[6] It is unlikely that the soldiers believed that there was a functioning brewery on the front lines no matter how quiet the sector, yet even the idea of shelling such a symbol of civilization seemed just so— distasteful. The men's reaction amused Truman, who didn't learn of the rumor until afterward. He later wrote, "It was with great regret that they pulled the trigger" that night, and that it was "quite a relief" to his Irish when they discovered that they hadn't dropped their poison gas shells on vats of fermenting spirits.[7]

Even before night had fully fallen, guns were rolled from cover and carefully positioned. A detachment from the 110th Ammunition Train soon appeared with the shells for the evening's fire mission—five hundred gas rounds. Slightly more than two-thirds of these were the deadly No. 5 "special shells" containing collongite (phosgene) with the balance made up of less effective No. 4 special shells filled with vincennite (hydrogen cyanide), a type which the French now considered ineffective because of improvements made to German gas masks. They no longer used the No. 4s and simply turned their stock-piles over to the eager Americans.

The fire plan Truman followed was exactly the same for all of the four 75mm batteries involved, and the two unused batteries, one from each battalion, were kept in readiness to respond to possible German moves against the American trenches. The battery fire schedule was broken down into five one hundred–round shoots: twenty-five rounds per gun firing at a rate of one round every eight seconds for slightly over three minutes in order to produce a rolling battery fire of one round every two seconds per battery. In order to make the best possible use out of the substandard No. 4 special shells, those would make up the initial eight rounds sent down range during the opening minute of each strike, hopefully catching some Germans before they succeeded in putting on or securely fastening their gas masks. Since a bombardment of this sort was most effective if a large number of shells released their contents on a target in a short period of time—quickly concentrating the gas to highly lethal levels and partially negating the effectiveness of even the new gas masks—all batteries would be focused on a single German position in order to saturate it before moving on to the next target. The four batteries combined would theoretically produce the detonation of two 75mm No. 5 special shells each second for three minutes.

The fire plan worked like this: Truman's men, handling a quarter of the American guns, would fire in five three-minute bursts of one hundred rounds, the first directed against the gas-retaining trenches that the Germans in the northernmost position were expected to flee to. After a five-minute suspension of fire, the second target, centered approximately 140 meters (approximately 150 yards) to the south, would be struck, followed by the third target (located near the first) being bombarded a scant three minutes after the shelling ended at the second. A full ten minutes after this ended, a fourth target would be hit in the same vicinity, and the fire ultimately returned to the original target after a final three-minute break. From the first shot to the last, thirty-six minutes would elapse. The thoroughly gassed Germans, meanwhile, would have no idea how much longer this might go on and that the Americans were using their indecision to make good their own batteries' exit from their temporary positions—except Salisbury's battery, of course, which would just have to hunker down and "take it" when the Germans fought back.

It was hoped that the seemingly irregular nature of the attack sequence would catch some German artillerymen without their gas masks as well as inhibit a quick counterbattery response by encouraging them to anticipate that the Americans were withholding fire until the Germans had moved back to their guns. Experience had taught the

Americans' French tutors that it was reasonable to expect no return fire for at least thirty minutes from the targeted Hun batteries because there would be a degree of confusion and disarray at their positions. The Germans would be forced to operate in protective gear at night with little light. They would suffer some number of casualties, would have to decide where to shoot, and finally, would have to compute and distribute targeting data to the possibly depleted gun crews. The Germans, as was their own practice, would then respond with a mix of both gas and high-explosive shells instead of setting up a bombardment of all one type or the other.

The American batteries opened fire at precisely 8 p.m. On Truman's command, Housholder ordered Dizzy D to commence firing, and the blast from Sgt. Ralph Thacker's No. 4 gun was followed by a ripple down the line. "Boy oh boy, it's a pretty sight," said Wooden; "the guns would throw fire out about 40 feet; sure looked nice."[8] The battery pounded its way through the fire program, its well-trained gunners and loaders quickly working up a sweat in spite of the cold. Truman, for the most part, stood well behind the gun line during the seemingly slow-motion strobe effect of the gun flashes, conducting its fire with the assistance of Housholder as well as Corporal Keenan and guidon bearer Evans acting as messengers. Chief Mechanic Wooden could be seen floating throughout the position like a ghost, and Truman called him over during a scheduled pause. "How are the guns performing?" asked the captain. Wooden's "Perfect, sir" was all Truman needed to know, and he dismissed the sergeant with a "That'll be all."[9]

A long blast of Housholder's whistle at 8:36 p.m. sharp ordered the final cease-fire of the night. Some 490 gas shells had been hurled at the enemy in fifteen minutes of actual firing time, a scant ten rounds short of what brigade orders had called for, because some now-forgotten problem had caused the No. 3 gun's section to fall behind schedule. First Sergeant Woolridge's detail had yet to return with the horses and limbers but were expected any moment, and the 75s were readied in anticipation of their arrival as the men laughed and congratulated themselves. Although the detail was supposed to arrive at 8:30, their absence was at first only an annoyance. After a short while, however, officers and men alike began to grow nervous, and a low-voiced "Where's Woolridge?" certainly passed more than one soldier's lips. The minutes were fast ticking by, and Battery D was arrayed in the open on an outer ring of a bullseye that the Germans had long ago painted on Battery E's old French gun pits.

With the exception of sending out one or two trusted men hopefully to find the wayward detachment and guide it in, there was absolutely nothing that Truman could do. If the periodic drizzle suddenly turned into a rain of steel, the wooded north-facing slope where D's men and equipment had been hidden that day was near at hand, but would offer no real protection, as it was open to the enemy. Likewise, to the east the men would need to evacuate all the way to the bottom of the precipitous drop-off in front of the guns to reach shelter, while, to the rear of the position, a roughly seventy-five-yard dash (in the general direction where the horses were to have been hidden) would bring them to the safety of the reverse slope. Each alternative would have required leaving the guns. To be sure, the mens' lives were far more important than weapons that the French could easily replace, but Truman likely would have rather had his right arm blown off than abandon his 75s—even temporarily—during his first action.

TEN, FIFTEEN, THEN TWENTY agonizing minutes had passed before the first sergeant made his appearance at roughly 9 p.m. The men were relieved to see him, but what Woolridge did next was unnerving. According to Sgt. Ed "Squatty" Meisburger:

> He came all right with all the horses and the drivers and he couldn't find his way, and he yelled something like, "I can't see you, where are you?" I was the [sergeant of the] First Gun Section, and I started up the road to show him where to come in. Then he pulled a flashlight out of his pocket and waved it around his head and said, "I can't find you, where are you?" Of course, when the enemy saw that flashlight they knew where the target was.[10]

In truth, it all happened so fast that the Germans would not have been able to use Woolridge's flashlight to target Battery D, but, if noticed, it certainly might have demonstrated that there was activity associated with E's position and conceivably spurred German artillery to move a little more quickly in response to the gas attack. The Americans needed no encouragement to move expeditiously, and the first two gun sections to get their animals in harness were sent galloping up the road with Lieutenant Jordan. Whether on Truman's orders or Jordan's, they stopped dangerously close to Salisbury's position to await the rest of the battery. Meanwhile, the leftover gas shells were loaded into the 3rd Section's limber, and the last two guns were ready to move when a series of inexplicable events occurred. Although ordered to pull the Nos. 3 and 4 guns out directly to the left, over firm ground, First Sergeant Woolridge apparently either believed that the firm ground was to the left front or was in some other way confused and ordered them out directly to the front and toward the forward slope. The lead animals started to pitch over the slope, and in the radical maneuvers to keep horses, caissons, and guns from careening down the hill, at least some horses broke their harnesses, and the 75s separated from the caissons; careening down the hill on diverging paths. Gravity did the rest, and they rolled merrily along until the suction of the soggy earth slowed them to a stop.

Captain Truman and his BC detail by the road immediately perceived that chaos was breaking out in the blackness to their front. Truman leaped upon his mount to ride straight for the commotion and found himself falling through the air as "she promptly stepped into a shell hole and fell down rolling over me. Luckily I had fallen into another hole." Lieutenant Housholder pulled Truman to his feet, and the detail sprinted en masse to the old gun line and beyond. "Two of my guns," wrote Truman, "had gone over a hill in front of the position and became mired in mud up to my ankles. . . . I ordered all the horses of the stalled pieces hitched to one gun, which made twelve horses on No. 3 gun; No. 4 was in so deep it looked as if it never would come out. About that time the German barrage started."[11]

First Sergeant Woolridge, thoroughly rattled by his nonstop stream of errors, finally broke under the pressure and bellowed out, "Run fellers! They've got a bracket on us!" practically in Truman's ear.[12] The drivers working to free the No. 3 gun—all ten of them—bolted into the night with the first sergeant, as did at least some of Sgt. Verne Chaney's cannoneers and virtually all of the horses, which scattered in every direction. Truman later wrote that only "six or seven" of the privates (some from his own BC detail, such as O'Hare, Gordon, and Woods) stuck by the gun instead of "distinguish[ing] themselves as foot racers" and in his later writing admitted that he unleashed a torrent of profanities that would have made his old railroad line gang blush.[13] "I got up and called them everything I knew," said Truman. "Pretty soon they came sneaking back."[14]

It was never clear who fled and who didn't. The cannoneers and BC personnel who were some distance away with No. 4 gun heard the commotion, but could see nothing and were not particularly aware of what was transpiring. They perceived so little threat from the German artillery that Chief Mechanic Wooden and gunner "Skinny" McNamara spent the entire show perched several inches above the oozing muck on their gun's trail waiting for someone to bring up the double-teamed horses that, unbeknownst to them, had scattered to the winds. The 1st and 2nd Gun Sections, standing on the road near the "gas-proof" bunkers to which Salisbury's men had wisely retreated, were probably the most vulnerable artillerymen in the area, but the Germans didn't launch a concerted effort to shell the old French gun pits until after Battery D had completed its passage through the danger zone.

Although Sgt. Paul T. Sieben, the gas NCO that went forward on the mission with Truman, detected no poisonous German shells falling near D's fractured position, some were detected to the southeast at E Battery, and a gas alarm was promptly sounded. The drivers and gunners on the road—including the diminutive "little [John] Higginbotham,"[15] who stood less than five feet tall—were struggling to place specially made masks to their horses in the dark when Lieutenant Jordan got wind of the troubles his captain was having, likely from one of D's stragglers. On his own initiative, Jordan detached all of his animals and galloped back up the road with them to provide some extra horsepower. Truman was impressed with the effort, but wanted him to lead his own detail to safety. Apparently Jordan was a little insistent with his captain that he "should pull me out," and Truman "had to order him off the hill."[16]

As for Nos. 3 and 4 guns, it was apparent that they were going nowhere for the time being:

> We covered up the two guns I had stuck with branches and things, and one of my lieutenants—Housholder is his name—and myself then collected up all the horses we could and got the men together, caught up with the other two pieces. . . . Four horses were killed, two of them outright and two had to be shot afterwards. . . . My greatest satisfaction is that my legs didn't succeed in carrying me away, although they were very anxious to do it. Both of my lieutenants are all wool and a yard wide.[17]

Very shortly after leaving Salisbury's position behind, Truman's column moved south past the fleeting position long since vacated by C Battery, commanded by his old friend Marks, then past the regimental headquarters at Payrou, where Truman left the march to report the loss of his 2nd Platoon guns to Colonel Klemm. Truman believed himself to be in utter disgrace over leaving them behind, and asked if he should turn around and retrieve them. Klemm offered no criticism and, with German fire increasing noticeably and no risk at all that the 75s might fall into German hands, told Truman to just go back the next night and pull them out. The following morning, Klemm would receive reports that both Battery C and Keith Dancy's Battery A had lost a gun apiece and some horses along the slippery mountain tracks during their withdrawals, although Marks's soldiers were able to retrieve theirs.

Truman had indeed gotten the men out in the nick of time, but it was his and the other units' excellent shooting that had bought him those precious minutes. The utter saturation of the most forward German batteries with poison gas had effectively rendered them incapable of responding. So many German artillerymen were either killed outright or incapacitated that counterbattery fire was not possible from these guns, and heavier weapons farther to the rear had to be brought into play, with all the attendant delay that required. Even then the Germans' initial probes in the direction of the single American battery site that they could confirm were tentative—twenty rounds plunging into the soft earth in the vicinity of D Battery by Housholder's count, and perhaps a similar number southwest along the ridge near Auf Rain. And then, of course, there was the ground at the bottom of the slope, blessedly sodden from periodic downpours and runoff. The same muck that held Truman's cannons fast greatly suppressed the blast of even large-caliber shells, and, in a letter written a few days later, he mentioned that "one exploded [with]in fifteen feet of me and I didn't get a scratch."[18]

Battery E was pounded throughout the night but suffered no losses, and the road where C's fleeting position had been located was given a very thorough going-over shortly after D passed it. Other heavy shells had overshot E, falling in the vicinity of a 130th Field Artillery battery, prompting that regiment to respond with its own big 155mm howitzers. This startled Truman's men, who were marching in front of them toward Herrenberg when firing commenced and hadn't known that there were heavies concealed in the woods.

Back at their original position, the two remaining 75s were manhandled into their camouflaged gun pits; then the 1st and 2nd Section limbers, the weakest horses, and extra phosgene shells were sent down to Kruth with Lieutenant Jordan. Food in ample quantities had finally been brought up during the men's absence, and the cooks prepared a hot meal, so thoroughly enjoyed that it is mentioned in nearly every commentary and oral history interview of men present that night, be they privates or sergeants, or their captain and his XO. Truman's pocket calendar notes that he slept from 4 a.m. till 4 p.m., but not before "busting [Woolridge] to private"[19] and promoting gas NCO Sieben to first sergeant. When Truman awoke, he was gratified to learn that "every man wanted to go along" to retrieve the guns that night, but Truman "took only the two sections who belonged to the guns"[20] as well as the strongest, freshest animals, and plenty of extra shovels and rope.

Dizzy D believed that the previous night's mission had been a resounding success. There were mishaps galore, explosions, panic, the shrieking of horses shredded by shrapnel, yet the battery had carried out its mission, and not one man was killed or injured. The men were convinced that their courageous captain was the key to it all and that theirs was a "lucky" unit. Claims and counterclaims as to precisely who stuck by Truman were the talk of the battery, and the good-natured squabbles quickly resulted in the affair being dubbed "The Battle of Who Run." But there was no disagreement when it came to Truman. Said newly promoted Corporal O'Hare, "We have a captain who cannot be beaten."[21] They would follow him anywhere.

CHAPTER 11

125 Miles of Mud and Rain

THE COUNTDOWN WAS ON for General Pershing's first great American offensive, a nine-division assault into the base of a giant bulge into the Allied lines at Saint-Mihiel, with three more divisions, including the 35th, in reserve. A success here would not only free the main rail link between Paris and Nancy from German interdiction, but also remove the Germans blocking the line running north to yet another—and much larger—American thrust north toward the vital communications center at Sedan. These twin drives were scheduled to take place back to back and be launched by a single formation, the U.S. First Army which would also have significant French forces under its command during the Saint-Mihiel operation. If successful, the First Army's launching of twin offensives would be a feat that no French or British army had been able to pull off during the war and would pave the way for an American-French drive into traditionally German territory in mid-November—carrying the war into Germany itself.

THE 35TH DIVISION WAS SLATED to take part in all three of these offensives, but in the immediate future it was envisioned that if the 35th was not called forward into the Saint-Mihiel fight, it would be one of the divisions launching the second assault. If it was pulled into the battle to pinch off the salient, it would be thrown into the meat grinder to the north at some later date after it had replaced losses in men and equipment. What this meant for Battery D was that it was ordered to turn its laboriously constructed position over to the French and move back to Kruth as soon as it retrieved its muddy guns. Once there, it and the gathering 60th Field Artillery Brigade would prepare for a series of grueling night marches spanning 125 miles, with only one brief rail movement that barely did anything to help preserve the strength of the unit's poor horseflesh.

Replacement and spare horses were taken in, and Woolridge, now a private, was booted out, landing in the 1st Battalion's Battery B, where Truman's old friend Captain McGee kept a wary eye on him. It was an extremely lucky break for Woolridge that Truman had been his boss, as Major Gates was ready to court-martial the man and prepared the groundwork for formal charges, informing Colonel Klemm: "After Captain Truman's report is made, I believe it will be necessary to take action in regard to his 1st Sergt."[1] Truman later explained:

> The Major and the Colonel wanted me to court-martial the sergeant. I didn't but I busted him and afterwards I had to transfer him to another battery. Later in the war, he stood firm under the fiercest fire. I didn't care for court-martials. I'd get myself back of a table and I'd look as mean as I could. Then I'd tell them, "You can have a court-martial or, if you prefer, you can take what [punishment] I give you." That worked.[2]

Unique among the writings Harry S. Truman left behind on his military service are two lengthy, detailed accounts of Battery D's movement to the Saint-Mihiel, then Meuse-Argonne, battlefields. The first was contained within the twenty-four-page November 23, 1918, letter to Bess penned after the lifting of censorship restrictions, and the other fills twenty pages in a handwritten, seventy-three-page manuscript titled, "The Military Career of a Missourian," which was believed to have been written during his first senatorial term. Although they parallel each other in both subjects covered and chronology, the later manuscript contains a very large number of additional details but labors under his third-person references to himself and the battery. The 1918 letter to Bess is the basis of the text that follows. Where appropriate, elements of the later narrative have been weaved in with the word "I" replacing cumbersome third-person references, usually "the Captain," as well as other modifications of Truman's third-person usage. Some place names have been added and, since the original four thousand or so words were broken into only eight paragraphs, the text has been further subdivided for clarity.

> We stayed in Kruth about two days and then got ordered to fill all our caissons and pull out of the Vosges and go back to the valley where we had detrained. On the 2nd of Sept. we entrained at Remiremont for Bayon. This was my first experience as the Commander of a train. It pulled out of Remiremont at midnight and I went to bed and supposing we'd ride all night, but I was woefully disappointed. About 3:30, a Lt. Col. woke me up and told me that in 18 minutes I would be unloaded at Bayon and that Bayon was under constant aeroplane bombardment. Well I was scared green. I was in command of the train, and there was absolutely no one to pass the buck to; I simply had to unload that battery and find a place for it under cover before daylight.
>
> At 4 a.m. someone came running down the track and told me that I was wanted up at the station where we were stopped. I ran up to the station and all out of breath and the Regulating Officer of the 35th Division told me that I would detrain in half an hour and be under observation of the enemy and maybe under fire. There were two dead horses at that station platform which looked as if we'd been shot from above so that the Regulating Officer's statement looked as if it might be correct. That Regulating Officer was Bennett Clark, now Senator.

While the fear of marauding German bombers was very real, there had been no air raids at all on out-of-the-way Bayon. Was Lieutenant Colonel Bennett playing a little joke on Truman, or was he using the dead horses, apparent evidence of an enemy attack, to bolster his calls for speedy exit from the trains? Whether by design or accident, they were a highly effective stage prop, not just for Battery D, but for all the units coming through.

> I told my outfit that it was evidently the work of machine guns from aeroplanes and they'd better speed up their unloading. The train pulled up to the station where the Battery was to unload, and they made a record in getting off that platform. Lt. Col. Bennett gave me a map and told me of a possible location if someone else hadn't beaten me to it. He also marked out for me a line of march. The train had arrived about 4:30 a.m. and at five o'clock the outfit was in a wooded pasture beside a beautiful little stream a half mile from the town and right on the bank of the Moselle River. I spent a very pleasant day snoozing and watching the men bathe in the river. I got up about noon and went up to the depot to watch Lt. Col. Elliott and the Supply Company detrain.
>
> I'd found out afterward that the horses had been shot by a veterinary because they couldn't walk. Bennett's joke had nearly paralyzed an Artillery Captain, and my only satisfaction was to tell Lt. Col. Elliott, whose train came in about ten o'clock, the story that the regulating officer had told me and point out the horses for evidence. I told him all the harrowing tales I could think of regarding the daylight attacks of Hun planes, showed him the two dead horses and invited him to draw his own conclusions as to how they'd met their fate and just what he could expect if a Hun plane came.

Unfortunately for Truman, he had done a little too good of a job spooking Elliott:

> Col. E. was duly impressed and as I had already preempted most of the woods, he was about wild trying to find a place to put himself and the Supply Co. He finally had me move over to one side of my good pasture and make room for him along side of my

battery, and he came piling in broad daylight. So I gained nothing but inconvenience for passing on a good lie.

By now, the rainy season lay heavily upon northern France, and Lieutenant Lee described it as a nearly continuous presence, be it "light, short sprinkles to heavy and long-drawn-out downpours," punctuated all too briefly by "periods of evanescent sunshine or moonlight as the case might be."[3] Although the published version of the 129th's regimental history does not present a systematic account of the weather, a quick examination of it and the other two 60th Field Artillery Brigade regiments plus several battery histories confirm no fewer than sixteen days of "Rain, Rain, Rain,"[4] "nasty cold drizzle,"[5] "driving rain,"[6] and "rain coming down in torrents"[7] during the first three weeks of September. Wrote Lee:

We sometimes went as far as 30 or 35 kilometers in a night; which wasn't so bad except when, as so often happened, obstructions or congestion in the road caused those long and tiresome, or frequent, fretful stops and starts. The wondrous fact of all these men over there made a vivid and solemn impression, whether marching in the moonlight, with the long line of horses, limbers, guns, caissons, and men stringing out interminably before and behind; or in the dark, cloudy, rainy nights, with only vague shadows immediately in front, and vague noises beyond; and in either case the silent, monotonous, steady forward movement of thousands of men, all alike in outward appearance of round-topped helmet and army raincoat; all with a common purpose and determination, but each occupied with his own thoughts; silent, spectral, inevitable. Once in a while one will address you; and the contrast, the sharpness of the break, almost startles you.[8]

Because of the wretched condition of the draft horses, only the minimum number of personnel required to keep control of the animals and rolling stock were mounted—and then only part of the time. Those assigned riding mounts, a much higher quality of horseflesh, generally rode throughout the march, but it is recorded that Truman on at least one occasion had his horse hitched to a limber to give one of the played-out beasts a rest. If the captain did this, it is certain that the other riders also were dismounted from time to time as their animals were rotated, if necessary, to help preserve the draft horses. The potentially dangerous practice of putting riding mounts into harness during a night march would not at all be a common practice, however, since by temperament and training, they were not suited to be limbered-up, and would require close, personal attention while in harness. Contrary to D Battery mythology, the riders and drivers stayed on their animals.

IN SOME VERY REAL RESPECTS, though, the men on horseback and the rolling stock had it little better than those marching through the boot-sucking mud and gravel roads. The old term "saddle sore" was given new meaning by the nearly continual rain. Lieutenant Lee, whose experience on this matter was both personal and direct, stated that "the short, skimpy rain-coats which had been substituted at Camp Doniphan for the really effectual 'slickers' first issued" to the Missouri Guardsmen offered "no protection," even to the thighs.[9] The inevitable result had been long foreseen. Drivers planted on the wet saddles of the caissons' horse teams and wagon seats, or the officers, NCOs, and common soldiers, like the BC detail orderlies and guidon bearer (all of whom acted as messengers), painfully bounced along for unending hours through the wet weather until their skin was rubbed raw. And at the end of every march, it was necessary to set up camp, carefully care for horses, and dig latrines into the sodden earth. Yet, the rain that plagued the soldiers from Bayon to the Meuse-Argonne also helped protect the men whose marches extended into daylight hours with disturbing frequency. German aircraft were grounded during such weather, and on the very rare occasions when one could be heard above the clouds, it was blind to the activity below.

For Truman and his men, the only option was to do their duty and persevere:

They changed my orders about four times that day as to where I was to go. About four o'clock in the afternoon orders were passed out directing the regiment to move out over certain roads to a little town called Coyviller, and my era of night marches began. Soon as it was dark the Battery started and overtook a regiment of Infantry. It was resting alongside the road and I asked a Lt. Col. of Infantry standing by the roadside if I could take my battery through the regiment and was informed I could.

I passed a whole regiment of infantry [that] was strung out for four or five miles and the battery was half through the second one when I ran into the brigade adjutant, a pompous important feeling major of infantry who wanted an explanation of this presence in the midst of an infantry brigade without orders, especially since the battery was from another division.* I explained my regimental orders and showed the pompous major my map and the town where I was ordered to go. It was only three or four miles away and straight down the road, in another hour the battery could get to the town. It was then 9 o'clock. This brigade adjutant made the battery pull over to the roadside and let all the infantry pass by. The battery stood from 9 o'clock until half-past 3 the next morning and then had to poke along behind that outfit until broad daylight even though it had been only one hour to good billets.

While the battery stood on the roadside we could hear Hun planes, and saw them bomb Toul, to the northwest, and Luneville, northeast on the opposite side of Nancy. Both operations were in plain sight. French anti-aircraft guns barked and spat nearly all the night through and I expected every minute that a stray bomb or shrapnel case would fall on my outfit. None did. We finally arrived at a patch of woods and put up for the day

---

*The unit that Truman came across was either the 9th or 23rd Infantry of the 2nd Division's 3rd Brigade. In his pocket calendar book, Truman expressed his intent to punch the offending officer: "I'll bust the Brigade Adj if I meet him after the war."[10]

under cover. With one exception, that was the worst night I ever spent in France. Some men let authority make fools of them, the adjutant of the 3rd Infantry Brigade was one of those men. If that ornery adjutant hadn't stopped me I'd have reached the town I was headed for by 2 o'clock and would not have had to make two nights of it.

The next night we pulled into a little old dirty place called Coyviller just at day light, and were placed in barns and haylofts. We were so tired and sleepy that after feeding the horses we immediately turned in and slept most of the day. When we had a chance to look the village over we found that it was situated in a valley some hundred or hundred fifty feet below the surrounding plain and that it could only be left by a steep climb up hill any direction you wanted to go. The village seemed to have more manure than anything else; piled it in front of every house down the one street and since Manuretown* was easier to say than the French name that's what the outfit called it.

Battery C from 1st Battalion was billeted in the same village, and I and the C Bty's Captain Ted Marks were the closest of friends. Two days after arrival Major Gates told us that we would pull out at dark. It was uphill, nearly straight up, every direction out of the place. [Because thick overcast effectively hid activity on the ground from the eyes of German airmen,] I decided to pull my guns up the hill out of town before dark and then go back after my trains and supply wagons, thus being able to double up the teams and get up the hill easily. But Marks tried to move all his battery out at once and naturally got stuck. I'd gotten my guns up and was half way out with my supply train when I found C Bty had

---

*Captain John H. Thacher recorded that in Major John L. Miles's 1st Battalion, Coyviller was referred to as "Stinkville."[11] The gathering of manure piles on village streets in this region was still a common practice during World War II, and has been referenced in a wide variety of oral histories and memoirs by soldiers who served in the U.S. Third Army and the European theater's communication zone.

pulled out while I was getting my supply wagons and that their supply train was stalled on the hill and couldn't move.

That split me in two, leaving my guns up the hill and my combat train kitchen, etc. behind C. We were both supposed to move out at 8 p.m. but it was 9:30 before Marks got up the hill and 10:30 when I got my battery all together. The road was so narrow, I couldn't pull around him and I had to wait. As usual it began to rain. The Major was very angry because D had to march at the tail of the whole brigade all night and it was broad day light when the regimental stopping place was reached. But I was lucky anyway because I got a better place to stay that day than any of the others had. The Colonel had some rather sarcastic remarks to make about Captains of Batteries who got lost, but nothing else came of the incident.

That evening, September 11th, we marched again and the route lay through Nancy. The town was dark except for a red light now and then in a doorway. Nancy was bombed regularly but escaped on this night. After going through the town the Artillery Brigade marched and halted, marched and halted all night. About eleven o'clock the big guns started a barrage off to the right; the beginning of the St. Mihiel drive. I have heard the first continuous roar of artillery preparation several times since but it's never sounded so big or so real as it did that night. It was dark as Egypt* and raining as usual and I had to ride behind the last carriage of the battery in front of me in order to see it.

The Artillery Brigade pulled into the Forêt de Haye, just east of Nancy and four miles south of the U.S. 82nd and 90th division's slice of the Saint-Mihiel front, and kept the horses harnessed day and night for three days but didn't get to fire a shot. It was such a walk-away that they didn't need us. We got credit for being in the drive, however because we were in reserve and ready to shoot, and spent the very pleasant time watching Hun prisoners go by.

---

* In Truman's calendar book, written six weeks before the November 23 letter to Bess, he used the phrase "dark as hell."[12]

Uncommitted at Saint-Mihiel, the still-fresh 35th Division was well-positioned to be one of the divisions leading the way during the Meuse-Argonne offensive. With a scant ten days till the jump off, Battery D marched out of Forêt de Haye on the almost singularly "bright moonlit night" of September 15–16. They could not reach their first destination before daylight—before noon in fact—but this was by design, because AEF headquarters was confident that the mass of activity associated with the current offensive would mask not just the regiment's movement, but that of several divisions through the general area. Soon, however, the return of heavy overcast and storms would provide some badly needed extra time in the mornings for units to arrive at their way points and set up camps under cover so that they could "grab a few hours sleep and march some more"[13] until the men got to the staging area for their firing positions. Truman continued:

> We marched for several days and on the twenty-third the regiment arrived at Aubreville. One of my Lts. went up to look over my position and I stripped the battery for action. I knew I was in for it this time because I [was ordered to take] only the firing batteries and just enough men to man the guns, and they for the first time were allowed to ride the limbers and caissons. On every other night march they had to walk and carry packs weighing from sixty to eighty pounds, depending on the number of souveniers [sic] in each pack. There was a saying that the Germans fought for territory, the English fought to control the seas, the French fought for defense and security, but the Americans fought for souveniers.
>
> I had all sorts of difficulties getting the battery up to the position it was supposed to take [after] getting out of the woods. One caisson got pigheaded and I couldn't budge the cussed thing with either prayers or "cuss" words. I tried both. Finally hooked all the men onto it with ropes and got it out. Well, I finally got my battery out on the main highway and headed for the front, and then and there began the wildest ride I ever hope to have.

It seemed as though every truck and battery in France was trying to get to the same front by the same road that I was going. I had twelve carriages in my column—four guns, six caissons, and two *fourgon* wagons, one of them full of instruments and one full of grub. I don't know which I'd rather have lost. I believe I could have gotten along better without the grub. Those devilish trucks kept trying to cut me in two. It was necessary to keep the battery moving all the way, and I had to ride the line to see that they stayed closed up. Every time I'd get a chance, I'd cut in ahead of a row of trucks and hold'em up until I got the whole battery by and every time a truck would get a chance, he'd cut through the battery. They didn't get very many chances because when we got the right of the road I made it a point never to let 'em through.

In one little old village we passed, we had to make a right angle turn around a curb, and one of these bloomin' trucks drove up just as close as he could while one of my carriages was going by and then he had to stop because I put my horse squarely across in front of him and held the whole train of a division while the battery went past. Every one of my carriages either hit that truck a jolt or smashed into the curb but I got them by and went on down the road at a gallop to find that my No. 2 gun had a horse down in the road.

It was raining as usual, and the road was as slick as glass. We finally got that horse up. It took us two hours of fast maneuvering and the hardest work to get that gun back to its place in column again. Every soldier and every train in France (American) were trying to get to the line by the same road it seemed and if a gun or a man became separated from his outfit it was just too bad. The gun finally caught up after I threaten[ed] to shoot a truck driver or two and had had words with one or two train commanders.

At this point in the narrative, Truman made a curious departure in the portion written well after the war and the 1925 suicide of Klemm, who used his old army revolver to shoot himself in his Kansas City bank office.

The Colonel was a West Pointer, class of 1907, who had left the Army when he was still a second lieutenant of cavalry and married a rich brewer's daughter. When the war came on he helped organize the 2nd Mo. F. A. [Missouri Field Artillery] and was elected its Colonel. He had German ideas about discipline and a superiority complex because of his education and his wife's money. He'd never associated with volunteer troops and didn't understand that nearly all of them were from good families, a number were college graduates and nearly all had high school training.

On the march out of the Vosges on Sept. 3 he rode up and down the line taking overseas caps away from privates and throwing them down the mountainside. The order was to wear helmets. But the organization commanders were the ones the Colonel should have bawled out, not the men. He'd promiscuously break sergeants and corporals and forget all about making the necessary order later. Whenever he found a man riding on a limber or caisson he'd almost throw a fit and by the time the entraining point was reached everyone was of the opinion that the Colonel was either drunk or crazy.

On the night of the 24th of Sept. however the Colonel was in an excellent humor. He rode up and down the line helping battery commanders untangle the batteries from truck trains and in infantry combat trains; encouraging everyone[,] and Captains really thought perhaps they had misjudged him on the Vosges march.

Truman may not have wanted to speak ill of the departed, but his men and a disgusted major in the 130th were less shy about filling in the back story. Said Sergeant McKim, "My overall impression was that he was a crazy man."[14] It was shortly after the 129th began its fatiguing series of soggy night marches that Colonel Klemm's behavior had inexplicably taken an irrational turn. Just over a week after the incident with the 129th's overseas caps, a bizarre repeat occurred on September 11 outside Nancy, as Klemm did it again to a unit not his own—and with Lieutenant Colonel Elliott collecting the caps as trophies! After the war, Major MacLean, commander of the 130th Field Artillery's 1st Battalion, published an account of his antics in their regimental history:

> On the way in, Colonel Klemm and his operations officer put on a show for the boys by riding along the line and taking the cap from the head of each fellow who was not wearing his helmet. The operations officer was riding along with his arm full of caps, followed by the black looks of the soldiers who had been robbed because they did not want to wear their helmets all the time.
>
> Klemm also double tracked [had the 129th get alongside] the 130th in getting into the woods, which was against the rules, and cut across so closely as to ruin a couple of our horses; but then he was a colonel and was undoubtedly in a hurry to get under cover so we could do nothing about it.[15]

Just over a week had passed when Klemm ordered that Battery D be punished because of its general failure to maintain proper march discipline. This happened on numerous occasions, and the veterans' memories tended to mash them all together when oral histories were conducted a half-century later. Thankfully, Truman's pocket calendar and extra-duty roster allow some of this to be sorted out, and Pvt. Floyd T. Ricketts explained the background to nearly all the events:

> [We had] about fifteen nights of forced marching. The weather was bad, rainy, and we would sleep in the daytime in thickets or in woods and then take off at dusk and march all night long. The next morning, of course, we would bivouac in another woods or forest. After about a week or ten days most of us were pretty well exhausted and that also went for the horses of the regiment. The horses were in bad shape. Every night it seemed we would lose one or two horses. They would just drop by the road exhausted and would have to be destroyed. And there was an order out that we cannoneers who were walking and following the guns were not to hold onto any part of the gun or the caissons so as not to put

any more burden on the horses. But walking along almost dead on your feet, you could hardly resist grabbing ahold of the caisson to help you along. I remember this one night, several of the boys were holding onto the caisson and Colonel Klemm rode by and noticed it and was quite upset.[16]

At Villey Saint-Etienne outside of Toul, some long-forgotten infraction or infractions led to the battery being ordered to march double-time up and down a nearby hill on the night September 17–18. Truman ordered the men, chests heaving under heavy packs and at the limit of their endurance, to fall out after one hour instead of putting them back into the line of march. "Truman took us off the road and we laid down and slept for a while, right in the ditch at the side of the road," said Sergeant McKim. "Then we got up and Klemm came back looking for us and he said, 'Captain, where have you been?' And Truman said, 'Carrying out orders, sir.'"[17] The hyperbolic former sergeant said that they had been double-timing an impossible four hours when Truman told them to call it quits (the captain's calendar book lists one hour), but the most interesting aspect of this confrontation that McKim brings to light is how Truman defied, apparently successfully, his colonel's orders by pretending to misunderstand them. Three days later on the road north of Loisey, Truman scored a long-remembered victory for his men, and unbeknownst to the rest of the regiment, them as well. And while Dizzy D didn't know how he did it, they were deeply grateful for the results.

ALONG THE LINE OF MARCH, straggling—a pronounced stretching out of the column—was becoming epidemic throughout the regiment as fatigued men and horses began to lag behind at various points, which forced following trains to bunch up behind them. There is no indication that units were not in the proper sequence or intermixed, but just a few hours after it had begun, the march was becoming more and more out of sync. Dizzy D, and probably several other elements as well, became the focus of Colonel Klemm's attention. He ordered Truman to "take us out of the line away from the caissons," said Ricketts, "take us up ahead of the Battery and give us a little double-timing as punishment." Squatty Meisburger, near the front of the Battery D train with No. 1 Gun, had a fairly good view of the proceedings, but could hear practically nothing:

> The colonel of the regiment, he came fluttering down the highway and complained about Battery D sort of straggling, and talked to Captain Truman. I don't know what the words were between them, but anyway, the colonel gave the order, "Call these men in and double time them up this hill." We were pretty tired by then walking, let alone doubletiming, and the captain said, "Yes, sir." But instead of following the colonel's orders, he ordered a "Column Right" and he took us off the highway into an inviting woods. And the orders were to feed the horses and tie them up for the evening and to bed the men down and to get a night's rest. . . . . The colonel sent for Captain Truman to come up at once and everybody figured the captain was going to get court martialed; but he came back grinning, and apparently won his battle. The result was the colonel called the whole outfit off the highway and rested them overnight and we took off the next morning.[18]

What exactly had transpired far from the men's ears? Lieutenant Lee confirms that the "whole outfit" was ordered off the road and into bivouac at 2 a.m., even though the regiment could have traveled for many more hours wrapped in a protective blanket of darkness. Truman, perhaps with the assistance of other officers, likely pointed out that pulling bone-tired men out of line to send them at a punishing trot was cruel—and absurdly counterproductive.

The men were already very well aware that Truman was diligently serving as a buffer between themselves and the erratic Klemm, such as when the colonel spied a soldier, Supply Sgt. James J. Doherty, seated beside a *fourgon* driver. Truman took seriously the directive against allowing unnecessary riders, as his extra-duty roster attests (ten Battery D men receiving a variety of disciplinary actions for the offense during the march—forfeitures of pay, extra duty, and a demotion for one soldier). But Sergeant Doherty had a twisted ankle and received his captain's permission to ride. "Klemm, seeing Doherty, flew into a rage and ordered him down," said author David McCullough. Truman informed his colonel that "as long as he was in command of the battery, Doherty would ride. Klemm, furious, turned and rode off."[19]

On another occasion Truman talked the colonel out of court-martialing a group of soldiers led by Private Leigh, who had moved out *ahead* to the battery bivouac point "rather than poke along [with] those horses," a sort of "straggling to the front."[20] Truman felt that the men deserved no punishment beyond a firm verbal reprimand:

> "Now, don't ever do that anymore." He said, "I understand what you were doing. I don't condone it, the Battery has got to be cohesive, you know, got to stay together. If everybody started wandering all over France, I won't have any Battery anymore. Don't do it anymore. That's all. Goodbye."[21]

The men knew that Truman would not hesitate to mete out deserved punishments but would fiercely defend them against perceived injustices. That night on the Loisey-Gery Road, Meisburger and others saw a victorious Captain Truman riding back down to his column, but the unseen battle with Klemm had included a vicious tongue-lashing as its price. Sick and tired of Truman's resistance (and likely understanding full well that the resistance had been justified in each instance), Klemm boiled over before harshly dismissing his subordinate. Truman's anguish—his anger—is plain in the notes scribbled into his pocket calendar under September 20: "The Colonel insults me shamefully. No gentleman would say what he said. Damn him."[22]

Private Harry S. Truman, Battery B, 1st Battalion, Missouri Field
Artillery, Missouri National Guard, 1905. Harry S. Truman Library
and Museum.

Corporal Truman, circa 1907. Harry S. Truman Library and Museum.

Lieutenant Harry S. Truman,
Battery F, 2nd Battalion,
2nd Missouri Field Artillery,
Missouri National Guard,
circa July 1917. Harry S. Truman Library and Museum.

The M1902 3-inch gun.
Author's collection.

A typical view of the 35th Division's layout at Camp Doniphan, Fort Sill, Oklahoma, 1917–1918. The tent in the foreground is of the same type that Lieutenant Truman shared with two other officers, and the frame building beside it is
of the same basic design as the regimental canteen and battery mess halls that he
managed. Harry S. Truman Library and Museum.

Truman and canteen staff outside of the 129th Field Artillery canteen, circa October 1917. The soldier to his left is canteen steward Pvt. Eddie Jacobson. Harry S. Truman Library and Museum.

Happy customers outside the canteen. Harry S. Truman Library and Museum.

Brigadier Gen. Lucian Berry, commander, 60th Field Artillery Brigade, United States Army, October 29, 1918. Berry's pronounced mustache prompted Truman to refer to him as "the Walrus" in numerous letters. U.S. National Archives and Records Administration.

A draft horse gives out. Despite the best efforts of Truman and his men, Battery D lost more than a dozen of the weakened French animals they received to fatigue. Author's collection.

A 35th Division ambulance company on one of the mountain roads that Truman's drivers found so treacherous during night movements. U.S. National Archives and Records Administration.

The night marches from the Vosges to the Meuse-Argonne were punctuated by hasty bivouacs alongside nearby woods so that the Germans would not detect the movement. Author's collection.

Although a good many of the men Truman recruited were enticed by the slogan "Join the Artillery and Ride," the appalling condition of the French draft animals necessitated that they march like regular infantry instead of adding to the animals' burden. Author's collection.

Captain Harry S. Truman's ID card, circa August 1918: a lean, mean, fightin'
machine. Harry S. Truman Library and Museum.

Loading horses into French boxcars. Harry S. Truman Library and Museum.

An eight-man machine gun section provided antiaircraft and close-in protection for artillery batteries like Truman's. A corporal and three privates handled each of the two M1914 Hotchkiss weapons that were mounted on carts or small *fourgon* wagons during battery movements, and commonly placed beyond the gun line's flanks when in position. U.S. National Archives and Records Administration.

At a typical battery position along a French tree line, the soldier in the foreground with a megaphone is likely the battery's executive officer. Harry S. Truman Library and Museum.

The enemy. Author's collection.

The other enemy: road congestion on the opening day of the Meuse-Argonne
Offensive, September 29, 1918. Author's collection.

A soldier struggles to get his animals to cooperate. Note the mule on his left in the rear rank. Author's collection.

The bridge at Boureuilles was opened on September 28, 1918, after extensive repair work by the 103rd Engineers. Two days earlier, the freshly-blown structure blocked the 129th Field Artillery's advance and forced the unit to cross no man's land and the German trench system. Author's collection.

A knocked-out German 77mm field gun. Battery D destroyed or forced the abandonment of twelve such weapons on September 27–28, 1918. U.S. National Archives and Records Administration.

A 155mm howitzer gun section of the 28th Division's Battery A, 180th Field Artillery, on the west side of Varennes, October 3, 1918. Author's collection.

A 75mm field gun of the 1st Infantry Division's 6th Field Artillery south of Exermont, October 4, 1918. Author's collection.

Truman's battery had a radio as a backup for maintaining communications with higher headquarters, but when he went forward to establish an observation post on September 27, 1918, it was with a team of four telephone men, principally to handle the communication wire. Author's collection.

A wartime cartoon of Truman in action was drawn by Pvt. Lyle E. DeTalent of the 129th's Headquarters Company, from the papers of Major John H. Thatcher. Harry S. Truman Library and Museum.

Battery D's sister battery in the 128th Field Artillery fires a rolling barrage from their "75s" during the 35th Division's jump-off on September 16, 1918. Truman's virtually identical gun line is approximately one thousand yards behind this one. U.S. National Archives and Records Administration.

Battery C, 130th Field Artillery, as seen from atop the ruins on the Aire River's west bank, September 28, 1918. Truman's gun position on the afternoon of September 27 is at the top left, along the edge of La Grotte. His position from the evening of the 27th until D Battery's withdrawal is farther up the Varennes-Cheppy Road at the center top. U.S. National Archives and Records Administration.

Soldiers scurry for cover on October 7, 1918, as German artillery begins a bombardment of Exermont, where the U.S. 1st and 35th Divisions suffered very heavy casualties. Author's collection.

Wounded are being treated in the 137th Field Hospital by the 110th Sanitary Train, 35th Division, which set up operations in a shattered church at Neuvilly, September 29, 1918. Author's collection.

Colonel Karl D. Klemm, commander of the 129th Field Artillery, and Lt. Col. Arthur J. Elliott, his executive officer. Harry S. Truman Library and Museum.

Gas masks for horses were not expected to save their lives, but hopefully preserve them long enough to accomplish a mission. During one gas attack, Truman's "Little [John] Higginbotham," perhaps a full head shorter than this soldier, scrambled to place these contraptions on his section's horses in the black of night. Author's collection.

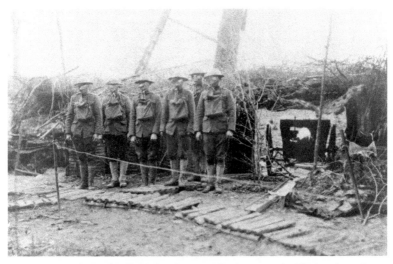

Artillerymen of the 15th Field Artillery, 2nd Division, on the Verdun front, later occupied by Truman's unit, pose next to their handiwork: a decoy position featuring a destroyed 75mm gun. Author's collection.

Battery D preparing to turn in its equipment, February 1919. Harry S. Truman Library and Museum.

Left to right: 1st Lt. Victor H. Housholder, Capt. Harry S. Truman, 1st Lt. Gordon B. Jordan, and 2nd Lt. Leslie M. Zemer. Harry S. Truman Library and Museum.

Sergeant William Tierney's No. 2 Gun Section, circa December 1918. Harry S. Truman Library and Museum.

The 129th Field Artillery's senior officers while quartered at the Chateau la Chesnaye, April 1919. Officers mentioned in this narrative: (7) Capt. L. Curtis Tiernan, (16) 1st Lt. Gordon B. Jordan, (19) Capt. Newell T. Paterson, (20) Capt. Harry B. "Pete" Allen, (21) Capt. Spencer Salisbury, (22) Capt. Harry S. Truman, (24) Maj. John L. Miles, (25) Maj. Marvin H. Gates, (26) the unit commander replacing Klemm, Col. Emery T. Smith, and (27) Maj. Charles E. Wilson. Author's collection.

CHAPTER 12

The Meuse-Argonne

THE 35TH DIVISION REACHED the Rembercourt area by early morning on Saturday, September 21. This far corner of the Verdun battlefield was the France that they had read about in the newspapers for years before Wilson's declaration of war, not the sanitized, geometrically precise trench systems of their training or the occasional cluster of wrecked buildings in the Vosges. Wide swaths of shredded ground and trees; Rembercourt itself rising out of the mud like broken teeth in a bloody mouth—these features brought to the forefront again the distant booming of heavy guns that had become such a normal part of the mens' daily lives that they didn't even notice it anymore. They did now, and it would be from their hidden bivouac that day that the gun crews would make a "wild ride"[1] past Aubreville on the "rainy, sloppy night"[2] of September 22–23 to their firing positions.

WHILE TRUMAN WAS STILL IN UNIFORM, he produced a superb series of longhand drafts, for purposes unknown, of his battery's operations once they reached the Meuse-Argonne. The draft written by a visibly unsteady hand and containing numerous cross-outs is presumably the first, and has a partially retyped and edited version associated with it. Another draft displays handwriting that is more uniformly and carefully set down. Both closely parallel each other, and while they agree in nearly every respect on times, dates, and places, each contains a variety of interesting details missing in its twin, and some structural differences. These form the basis of the narrative in this and the following two chapters, and are bolstered by useful comments in his November 23, 1918, letter to Bess; "The Military Career of a Missourian"; three lengthy, no-frills operations reports; battery and battalion records; as well as observations in several notebooks. A small number of useful details also appear in Volume 1 of Truman's *Memoirs*.

In some of Truman's writings, set down at different times between roughly fifteen and thirty-five years after the events, he sometimes put down the wrong dates. In all cases, I have adjusted them and various times to conform with battery and regimental records, as well as the calendar book he carried in his pocket. Similarly, Truman's memory during the 1930s was far off the mark when recalling Battery D's ammunition expenditures and rate of fire at the opening of the Meuse-Argonne offensive. The data used here is from the notes, operations reports, and ammunition reports produced by Truman and Lieutenant Housholder in September and early October 1918.

The 129th F.A. moved into positions in the Forêt de Hess on the early morning of Sept. 23, 1918. The regiment had been marching every night since the Battle of St. Mihiel where it had been in reserve a short distance north of Toul in the Forêt de Haye.

The night of the 22–23rd was cold and rainy and the clouds seemed almost within reach. The regiment had spent the day in the woods just west of Rarecourt. The Battalion Commanders, Major Marvin, H. Gates and Major John L. Miles had gone forward in the afternoon with their details to reconnoiter positions for their respective battalions. As soon as it was dark enough, the regiment pulled out on the road (which was easier said than done because the wood in which the day had been spent was really a mud hole), and started on the wildest ride it ever experienced in the whole year it was in France. It was dark as Egypt except for occasional flares from the front line and flashes from active enemy artillery.

The road was very slick making it very hard for the horses to keep their feet. It seemed as if every American truck train in France was trying to get to the front on that road. It was necessary for the Artillery to thread its way in and out of these truck trains, sometimes going all the way into the field to get around stalled or overturned trucks. It was a wild ride always at a trot and sometimes a gallop. The cannoneers rode on the seats provided for them—the one and only time they ever did by authority while on the front.

Platoon and Battery Commanders had all they could do keeping the column closed up. If a carriage dropped out because of a fallen horse it was almost impossible to get it back to its place in line. Each Battery had a carriage or two at the rear of the columns. Battery F had its instrument wagon upset and one of the men on it broke a leg. Whenever a carriage got behind it was a headache job to catch up again. Col. Klemm was all along the line encouraging the drivers and battery commanders to do their utmost to arrive with the units complete.

By now, it had become obvious to the Germans that the *Amerikaners* were shifting troops to the French lines between the Argonne Forest and Verdun, but the Germans did not recognize the nature and scale of the buildup. The U.S. First Army was having a high degree of success in hiding away the men and equipment, and any suggestion that the inexperienced AEF command would consider launching a second—and even greater—offensive immediately after Saint-Mihiel was unimaginable. Still, it was difficult to hide the big French-made railroad guns that the Americans had hauled up to Aubreville. They were attracting sporadic fire from the longest-range German 130mm and 150mm cannons even as the 129th Field Artillery clattered through the streets. Soon the regiment was within the reach of shorter-range heavies, but, as yet, the Germans were not directing fire at them or seemingly anything other than known road junctions such as Neuvilly, which the regiment was anxious to get through as quickly as possible.

About 2 o'clock on the morning of the 23rd the column reached Neuvilly. Heine [slang for German] was sending over 150s and 210s at regular intervals and we didn't tarry long in the town. The Majors directed the Batteries to their positions. Bty D went into position about a mile from the road across a muddy field, in some small timber clumps just off the Foret de Hesse. [This was] about a couple of hundred yards from Hill 290 on the French map. Well naturally, after all that wild ride, I had to get two caissons stuck and at regular intervals[, and] Heine would drop a shell in that neighborhood just to let us know he was there.

It was a heartbreaking job. The fields were muddy and full of shell holes. Carriages would get stuck and horses fall down; men would slip into shell holes half filled with water. By putting twelve horses on each gun and having every available man push, we finally got into position. At 3 a.m. everyone was under cover. The horses were sent back to Aubreville with the limbers and the combat train under Captain Bostain finally got the position set up by daylight. The cannoneers dropped down by their pieces and tried to get a little sleep, and I went up on the side of a hill with two of my lieutenants to some woods on the edge of Hill 290 to the right flank of the Battery and went to sleep.

Approximately a half-dozen batteries of French 220mm guns and 155mm howitzers had already been carefully scattered throughout the area when the 60th Field Artillery Brigade's regiments began to fan out south of the dubious screen provided by a low ridge called les Côtes de Foriment. North of the ridge and in view of the forward trenches, nine French batteries of 75mm and 105mm guns lay silent and camouflaged along the narrow tree lines of two roads.

The 128th's 2nd Battalion was farthest west of the 60th's regiments, just off the main north-south highway called the Route Nationale, and its 1st Battalion was positioned nearly a mile to the east. The 130th with its big 155mm howitzers was concentrated between them and slightly north. The 129th's spot at the base of Hill 290 was directly south of the 128th's 2nd Battalion, with the 2nd Battalion's F Battery anchoring the left flank, the 1st Battalion arrayed in a line to the north east from F, and the rest of the 2nd Battalion extending southeast from F Battery. Truman's unit was at the end of the westward-pointing V's southern arm, and thus was the farthest to the rear of any artillery battery—French or American—in the brigade sector.

Got up about 3 in the afternoon [September 23] and picked out another place to put my cot which was very lucky for me because that night my first choice was unmercifully shelled, and I'd be in small pieces now as would half my battery and my lieutenants if I'd stayed there. We spent the rest of the day, which was the 24th, in digging trenches and preparing shelter for the men and figuring out ranges to different places to fire on. When it did finally come time to fire, they gave us targets of course that we'd never figured for.

That night Heine shelled all the surrounding territory but missed me. Two lieutenants and I bedded down in the woods and slept until 5 a.m. Sept. 25. We arose and went down to the Battery and about that time several German shells came down where we'd been asleep. The same thing happened to Captain Pete Allen of Battery F who had his headquarters destroyed by an exploding shell that hit his bed just after Pete had gotten out of it, and a shell blew out Battery E's ammunition dump, killing a man from Salisbury's outfit. D Bty set up a kitchen a short distance from the Battery position. About nine o'clock an enemy shell burst in the neighborhood and blew up the food on the field range, knocked a hole in the stove pipe and almost ruined the messes of an excellent cook.* The kitchen was moved back to Aubreyville, and rations

* According to "Squatty" Meisburger, the only reason that Mess Sgt. Lee Heilman escaped serious injury or death was because he was away gathering firewood. (Edward M. Meisburger, "20 Years Ago K.C. Men Made Argonne History," Kansas City Journal Post, September 25, 1938, 1.) This, presumably, was also true for the other cooks, Pvts. Chester Gibbs, Daniel Statzel, and Harold West, who also doubled as one of the buglers.

were brought up by ration cart as regularly as could be expected after that.

On Saturday Sept. 25 evening about 5 p.m. orders came for an officers meeting in two hours at the Colonels dugout. He told us that a drive was to start from the North Sea toward the Adriatic at 5:30 a.m. the next morning Sept. 26, 1918. He told us that the 129th F.A. would begin wire cutting operations at 4:20 a.m. and that we would fire a rolling barrage at 5:20 to 7:41. He then remarked very casually that one of the Batteries would be the Infantry Battery and would march up with the Infantry, go over the top as close as it possibly could to the Infantry and fire on targets designed by the Inf. Commander, after it had fired the usual barrage that all the rest had to fire.

All the Bty Commanders simply held their breath waiting to see who would get killed first. Finally Battery C's commander Capt. Marks was informed that his would be an Infantry Battery when the move forward began, and was heartily congratulated by all the others because of the honor, and a feeling of great relief was felt by the other five B[attery]. C[ommander]s. The Colonel asked us if we understood [our orders] and when everyone said he did we were dismissed and told to hop to it.

In keeping with the tactics advocated by Colonels Danford and Burleson, Colonel Klemm had instructed Marks to attach his Battery C to Col. Clad Hamelton's 137th Infantry in order to provide direct and immediate support of the doughboys. Although there would have been apprehension about being up front and likely having to set up his guns in the open, Marks would have indeed taken the assignment as an honor and felt the military man's eagerness to "get to it." Yet this story all but disappears beyond this point. There is no evidence in the C Battery and regimental histories, or the oral histories of all the officers involved, that a link-up of any sort took place or that soldiers from either unit were sent to establish a liaison. The only item that displays a serious intent to detach C Battery to the 137th comes, inter- estingly, from a fleeting reference in one of Truman's accounts, which

lists the 129th's march order out of the Forêt de Hess. Battery C, a
1st Battalion unit, did in fact lead the parade north, followed by the
2nd Battalion, and then the balance of the 1st Battalion, far removed
from Marks. If there was any effort to establish meaningful contact
between the infantry and artillery formations—and the 137th would
have been anxious to have the support of Marks's guns—it remains
hidden. This curious footnote to operations is mentioned because
Captain Truman and Major Gates would very soon find themselves in
the same situation as Marks.

SERGEANT MEISBURGER, chief of the First Gun Section, describes
Truman's activities and his headquarters setup at this crucial time:

> At 2:30 on the morning of the twenty-sixth, the gunners were
> aroused and the gun sergeants were called to Captain Truman's
> headquarters, which had been established in a covered supply
> wagon. While the sergeants were in there getting instructions
> and firing data for the barrages, the cooks were passing out a real
> breakfast with plenty of bacon and coffee.
>
> Sgt. George Brice was there in charge of the telephones and
> other signal equipment. He and Fred Weidenmann already had
> strung a line to the observation post up front where Captain
> Truman would stay to direct the fire he had already figured out
> on the firing maps.
>
> The line officers and the sergeants were told by Captain
> Truman on what a large scale this offensive was being undertaken
> and what it would mean if it were successful. The sergeants then
> had their luminated stop watches synchronized (watches which
> the captain bought us in Paris*); received their barrage sheets
> containing the zero hour and range and elevation information . . .
> passed out [at] the wagon.

---

*Meisburger assumed that the stopwatches for the timing of battery fire were
purchased in Paris, but it is more likely that Truman acquired them in Angers
while the unit was training at Brain-sur-l'Authion.

Just outside the headquarters wagon (the moon was shining now) was Capt. L. Curtis Tiernan, chaplain of the 129th field artillery, seated in a chair, hearing confessions of men of his faith.[3]

And from Truman:

All was bustle around the battery positions. Lt. Jordan, ammunition officer for the 2nd Bn.,* spent the night hauling ammunition. He succeeded in getting the full quota for each battery without accident or casualty by 2 a.m. although the roads were constantly harassed by enemy artillery and the [main] dump itself was shelled intermittently. The figuring of a barrage of the size of that Sept. 26 one was a task. The Captains and their B.C. details stayed up most of the night doing the figuring and making out the barrage sheets for each gun and getting things shaped up for the move forward. No one slept. There was too much excitement. The Chaplain, Lieutenant Tiernan, was busy all night hearing confessions and encouraging the men to do their utmost on the march.

At 2 a.m. the heavies opened up and by 4:20 several hundred 75s joined the serenade, firing on barbed wire entanglements in front of Boureuilles for one hour. The rolling barrage started on Vauquois Hill at 5:30 hour and continued until 7:41, the range being increased 100 meters every four minutes. There was more noise than human ears could stand. Men serving the guns became deaf for weeks after. I was as deaf as a post from the noise. It looked as though every gun in France was turned loose and the sky was red from one end to the other from the artillery flashes. It was like a continual play of lightning or the flashes of that artillery preparation—a continual explosion of guns and shells interspersed with the typewriter staccato of machine guns further up front.

---

*Lieutenant Gordon B. Jordan served in this capacity as well as his Battery D duty in charge of the unit's rolling stock, horses, and ammunition train.

The 129th F.A. fired about 13,000 rounds that morning. The guns got very hot. Four hundred gallons of water were used on gunny sacks to cool the guns in just Bty. D. When a gun was taken out to cool it would be swabbed with salsoda* and water and covered with wet gunny sacks. Steam would arise just as if an engine were underneath letting off surplus driving vapor. Daylight came about 6:30. It was a smoky, foggy morning and we could see our sausage balloons beginning to go up behind us. There was a row of them all ascending together and they were so evenly spaced that they looked like the floaters on a fishnet. The barrage ceased at 7:41 a.m. and everything became as quiet as a church except for a smattering of machine gun bursts. Some German aviators flew across and sunk a couple of the American observation balloons and calmly went back to their countrymen.

Battery D's share of this onslaught was 2,018 rounds—720 during the wire-cutting, following the standard French program of one round every fifteen seconds from three guns while a fourth gun was out on rotation to cool, and then 1,298 during the rolling barrage. There should have been 1,572 rounds fired at the Germans during the latter phase, but either there were problems getting some of the gun barrels cool enough to safely resume firing after rotation, or some of the gunners were having difficulty keeping up with the changing fire plan, which marched the barrage north in stages ahead of the foot soldiers' advance. Three of Battery D's guns fell behind schedule (Meisburger's No. 1 Gun lagged the farthest, shooting only 447 of the planned 524 rounds per gun during the rolling barrage), while Sergeant Thacker's No. 4 Gun sent 562 rounds down range. Thacker's gun crew included the battery

---

*Salsoda is a transparent, crystalline, hydrated sodium carbonate. Today, the most commonly used salsoda cleaning product is Arm & Hammer Super Washing Soda. Late in the firing program, Chief Mechanic Wooden found it expedient to swab not just the guns rotated through the cooling periods, but also the ones firing. This was done every second or third shot after pouring a bucket of water straight down the gun tubes and out their open breeches.

hot shot, Cpl. James T. "Skinny" McNamara, who Chief Mechanic Wooden later stated "was awfully fast . . . about the fastest one in the regiment at [adjusting] the range and stuff like that."[4]

> Battery breakfast was served at 8 o'clock and our orders were to pull out as soon as ready afterwards. At 8:26 the 2nd Bn. was ordered to move out with F in front followed by E and D in the rear. Bty D got ready to pull out first so D was ordered to lead the Battalion which it did at 9 a.m. The road was muddy and it was a hard pull. The artillery had to use a road winding through the Forêt de Hess because the Route Nationale from Neuvilly to Varennes was reserved for supply and ammunition trains. No man's land was reached about 1 o'clock.

These supply and ammunition trains, however, were going nowhere. When the Germans stormed through the area in 1914, the retreating French detonated several tons of explosives packed into a highway culvert south of Varennes, blowing a fifty-foot-deep, one-hundred-foot-wide crater in the earth. The Germans subsequently pulled back, and their defense line incorporated the crater. It and the Route Nationale south of the town were solidly in the operational zone of the 28th Division, on the left flank of Truman's division, and the highway ran straight as an arrow nearly two miles north up the Aire River valley till cutting back northeast across the river and into the 35th Division's zone at Varennes. Terrain dictated that both the Pennsylvania Guardsmen of the 28th as well as their Kansas-Missouri colleagues would have to use this single road—barely wide enough for two vehicles to pass each other—as their principal supply line. Yet, until army engineers either filled in enough of the hole to create a passable roadway through it, or skirted the outer rim with a bypass through the trenches, barbed wire, and minefield, American infantrymen would be almost on their own.

THERE WAS NO ARTILLERY SUPPORT for the doughboys at this time because elements of the 60th Field Artillery Brigade were in the process of displacing forward, and the designated French artillery had no dependable way of knowing where the lead American elements, by now more than three miles past the crater, were located. This situation had been anticipated by AEF headquarters, which did not expect that its divisional field artillery brigades, with the exception of a handful of designated infantry batteries, would be engaged between the end of the rolling barrage and the following morning, D-plus-1. The infantry batteries could not keep up, however, and what fire support the infantry would have during this first day's advance was to come from a relatively new battlefield weapon—the tank—and specifically the 140 light Renault machines of the 344th and 345th Battalions organized into a provisional tank regiment under Col. George S. Patton Jr.

As for the 129th Field Artillery, its elements were instructed to push ahead along the extremely poor road zigzagging around the low ridge at Les Côtes de Forimont and through the Forêt de Hess instead of waiting for any of its rolling stock that had gotten stuck in the mud to be freed. Consequently, all of the C Battery guns and limbers that bogged down along the way were passed by Truman's unit, which was itself shedding gun sections that were likewise losing battles with "General Mud." Directed onto the original road into Boureuilles that paralleled the Route Nationale barely two hundred yards to the east, Truman and Major Gates, now at the lead of the 129th Field Artillery's struggling and badly strung-out column, arrived at the town with the one and only gun section to have made it that far. At the outskirts of Boureuilles they turned left down a short lane that brought them to the highway and well above the crater before continuing north through the devastated town toward the Aire and Pointe Boureuilles, a small portion of town that lay across the river. But they could go no farther. A large stone bridge with a span blown out blocked their path south of Pointe Boureuilles's jagged ruins. It was here, and with not the slightest clue beforehand that they were to act in concert with Patton, where Gates and Truman were informed that they were to find him—or really any tank unit commander that they could liaise with—and provide fire support for the armor.

At about 1 p.m, Battery D reached No-Man's Land and reported to Colonel Klemm who was sitting along side the road with Captains Andre Fouilhoux and Paterson, and holding his horse beside a little bush. The Colonel asked if D was up and ready to fire on the Germans. I said "Yes, Sir" but only had one gun and two caissons. The others were in the mud somewhere but were slowly coming up.

Colonel Klemm could not have been terribly pleased at seeing his regiment reduced (at least temporarily) to a single gun section, the major's small detail, and the few members of Truman's BC detail not sprinkled along the trail trying to help get the guns out of the mud and ditches. He had no option other than to accept the officers' assurances that more men and equipment would be arriving shortly.

Across a bridge destroyed by the enemy on the Aire River was a ruined town called Boureuilles. The engineers reported that it would be about three or four hours before the bridge could be fixed, and the Colonel ordered Battery D to go into position for action behind a hedge to the right of the road, just south of town. The Colonel told us to make a reconnaissance for targets along the edge of the Argonne Forest to our left, and find out if some enemy machine gun nests across the Aire, which were evidently holding back the tanks, could be silenced.

Major Gates, Lieutenant Jordan, and I, plus several BC instrument personnel and runners, walked up the road to where the bridge over the Aire River (Creek it should have been called) was out. We waded the stream and went further up the Route Nationale toward Varennes to find the infantry commander or the commander of the Tank Corps. Some machine guns opened up. We sat down behind a bank on the side of the road from which the fire was coming and discussed the situation. Word was sent back to the Battery to get into position as quickly as possible at a point that had been fixed before we started.

Just then some Brigadier Gen. of Infantry came riding down the road on a fine horse with an orderly following him like he was on parade. Major Gates and I persuaded him to alight and send his horse back to Boureuilles which he did in somewhat of a hurry when more bullets began traveling over the road. We went almost to Varennes but no infantry commander or tank commander could be found. A lieutenant from the Tank Corps informed us that there was nothing that we could do at that time. Finding no available targets and not being able to communicate with the Battery, we turned back around 2 o'clock.

From the elevated ground along which the Route Nationale was built, Major Gates and Truman looked beyond the roofs of Varennes to the big hill more than a mile due north of the town, where their division's 139th Infantry was engaged after passing through the 137th. Only slightly behind them on the 28th Division side of the Aire, the 110th Infantry was wrapping up the day's bloody business. Stretching to the right of these two formations and hidden in the haze of battle, the initial surge of the seven American divisions attacking abreast between the Aire and the Meuse had formed a generally uniform penetration three and one-half to four miles deep. The only exception was in the very middle of the line, where stiff resistance on the slopes of Montfaucon would hold up several regiments for another day. Beyond the 28th Division's right-flank regiment, however, the dense tangle of the Argonne Forest, running right up to the bluffs over the Aire Valley, had severely limited the gains of the 28th's other regiments, resulting in the American front suddenly dropping back nearly two full miles. The division on the 28th's left had made even less headway, further hindering the advance of the Pennsylvanians.

FORWARD MOMENTUM WAS PETERING OUT by the time that the artillerymen reached the low rise overlooking Varennes around 2 p.m. Soldiers were milling about in the town while long lines of other doughboys, probably the 110th's 1st Battalion, marched past them on a valley road and still more moved up the Route Nationale past Gates's little detachment. A score of tanks was also scattered close below—some moving about, some not—and more could be seen perhaps a mile to the north, where the 110th was consolidating its gains. Many more were across the river in the detachment's own divisional area and seemingly a long way off. Despite Klemm's orders, there appeared to be no reason to be wandering around in another division's sector, and they were just getting farther and farther from their own guns. A halfhearted effort to coordinate with the nearby tankers was initiated and quickly abandoned. The detachment turned on its heels to retrace its route to Boureuilles. Although Truman did not mention it, he and the others would have taken note of the total absence of 28th Division artillery anywhere along their route. That, however, was not their problem—at least not yet.

CHAPTER 13

"Go to Hell . . . But I'll Try!"

At 3 o'clock we returned to the battery position and found that the Colonel and his staff were gone and the regiment had moved. Col. Klemm ordered it to countermarch and cross No Man's Land at a point further to the right above a ford in the river where some tanks had gone through and made a sort of temporary road. Lieutenant Housholder had been left in charge of Battery D's position and the other guns had come up so that I had a four gun battery when we got back.

Colonel Klemm left orders to take the battery east into No Man's Land and join the regiment as quickly as possible and take up position in a wood back Vauquois Hill. I found that the Hun had a bracket on me—that is an over and a short—and decided that I should get away from there as quickly as the Lord would let me. The Colonel had ordered my Lieutenant to limber up and I got hooked up before Heine started his "fire for effect" and started across No Man's Land crossways trying to get to Rossignol Wood.

The march away from Boureuilles, where the 103rd Engineers were only now getting started on rebuilding the bridge,* was in the reverse order of how the regiment's scattered elements had been hastily reorganized on the side road. Thus, when the units were ordered to turn around in-place and backtrack to where they would leave the road, the rearmost elements in the regimental column now found themselves leading the difficult overland march. Because the battery that ended up behind Battery D, Capt. Harry Allen's Battery F, had only just left, Truman's men had little trouble catching up. Gates galloped on ahead to find Captain Paterson, and Battery D was now bringing up the rear of the regiment, which, by the map, only had about a mile and a half to go before reaching the safety of the woods. The limber and *fourgon* drivers navigated their teams across the shell-pocked terrain as carefully as was practical, but there was no steering around the mud that oozed to the surface as soon as the first horse team and wheels squished across the rank, knee-high grass and progressively deepened as more and more horses, men, and equipment struggled over and through it. This, however, was only a brief prelude to the most grueling part of the march.

> It was necessary to cross a deep hollow in order to arrive at the proposed battery positions behind, north of, Vauquois Hill. The enemy kept up a constant harassing fire in the vicinity of the column but luckily only two casualties occurred. As usually under such circumstances, I got stuck and had to hitch in the men. We finally caught the rest of the column and the Hun began to shell again. Captain Paterson's horse was killed and they got a direct hit on Captain Salisbury's instrument *fourgon* which blew up. It was afterwards discovered that Capt. Salisbury

---

* The platoon of 103rd Engineers that had suffered heavy casualties at the bridge earlier that morning was replaced by Company B of the 27th Engineers, who constructed a temporary wooden trestle bridge, completed late on D-plus-2, before tackling the major repairs needed on the large stone bridge.

lost enough equipment in that *fourgon* to outfit a regiment. Several men were wounded in headquarters company and a great many had narrow escapes both from gas and high explosives [other soldiers were wounded in A Battery, one later dying, and a horse was killed]. One of my men was sitting in a shell-hole and a dud lit right between his legs: If he hasn't a charmed life, no one has.

About 5 p.m. the enemy bombardment finally got so bad we had to unlimber and wait for it to quit. The enemy artillery had evidently gone into position and obtained observation of the regiment because a bracket was obtained. Just like earlier on Battery D in its position behind the hedge, Fire for Effect for some reason was not used or the whole regiment would have been destroyed. The Battalion Commander ordered the horses unhitched and placed behind the crest of the hollow where they'd be out of range. In about an hour orders to hitch up were given and a real piece of labor began.

Truman is likely wrong here, since what he perceived as being bracketed was more likely the random fall of shot instead of targeted "overs" and "unders" as the German gunners fine-tuned their aim. This is borne out by the fact that the Germans did not follow up the "bracketing" of the battery both near Boureuilles and in no man's land by an intense barrage—"firing for effect"—on the exposed artillerymen. More likely, the speed and depth of the American penetration that morning had dislocated the German observation system, forcing them to fire blind on a series of pre-registered locations as the German gunners saw fit. The moderate but still dangerous shelling that occurred around 5 p.m. thus appears to be what French and American artillerymen called a "normal barrage," which was conducted for a time at that location before being directed to any one of several "eventual barrage" targets. If the Germans had had enough cannons available (and on D-day they didn't), they would have shelled the bottlenecks at the Route Nationale crater and blown the bridge at Boureuilles in a more concentrated and systematic manner—an "interdiction barrage." While none of the German fire came even close to the volume dished out by the Americans and French that morning, it was only sheer luck that the 129th did not suffer heavy casualties.

By 6 p.m. it was dark enough for the horses and men taking refuge in the hollow, Batteries D and F, to go back up to the caissons, guns, and wagons, and ready themselves to move, unseen by enemy eyes unless a dreaded star shell revealed them to the Germans. Now it was necessary to move the equipment through the hollow, with mud on the way down, mud at the bottom, and mud ahead of them. In the lazy days of peace, the gentle incline would have been little challenge for a wagon and a pair of pokey draft horses. On this night it was a formidable uphill pull across a virtual quagmire and, to add insult to injury, the ground was a forward slope that had been pitted by the 129th's own 75s during the rolling bombardment. And then it started raining.

There was a little hollow we had to cross when it finally got dark. This was done after much difficulty on account of mud and shell holes. The horses were very tired having been in the harness since 2 a.m. Some of them since the evening of the 25th, and the men were just about worn out, most of them having been up since early the morning of the 25th. The horses were taken from one carriage and hitched to another, 12 horses on a piece, and every available man was used to push this carriage forward some way or other until it got across. Then the next carriage would be taken in charge and brought forward in the same manner. Guns and caissons were mixed in a promiscuous mass at the top of the hill where the horses and men worked so hard to get them across.

Battery E being in the lead after the regiment counter marched, succeeded in getting across the ditch before dark and arrived in position in the Bois de Rossignol. Batteries A and B managed to get into position about 10 p.m. I went back myself after No. 1 gun[,] the next to the last carriage brought in, and the last one was brought in by Lt. Jordan. It was 3 a.m. on the 27th when I had finally gotten all my carriages but two into that wood. Those two [one of them the "rolling kitchen"] are out in that no man's land yet, I guess, because I never did get them because of the mud, shell holes and tired horses and men. That was the worst night I ever spent. Men went to sleep standing up and I had to make them keep on working because I had to be in position to fire by 5 a.m.

Once all of the battery was across and assembled after midnight, it was almost halfway to Rossignol. Their next obstacle, the three-layer German trench system code-named Balkan Trench, proved to not be an obstacle at all, as a battalion of the 35th Division's 110th Engineers had filled in the gaps and removed barbed wire from a reasonably good north-south road that formed the final haul before the bleary-eyed battery pulled off a few hundred yards to the right and into its position. It had been twelve hours since Truman got back to Battery D's firing position from the reconnaissance toward Varennes.

AEF AND CORPS HEADQUARTERS' COMMUNICATIONS with the 35th Division commander, Maj. Gen. Peter E. Traub, had broken down almost as soon as the first lines of infantry went over the top with Traub following close behind (and the chief of staff, Col. Hamilton S. Hawkins, being forced to try to find him plus carry out various tasks on the battlefield). Simultaneously, reliable communications among the division, its four infantry brigades, eight infantry regiments, and two of its three artillery brigades (the 128th and 129th) could only be described by the word "sporadic" if one was feeling exceptionally generous. It was impossible to maintain either radio or wire connections once the division lunged forward, and communications could only be maintained through use of runners scurrying about under fire to find the various colonels and majors in their ever-shifting shell-hole command posts. It also didn't help, of course, that, in perfect Great War tradition, the headquarters above the 35th Division, I Corps, governing the 35th Division and the two divisions to its left, was still learning the ropes; had not absorbed the practical realities that forces a sort of natural sequence to field operations, or "battle rhythm"; and was issuing a series of nonsensical attack orders from its chateau far to the rear. For example, at 2:45 in the afternoon of D-day, it ordered an evening attack—supported by artillery that was everywhere but in position—to commence at 6:35 p.m., then a night attack at 11:10 p.m., then at 1 a.m. on September 27 ordered a dawn attack for 5:30 a.m.

THE HASH THAT WAS MADE of the morning's operations, as well as the next several days to come, has been examined elsewhere,[1] and, as the reader might suspect, the finger-pointing and excuses by Regular Army officers principally settled on National Guard officers and men as the *dummkopfs* responsible. The short version is this: When the division staff realized there was not enough time available to notify and coordinate the artillery for a 5:30 assault, Colonel Hawkins, in General Traub's absence, countermanded the corps' orders and sent out to the brigades a directive to begin the attack at 8:30. Traub found this out when he returned to headquarters and countermanded the countermanding order, stating, "It is General Pershing's order; it must be done."[2] Faced with the fact that this would send in the infantry completely naked of artillery support, Traub then allowed for a one-hour delay in the infantry's jump-off. Whatever artillery was available would fire. The staff, and certainly the general as well, must have understood the artillery fire would be unfocused, uncoordinated, and directed upon positions far in the German rear in order to not risk killing American troops whose positions were relatively unknown. The "artillery support" was really nothing more than "moral support" and was ordered just so that Traub could demonstrate that it had been done.

In the meantime, orders for the 8:30 advance—requiring a three-hour artillery preparation that many batteries could not immediately comply with but which all could eventually take part in before the jump-off—were floating around the battlefield and looking for places to land. Now the runners were also attempting to deliver the message countermanding the 8:30 jump-off and redirecting it to 6:30 after one hour of preparation. Both of the division-generated orders directed that artillery preparation begin at 5:30, but while the 8:30 attack would have eventually enabled all the batteries to come into play, the 6:30 attack meant that many (and, as it turned out, most) guns would never fire a shot. And the question now was, which units received what, if any, orders? Captain Truman describes how the soldiers at "the pointed end of the stick" tried to make the impossible-to-carry-out fire mission work:

> At three A.M. on the 27th the last carriage was in the position designated. This distance [traveled] was only about a mile and a half but it was nothing but a bog. Mud, mud, mud. The mud was worse than the guns and cannon* firing at them. Men went to sleep standing up trying to get the pieces across the shell holes and over the ditches. At last they lay down for a few winks and at five o'clock the operations officer of the regiment, Captain Paterson, came to my sleeping place under a bush with orders to fire another barrage in ten minutes. I told him to go to hell, that I could not figure a barrage in ten minutes, but I'd try!
>
> I was rather sleepy but arose and tried to figure a creeping barrage for the infantry beginning at 5:30 a.m. This barrage was to be fired at an initial range of 4000 meters and to increase 100 meters every 2 minutes for an hour. It was an impossible task. The order was one hour late arriving and by the time data was figured and trenches dug for the gun trails, the time had elapsed for firing. At seven o'clock we were ready to fire but the guns

---

*American soldiers of this era occasionally used the word "cannon" when, as in this usage, referring specifically to howitzers. Generally, though, the word was used to mean any artillery piece, whether a gun that fired in a relatively flat trajectory, like the French 75mm, German 77mm, and numerous heavier-caliber weapons, or howitzers like the French 155mm and German 210mm, which fired rounds at a high angle and were particularly effective when used against trenches and bunkers.

wouldn't raise up high enough to fire at the range necessary for safety to the infantry.

Batteries C, D, & F did not fire a shot for it was physically impossible for them to sink the trails fast enough to catch up with the barrage. Batteries A and B [of 1st Battalion] had taken up position on the slope of Hill 221, and were able to begin firing at once. Battery E succeeded in getting a gun into action by putting the trail into a convenient shell hole and fired several rounds at the extreme elevation in the general direction of Germany. That Bty. got credit for firing the barrage! The others [in 2nd Battalion] caught hell for not being able to fire.* This is the only time in the whole drive that the regiment did not fire every time it was called on to do so.

Major Gates was ordered forward at 9:30 a.m. to find positions, for the 2nd Bn. in the vicinity of Varennes and Cheppy, and Capt. Salisbury was left in charge of the Bn. with orders to bring it forward as quickly as possible. Breakfast was eaten about ten o'clock while the men were hitching in. The second battalion was ordered to take up positions north of Varennes on the Route Nationale and be ready to fire as soon as possible. The Bn. pulled out at 11 a.m., E, D, and F going east to the Cheppy road. The ground was strewn with hand grenades, abandoned Boche machine guns, and dead Germans. It had been badly cut up by our barrages of the day before and it was a heavy pull getting out to the road.

The battalion was halted about a kilometer from Cheppy where the road forks for Varennes. There were three trees at this point and they had evidently been used to conceal a Boche

---

* Although the initiative taken by one of Battery E's gun sections so impressed Truman that he mentioned it in no fewer than five of his various accounts, so few rounds were fired (probably because of the inability to accurately calculate the trajectory for the unusual setup in the available time) that Major Gates did not include this effort in his October 8, 1918, "Operations Report covering the September 25th to October 2nd period."

machine gun because there was a pile of dead American soldiers in all sorts of ghastly positions at the fork of the road. There were seventeen of them and nearly a dozen more and a line of them lying head to heel down the road shot in the back. It was evident that the Hun had let them go by and then sprayed them with bullets. One or two had their heads completely severed and one was simply sawed in two at the waist.

The Battery had been clattering and carrying on as they usually did when on a road march and when they saw this spectacle everything became quiet as a church and a hard boiled sergeant remarked "Now, you so-and-sos, I guess you'll believe you're in a war."

An officer with the 110th Engineers later described this area and the ground running to the west along the Germans' "Scorpion" trench system as "a cemetery of unburied dead."[3] A few hundred yards to the left of the road junction was where Colonel Patton had been shot down while organizing an ad hoc infantry assault the previous day (and roughly two hours before Gates and Truman had been sent looking for him even farther to the west). From its position in the Rossignol Woods, Gates's 2nd Battalion had leapfrogged those of the 128th's 2nd Battalion and the 129th's 1st Battalion, which straddled the road to Cheppy, and continued firing their barrages in support of the infantry throughout this period—in the case of Major Miles's 1st Battalion, right over the heads of Truman's and Gates's men.

Past the crossroads, the battalion soon came to another at Cheppy and pulled west toward Varennes before turning north again. After moving approximately three hundred yards, Batteries E and F turned right again (east-northeast) up a tree-lined country road and deployed with a broad field to their front. Battery D was directed to the left flank, a peach orchard on the opposite side of the highway in the narrow area before the land dropped off into a wide depression called La Grotte. So while the rest of the battalion had an unobstructed field of fire and could go into action almost immediately, Truman's men had to first chop down several rows of trees and drag them away from their flat-trajectory guns.

> The enemy artillery was playing on Cheppy and we had to wait until a lull before we could go through. At 1 p.m. the batteries went into position on the Route Nationale about a kilometer north of Varennes. Battery D in an orchard on the left of the road. Batteries E and F on the right under some trees and Boche camouflage. Orders were received at 1:15 to open fire on Charpentry at once. At 14:30 hour [2:30 p.m.] the three batteries began a harassing fire. Major Gates ordered me to go forward and observe the effect of the fire on Charpentry and to get into communication with the Infantry commanders of the 69th Brigade and the 138th Infantry.

As described in the opening passages of this book, all of the 2nd Battalion guns were in action by 2:30, but only after Truman's, according to the regimental history, had belatedly joined the 75s that had begun firing a full hour earlier. Truman appears to have been a little sensitive to this, but D's delay was not something that could have been avoided.

FURTHER DELAY WAS CAUSED by an air attack on D from a German two-seater reconnaissance plane that took the opportunity, when scurrying back home, to machine-gun and drop a small bomb, killing two horses and destroying some telephone equipment, including a headset snipped right off 2nd Lt. William L. Eagleton's head. The lucky fellow was uninjured, but Pvt. Lawrence Edelman, a battery farrier, scared the wits out of some cannoneers who feared him more than the enemy aviators. As the low-flying biplane was making its escape, Edelman had to return fire almost horizontally—right over part of the battery—from one of the *fourgon*-mounted Hotchkiss machine guns, causing Sergeant Meisburger's gun section to dive for cover, including Private Leigh under a fully stocked ammunition caisson. Meisburger remembers "Major Gates coolly smoking his pipe"[4] throughout the attack, which lasted perhaps a minute from when the aircraft was first spotted to the last rounds leaving Edelman's Hotchkiss.

While this was happening, Truman's reconnaissance party was heading northwest up the Route Nationale, then north up a dirt road that ran straight over the top of a gentle forty-five-foot rise, Hill 202, before curving down onto a small plain and then dropping steeply at a reverse slope, providing good cover for the German defenders opposite Charpentry on the far side of Buanthe Creek. With him was a musta-chioed young second lieutenant assigned to D just before the offensive, Leslie M. Zemer, and a good percentage of Truman's BC detail: the redoubtable Cpl. Bill O'Hare, Instrument Sgt. Harry Kelley, and four telephone men who also served as runners. Captain Truman would soon praise Kelley as a "very, very bright, excellent soldier," and maintain that he was "my right hand man from Sept. 26 to Oct. 3." Said Truman, "He figures my firing data as well as I do it myself."[5]

After laying the battery I was sent by Major Gates to observe the effect of the fire of the Second Battalion on Charpentry. I went forward with Lt. Zemer, Sergeant Harry Kelley and Corp. Wm. O'Hare down the Route Nationale and over the hill to a point at about 3161, about 700 meters south of Charpentry. The German front line at that time was about 100 meters south of Charpentry at the foot of the hill. The town was plainly visible from the point where we were posted, and shots from the Second Battalion falling in Charpentry were plainly visible. I got in a shell hole to observe fire. Communication could not be maintained because the infantry kept breaking the telephone lines. Bursting shells also made it hard to keep the phone lines intact.

About 3 p.m., or 15 hour, three American tanks went into Charpentry and were driven out by the enemy. A couple of [other] tanks were operating in the field to the left of Charpentry. They were greatly hampered by artillery fire from the Argonne Forest on the left. We located two batteries

evidently of heavy caliber about 2,500 hundred meters west[6] of
the German OP at Chêne Tondu. They were out of range of our
75s and were doing some execution on our front, firing on these
tanks and also on the American infantrymen in the open field to
the right of the Route Nationale.

Both groups of tanks were temporarily beyond the reverse slope
where numerous German machine gunners had taken cover from the
2nd Battalion shells and then returned. The infantry did not move
forward with the armor, which destroyed few if any of the machine guns
firing on the infantry. Because of the intermixing of units on the 35th
Division's left, it is impossible to say if these were soldiers of the 137th
or 139th Infantry; perhaps both. More tanks under the command of Lt.
Joseph R. Younglove came up the road, and Truman briefly discussed
the situation with him as they watched the men "hit the ground" when
German artillery played through the area to his front. Pulling forward,
Younglove was later told to "get those damn tanks away" because they
were "drawing fire."[7]

Truman had no way to communicate any of this back to Gates. The
telephone wire was run where it was thought that tanks were unlikely to
travel, but tramping feet and exploding rounds prevented communication except for frustratingly brief periods. The most forward American
elements on the 35th Division's left were in a precarious situation.
Unnoticed by Truman's party, some "shifting and straightening"[8] of the
infantry's lines had begun. The result? Truman's shell-crater observation post was now nearly two hundred yards *in front* of the reforming
137th–139th lines. So intent had he and his small group been at
observing fire and setting up wire communications, that they hadn't
recognized the full-blown pullback in the smoke and confusion, and
potential disaster was averted only when one of the last infantrymen
out warned them of the move.

About 3:30 p.m. (1530) the American Infantry fell back 200 meters
to reorganize and left me there. I was beyond our front line, and I
didn't even have a pistol. Lt. Zemer and I fell back also. Strenuous

efforts were made to establish communication. The brigade commander could not be located, [and] a French officer at Brigade Hqtrs informed me that the brigade commander had not been seen that day. The regimental commander of 138th Infantry could not be found, nor could the platoon commander of the leading platoon. We established an OP at a tank headquarters, at point L3252 above Montblainville and spent the rest of the afternoon in an endeavor to get into communication with the battalion.

Apparently, either direct observation or a check of a terrain map revealed to Truman that setting up a new artillery observation post farther back (south) on Hill 202 would produce blind spots along the most likely axis of advance used by German reinforcements—the Route Nationale. Truman instead selected a position somewhat down the western slope and on the left side of the highway, where he could obtain excellent observation of both the entire length of the road and the Argonne Forest, which ran all the way up to the bluffs on the other side of the Aire River and which faced the wide-open 35th Division flank. As it turned out, the Germans principally used other routes for their final approach to the battlefield, but there was plenty to keep Truman busy to the west in the 28th Division sector.

AMERICAN PLANNERS AT FIRST ARMY had long understood that, with the exception of a small number of batteries with specific missions like Truman's intended support of Patton, their divisional artillery would be largely out of action after about 7:45 a.m. on D-day as it displaced forward. But they also believed that most units would be ready for action the following morning, D-plus-1. What they did not anticipate was just how clogged most of the roads would become, even further delaying units that didn't get off to the fast start of the 60th Brigade's 75mm regiments. And there was absolutely no way that they could have imagined the bizarre series of events centering around some of the 28th Division's senior artillery officers which, together with the traffic jams, immobilized the bulk of its artillery for nearly three full days.

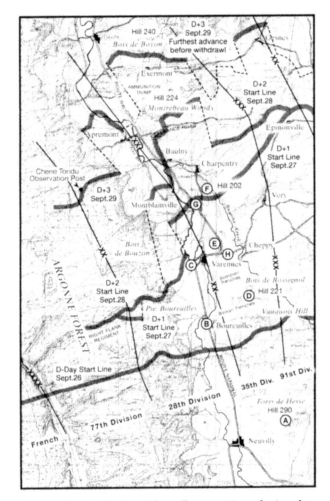

2nd Battalion, 129th Field Artillery positions during the Meuse-Argonne Offensive, September 26–October 2, 1918

A: September 26, morning—Battalion position during opening bombardment

B: September 26, early afternoon—Battalion elements gather to the rear of Battery D's firing position

C: September 26, early afternoon – Furthest point reached by Major Marvin H. Gates and Captain Harry S. Truman when searching for Colonel George S. Patton Jr.

D: September 26-27, night—Battalion lager

E: September 27, afternoon—Battalion position

F: September 27, early afternoon—Battalion observation post of Captain Truman

G: September 27, mid afternoon to evening—Battalion observation post of Captain Truman, and September 28, Major Gates and Captain Truman

H: September 27-October 2—Battalion position

Distance Scale: Each grid square measures 1 kilometer (1,000 meters) deep by 1 kilometer wide. A kilometer equals 1093.6 yards or slightly more than 6/10 of a mile. The maximum effective range of the 75mm gun is almost 7 kilometers or 4 1/3 miles.

Due to road congestion and the inability to obtain reliable information on the precise location of the 28th Division's forward elements, the 109th Field Artillery provided very little fire support before the morning of D-plus-3. This even included the battery tasked with following close on the heels of the infantry, which had likewise become stuck in traffic below Boureuilles and was forced to remain there for two full days. Elements of the regiment had to content themselves with firing on the occasional bypassed machine-gun nest until it was finally able to a position in the bottomland northwest of Varennes on Sunday, September 29. The lack of operationally useful information on the whereabouts of both friend and foe affected the stationary French artillery units as well when troops were on the move. And then there were the basic tactical constraints imposed by the Germans' stubborn defense of the Argonne itself.

While Truman and the rest of the 129th were able to head off laterally across no man's land and then north, the 109th had virtually no room to perform such a maneuver. The 28th Division's lines were bent far back to the rear beyond the left of the hard-charging 110th Infantry because of the center regiment's inability to make much progress in the forest during the early stages of the offensive. The situation was even worse on the 28th Division's left, where the 77th Division made no gains at all for a time, with the result that the western half of I Corps' line resembled a descending staircase, with the 110th Infantry as the top step. Through September 29, this "staircase" on the left generally moved apace with the 35th Division and the 28th Division's right.

In and of itself, this came as no surprise to any of the senior commanders at brigade level and higher, since the campaign plan did not call for a strong effort against the forest defenses. The mission of the 28th and 35th Divisions was to plunge ahead as far and as fast as possible to the right of the obstacle so that the Germans in the Argonne would be compelled to withdraw on their own or be cut off. But as the Romans had learned in the time of Caesar (and the Allies would learn twice in the Ardennes two decades hence), the Germans were not shy about pushing forces into such terrain and fighting it out.

The 28th Division's other 75mm outfit, the 107th Field Artillery, reached Varennes the night before the 109th after being delayed not only by traffic, but extremely severe problems within its leadership. First, "Major William T. Rees, commander of the [107th's] First Battalion, went to the hospital sick,"[9] a half hour after receiving orders on D-day morning to push off; his replacement, Capt. Samuel A. Whittaker, was relieved the following day for not getting the unit moving. Colonel Burleson and the executive officer, Lt. Col. Albert V. Crookston,* closely escorted the road-bound unit in an effort to provide enough authority to move it through and around congestion on the Route Nationale but were nevertheless unable to make significant headway along the clogged road. Command of the 1st Battalion was turned over to one of the battery captains, Clinton T. Bundy, until yet another more senior officer, Maj. Walter W. Hess Jr., could be brought up on D-plus-3.

Both divisions' medium artillery battalions—almost totally road-bound during the rainy weather—eventually worked their ways up the hard-surface Route Nationale and deployed on each formation's side of Varennes. Characteristically, while all elements of the 35th Division's 155mm battalion were in place and firing by 5 p.m. on D-plus-2, the 28th Division's mediums, of the 108th Field Artillery, could not supply a concentrated effort until D-plus-4. French light batteries, though not yet in action, were also beginning to displace forward on D-plus-2. More importantly, though, it must be noted that corps artillery at *this* point in the Meuse-Argonne Offensive operated

---

* In yet another indication of tension within the command, Lieutenant Colonel Crookston, a longtime Pennsylvania Guard officer, had served as regimental commander until Col. Richard C. Burleson, a Regular Army officer and West Point graduate, was placed in charge for the Meuse-Argonne Offensive. Crookston later resumed command and, as editor of the portion of the 28th Division history covering the operations of his regiment, saw to it that Burleson's tenure with the regiment was erased from the text, which stated that Crookston was in command throughout "much" of the period. Burleson, who died in 1960, had a long and distinguished career in the army, as did his stepson, Gen. William A. Knowlton, and Knowlton's son-in-law, Gen. David Petraeus.

under the restriction that it could fire on targets no closer than four miles from the infantry's frontline positions without specific authorization to do so. Yet, even if the 28th's artillery was able to array for battle, its inability to place artillery observers on high ground and the inadequacy of aerial spotting in 1918 meant that the guns were largely limited to firing at either German elements that were in direct contact with its infantry, or at targets long known and well plotted by the French.

The net result of all this was that there were almost no American and French shells falling into the wide expanse of forest on the 35th Division's ever-lengthening left flank until D-plus-3: a flank that, despite the presence of the 110th Infantry, was completely open to German observation and directed fire. As for the 28th Division, the battlefield topography tended to mask its lead elements from enemy artillery observers until the Pennsylvanians reached the Apremont area and started to receive their full share of Teutonic abuse.

Artillery elements of the three German divisions sent to confront the 28th and 35th Divisions were arrayed in the conventional manner designed to support their frontline troops, but what was the German reaction to this gift along the Missourians' flank? According to the German XVI Corps chief of staff, Maj. Herman von Giehrl, they did not withdraw for fear of encirclement and capture. Instead, they poured a significant amount of their available light artillery into the area, ensuring that, "The enemy infantry suffered particularly from the flanking fire of thirteen field batteries, which, from their position on the eastern edge of the Argonne, constantly held up the advance."[10] The dastardly Huns, displaying no respect for American divisional boundaries, directed a murderous fire into the 35th Division, whose infantry regiments frequently complained of being shelled by their own units because a significant amount of this German fire was literally coming from behind them.

Back at Truman's new observation post, breaks in his telephone wire were still causing a good deal of trouble, but the line detail was managing to keep communications with his battery relatively open. By now it was late in the day, and Truman was principally concerned with the Germans' Route Nationale approach in his own division's sector. He also had an excellent ringside seat to the 28th Division's activities in the Aire Valley—a better one, in fact, than the German artillery spotters on Le Chêne Tondu until the Pennsylvanians moved into higher, more open ground farther north. About this time, Truman noticed that American reconnaissance aircraft had dropped a flare just to the west of his position. Turning his field glasses to the spot, he saw a battery of German 77mm guns setting up a little more than rifle distance away.

CHAPTER 14

Scratch Two Boche Batteries

TRUMAN HAD UNDOUBTEDLY REPORTED the coordinates of the heavy batteries and observation post that were outside of his divisional area during one of the periods when his line wasn't dead. It must have also been more than a little disconcerting that his enemy counterparts on Le Chêne Tondu were not taken under fire, but there was nothing more that he could do about it, as it had been drummed into him and all American artillerymen that you do not fire out of your division's designated sector. It was obvious to Truman, however, that these gunners across the river would soon be firing rounds right into the 35th's infantry formations that were, in effect, passing by the Germans' front.

Two American aeroplanes flew over Montblainville about 6:00 and dropped flares on a Boche [derogatory French slang term for Germans] machine gun nest and a battery west of the town at point L1455, but the telephone detail of Battery D was having a hard time establishing communications with the OP. As fast as they would get the telephone line laid it would be broken either by shell fire or infantrymen walking over it. Finally through the efforts of Corporals Schmidt and Samson, and Privates Harry Dabner and Fred McDonald, the line was gotten into working order about 5:30 (17:30) and I secured permission [from Major Gates] to fire on the battery and on OP Tondu. The battery was fired on but it got too dark to see before the OP could be fired on.

The Germans were just as ignorant as the Americans of where the fluid front lay. The six-gun German battery and machine guns (presumably there were more than the one Truman saw) had approached Montblainville from the west and deployed on high ground at the edge of some woods about four hundred yards short of town. This was a dangerously vulnerable location if any sharpshooting Pennsylvanians started to take them under fire. The road running through Montblainville marked the junction point between the stretched-thin lines of the 110th Infantry (now well beyond Montblainville and oriented to the north) and the 109th Infantry (oriented to the west). But although the town was reputed to be occupied by elements of the 110th at this time, the Germans establishing their position were unmolested for a full half-hour before Truman took them under fire, according to the 73rd Engineers rebuilding the river crossings. Truman didn't want to commence firing until the horses had been led to the rear, rendering the guns immobile, but if his men didn't start pumping out rounds soon, it would be too dark to observe and adjust fire. The removal of the horses made the decision for him.

The sounds of battle had sunk back into one of their periodic lulls, so if the wind was right, the nearly horizontal, high-velocity stream of shells passing exactly a half mile to the south might have even reached the ears of the men at the observation post. They certainly would have heard the close-in detonations across the Aire seconds after the earth and smoke shot skyward, and Truman later boasted, "I'm the only battery commander in the 129th who ever saw what he fired at and I think that is some distinction."[1] So accurate were Truman's and Kelley's computations, and the work of the 2nd and 3rd Gun Sections, that Dizzy D only fired 49 rounds at the target, with perhaps the last half-dozen or so hanging in the air, when Truman ordered a cease fire. Scratch one Hun battery.

By "The Book," roughly five hundred rounds was considered an "average expenditure" for the destruction of an enemy battery, but the task had apparently been accomplished with just a fraction of that number; night was closing in; and Truman would order no unobserved firing on a site so near to American troops. Before the U.S. 109th Infantry solidified control of the area that evening, the onset of darkness allowed the Germans to recover three guns they judged to have survived the barrage. After the war, the 28th Division history inadvertently provided an amusing postscript to the twilight bombardment in a passage describing the movement of the similarly named 109th Field Artillery's Battery E to the front. Some infantrymen apparently alerted the unit to the abandoned guns, with the following result: "The battery, in addition to establishing itself well in front with the infantry, had the proud distinction of capturing a battery of three German 77mm guns,"[2] and one of the guns, having received little or no damage, was subsequently used against its former owners.

Truman's personal postscript to the destruction of a German battery was somewhat less humorous. Upon his return to the battalion gun line, Colonel Klemm "threatened me with a court martial for firing out of the 35th Division sector!"[3] Truman certainly didn't take the reprimand too seriously, having obtained permission from his commanding officer to fire on an out-of-sector target that directly threatened American lives, but Klemm's marionette-like adherence to orders made obsolete by conditions in the field and his manifest detachment from what was happening to the frontline troops must have been shocking. The incident, which likely followed an even stronger rebuke of Major Gates, also seems to have marked a change in Klemm's physical presence among the troops. Whether it is the regimental history, Truman's letters, or the oral and individual battery histories, Klemm seems to have become nearly invisible during the balance of combat operations. With the exception of a quick inspection of the Charpentry and Very areas on the morning of D-plus-2, no mention has surfaced of any other inspections by Klemm of the front or even visits to the firing batteries. Moreover, no initiative of any sort seems to have emanated from regimental headquarters beyond the supervision of supply matters, as Klemm's command post became solely a clearing house for brigade orders.

The response of Gates and Truman to their colonel's threats of court-martial for firing out of sector was to organize another reconnaissance party to follow the wire out to Truman's observation post before first light. And Gates, accepting the battalion commander's prerogative of observing from the forward OP, would accompany Truman's party. Considerable attention would be paid to the Route Nationale, of course, but if the 28th Division's cannonneers had not eliminated the Germans directing fire on the 35th Division's flank from Le Chêne Tondu, or it looked like the Pennsylvanians would not soon be overrunning the heights, then Truman would bring down fire smack dab in the middle of the 28th's sector, after Gates personally put his eyes on the target and approved its destruction.

AN URGENT MATTER had to be attended to long before Gates and Truman hurried off to the observation post. The regimental history noted:

> During the afternoon a German airplane flew over the battery positions, dropping several bombs near them but causing no material damage, except to destroy some telephone equipment at Battery D's position. Because this airplane had located the battery positions, the Battalion Commander deemed it wise to move their positions about 100 meters to the right and 200 meters to the rear of the ones they then occupied. The move was accomplished about 10 p.m., and the whole battalion was put into position on the road between Cheppy and Varennes.

Battery D was now located along a cut in the road, with room for the passage of vehicles behind the guns and, according to chief mechanic Wooden, enough clearance for "the muzzles of the guns [to] just swing over the bank."[4] The move turned out to be "none too soon" according to the regimental history, "for a heavy bombardment of the abandoned position followed soon after the movement."[5] Although the entire battalion had displaced, the men of Battery D were convinced that their captain was responsible for the move, and in later years it was trumpeted time and time again as yet another shining example of Truman's superb leadership. The switch to the Varennes-Cheppy road also saw a curious incident that was to become one of Truman's favorite war stories: "In going into position I rode my horse under a tree, and a low-hanging branch scraped my glasses off. In desperation I turned around, hoping to see where they could have fallen, and there they were, on the horse's back, right behind the saddle."[6] Truman added, "No one would believe a tale like that but it happened."[7]

The displacement to the road behind them put the battalion back into the area described earlier as "a cemetery of unburied dead," and another Truman story, this one involving First Sergeant Sieben as well, was sobering:

[We] went on a search for a safe place to put the horses and limbers for the regt. A sunken road or lane was discovered just west of Cheppy with a hedge on each side of it, but it contained so many dead Huns that it could not be used. An orchard just east of Varennes and back of the new battery position was finally spotted and used for a horse line until the regiment was relieved. The night of the 27th was very dark, the only light being made by flares from the front line, but was quiet except for a few enemy shells and a gas alarm or two in Varennes.

Battery D, with Major Gates's command post to its rear, was at the crest of the low north-south ridge with the other 129th Field Artillery's batteries farther down the road and extending almost into Cheppy. Major Miles's 1st Battalion was by now preparing to leapfrog ahead and set themselves up in the bottomland south of Charpentry, seized the previous evening. The 128th Field Artillery Regiment and French 219th Artillery Regiment were generally settling into the area between Miles's new position and Gates after pushing their own 75s forward. To Truman's left, through a wooded area and down into La

Grotte, the 155mm howitzers of the 130th Field Artillery were massed and firing from the east side of Varennes, as was the lead battery of the big howitzers belonging to the 108th on the other side of town.

SOUTHEAST OF THE HORSE LINE scouted by Truman and Sieben, on the road running south from Cheppy, was the 35th Division's dressing station, or field hospital, which did what it could for the wounded streaming in, and was sorting out the hopeless from those that could be saved and sent back to Neuvilly for more treatment and evacuation to the rear. However, the extreme number of casualties combined with the general lack of ambulances and clogged roads essentially froze nearly all traffic to and from these sites. No one had expected things to work perfectly, but it quickly evolved into an intolerable situation that would later be the focus of congressional hearings.

Captain Harry R. Hoffman, a doctor attached to the division, described the conditions on September 27 and on the 28th as the rain picked back up again:

> Imagine the plight of our wounded. There were 800 at the advanced dressing station; 1,400 more at the triage, just back of the fighting lines. Some were legless; others armless; many with sides torn out by shrapnel. All, practically, were in direct pain. It was bitter cold. The mud was knee-deep. A half sleet, half rain was beating down mercilessly. And for 36 hours those 2,400 men were compelled to lie there in the mud, unsheltered. We had neither litters on which to lay them, nor blankets to wrap around them....
>
> On the 27th, Maj. W. L. Gist, director of the Sanitary train, consisting of the ambulance companies, sent a runner to Col. [Raymond C.] Turck, the divisional surgeon, saying, "For God's sake send us something—blankets, litters, food." Col. Turck sent back word, "Received your report. Can't do anything; roads blocked."[8]

Many of these men walked or were carried past Battery D's positions near Varennes in a nearly continuous stream. "The procession of wounded took up the whole road," said Sergeant Meisburger. "One smiling, freckle-faced doughboy, with his leg blown off near the hip, sat on a horse rolling a cigarette. He died just as he reached the dressing station at the foot of the hill."[9] There was some reason to hope, after the Germans pummeled the wrong coordinates, that the battalion's soldiers might not have to make the same trip down the hill if the Germans continued to believe they still occupied the original position. And the lay of the land seemed to work to their favor.

> It was a very good place for a battalion of artillery. There was a road about 200 meters in front and a hedge about the same distance behind the road the batteries were now on, and enemy observers could not tell from which of these places our fire was coming.

The movement after dark to a different location had spared the 2nd Battalion from a thorough pummeling by the German gunners the night before, but it could well have turned out to be only a temporary reprieve. Sooner, rather than later, the enemy artillery spotters ensconced in the abandoned mill high atop Le Chêne Tondu would detect the subtle shift, and the German batteries would adjust their aim accordingly. Other points from which the 2nd Battalion might be detected were situated at approximately the same height above the valley as its gun line or slightly lower. Thus, the removal of the Chêne Tondu observation post from the equation would have greatly benefited Gates's men, because while the German observers at other observation posts could tell that American artillery fire was coming from that general area, there was a very good chance that they would not catch on that Gates's batteries had just displaced from where the reconnaissance aircraft had spotted them.

It is unlikely that Gates and Truman thought specifically in terms of protecting their own soldiers and guns when they left for Truman's observation post that morning, but if they were successful in knocking out the Chêne Tondu observation post, the chances of their men's survival would increase markedly. Having already taken Lieutenants Zemer and Jordan with him on reconnaissance missions, Truman this time brought Housholder, with the rest of the detail filled out by Kelley, O'Hare, and some telephone men. What Truman found when they reached the observation post and looked out across the Aire was that there were no American troops currently threatening the German observers, who continued to go about their business undisturbed. Nor was the 28th Division's artillery targeting Le Chêne Tondu. Gates and Truman knew what to do in spite of the warning from their colonel the night before. They took the range and elevation, computed fire data, and checked and rechecked, and at 9:30 a.m. sharp, Battery D gunners rapidly pumped out sixty-four rounds within the space of just a few minutes. So much for threats of courts-martial.

The officers observing fire through a BC (scissors) scope and field glasses were gratified to see the old mill "promptly abandoned by its occupants who could be seen scurrying from it."[10] The fire for effect was timed to be carried out immediately before the 35th's infantry regiments surged forward with tank support to seize Montrebeau Wood plus the open country to its right. With the exception of the 129th's 1st Battalion galloping up Hill 202 just east of Truman's observation post on its way to Charpentry, the rest of the artillery ostensibly supported this assault but was limited to firing at such things as roads and areas where Germans were likely to congregate because, even at this late date, little effective communication existed between the infantry and artillerymen. Meanwhile, Truman's little band kept an eye on Le Chêne Tondu in case the Germans returned, but there was no attempt to reestablish the observation post. Other activity at nearly the same spot soon caught their attention:

> At 11 hour a German battery moving down a road at point 8666, to the left of O.P. Chien [sic] Tondu, was fired on by Battery D. Forty-three shells were dropped on this battery in less than two minutes, causing the enemy to desert his guns and leave them on the road. No further traffic was observed on this road during the day. About 11:30 hour, orders from Col. Klemm were received to cease firing because the 140th Infantry reported that they were being fired on from the rear.

The German battery had just begun pulling out of position and, because of some scattered woods (unmentioned by Truman but apparent on the French maps), only three limbered guns could be seen from his observation post. Truman wasn't sure how successful they had been, but when he later mentioned the flagrant disobedi-ence of Klemm's orders to Colonel Burleson, then commanding the 28th Division's 107th Field Artillery, Burleson responded, "You got'em all right; for when we later came up that way, there were six abandoned guns beside the road."[11] Shortly after Truman's forays to the west, Captain McGee's B Battery, at the direction of the 1st Battalion commander, Major Miles, also engaged German guns in the 28th Division's sector opposite Baulny shortly after noon. An I Corps liaison officer who was present cheered the battery on even as they did it. But whether or not Colonel Klemm was aware that Battery D, with its battalion commander's wholehearted approval, was shooting up more targets in the Pennsylvanians' sector—literally miles away from the 140th Infantry attacking east of the Montrebeau Woods—Klemm's unexpected cease-fire order applied to the entire battalion, and Battery D complied as well. The regimental history later explained:

A shell fired by a hostile battery such as one near Montblainville, almost directly from the south, coming thus apparently from behind them, would naturally be a source of disturbance to our infantry, and, in the absence of more accurate knowledge, might even make them feel that their own artillery was firing "short." In this particular situation there was ample opportunity for such misunderstanding. The 28th Division was fighting along the edge of the woods of the Argonne Forest proper, which was honeycombed with machine-gun nests. Against these the 77th Division, in the forest itself, was making very slow progress, and a rapid advance by the 28th seemed to be impossible. [Even] with the most heroic work on their part they fell far behind the line of the 35th Division front, and our infantry was never at any time during the advance entirely free from flank fire. The 91st Division, on our right, was also slightly behind the 35th at first, but advanced rapidly, and was soon on substantially the same line.[12]

The matter was cleared up with the infantry, and Battery D joined the others in providing fire against the Exermont area, where German resistance was beginning to build. Between 3:50 and 4:15 p.m., D joined the ongoing bombardment and fired a furious, 715-round barrage (three guns firing at any time at an average rate of 9.5 rounds per minute) starting on the Exermont Road near the point where it entered the Route Nationale, and then dropped it four hundred meters to target, probably uselessly, a deep draw that harbored a long-established forward ammunition dump and a relatively protected route that the Germans could use to get within dangerous striking distance of the Americans holding the northern edge of Montrebeau Woods. Truman then pulled the fire back half the distance between the draw and the road, where he ended Battery D's shooting of the day.*

The prohibition against firing out of sector was also dropped. In the beginning, the restriction had been an eminently practical one. Although, as noted earlier, training within the AEF for a war of movement had been woefully inadequate, this was exactly the kind of battle that General Pershing desired. American divisions were to violently push north with all possible speed, giving the Germans no

---

*The regimental history refers only briefly to this barrage, and Gates's operations report provides few details. Thankfully the battalion's activities can be pieced together from Truman's notes and the short, daily summaries and ammunition reports provided by the three batteries. In a separate Battery D operations report for the September 26–October 3 period, typed up by Sergeant Keenan but obviously approved by Truman, the main target is referred to as the Espérance Road in both drafts, but this is an error. The abbreviated 9797 coordinates demonstrate that the Exermont Road just east of the Route Nationale was the focal point of Battery D's efforts on the evening of September 28. Battery D and the rest of the battalion fired on and near the Espérance Road on numerous occasions the following day, and the confusion likely resulted from the similarity in names.

time to consolidate, and the field orders issued from I Corps to both the 28th and 35th Divisions left no room for ambiguity when they directed that the advance was to be made "without regard to progress made by those to the right or left."[13] In such a situation, with units not necessarily advancing at the same pace—and effective liaison and communication little more than wishful thinking until the front stabilized—the surest way to ensure that a formation did not accidentally kill Americans on its flanks was to confine all of its fighting within an assigned zone of advance. However, the situation, as it developed along the 35th Division's left flank, made strict adherence to this directive a costly, even suicidal, tactic.

The insistence at divisional headquarters down through the brigade and regimental artillery headquarters that there be strict adherence to this First Army directive was obviously being ignored at battalion and below. Although Generals Traub and Berry may not have known of the out-of-sector firing at midday on D-plus-2, they certainly would have found out soon after. The 1st Battalion's Major Miles and Captain McGee would likely get off with only a severe tongue-lashing; the 2nd Battalion's Major Gates and Captain Truman, having already been warned in the strongest of terms and suffering under the weight of being National Guardsmen, risked being relieved of command and replaced by officers who "knew how to take orders." This never happened, in large part because, unknown to the two soldiers, they received some timely fire support from a brother officer who had been engaged in hot actions at places like San Juan Hill and Mount Bagsak.

ALTHOUGH TRUMAN AND HIS MEN had removed two batteries from the Germans' order of battle and his old friend McGee a third, the 35th Division was still suffering grievously. The First Army's operations summary for September 28 states the situation plainly: "An advance was ordered and was carried out under heavy [enemy] artillery fire, the fire from the left flank across the river being particularly deadly as it was necessary to cross open fields in full view of the enfilading batteries."[14] Hearing reports of heavy losses and concerned that the division was in danger of getting bogged down, General Pershing went forward on D-plus-2 to observe for himself what was going on—a move which, incidentally, prompted MPs in the 28th Division's sector to "completely shut off traffic and [hold] the road open for the general's party"[15] for nearly three hours and prolonged both divisions' lack of artillery support.

General Traub detailed the terrible flanking fire from Apremont and the Argonne Forest and explained that he was unable to respond because of the First Army's standing order that forbade divisions to fire on points outside of their own area. An aghast Pershing responded, "But surely you do not obey that order?" to which a confused and defensive Traub replied, "It is the order."[16]

Yes, it was "the order," but the boilerplate directive was not intended to be a suicide pact between unthinking subordinates. Traub had never informed his corps commander that the Germans, rather than being intimidated by the American's rapid drive up the east side of the Ardennes, had instead reinforced it with all the light artillery they could muster, intent on savaging the drive's flank. I Corps and the First Army would have immediately understood the significance of the German move if Traub, either on his own or at the insistence of the equally mum Berry, had been willing to report bad news. It literally took the AEF's four-star commander personally going forward to a division headquarters to discover what the Germans were up to.

This singular fact was completely swept under the carpet during a hurried investigation carried out by the I Corps inspector—before the guns had even cooled. Traub received no direct criticism in the report by Col. Robert G. Peck, which came to the conclusion that it was the inefficient leadership of lackadaisical and ill-trained National Guardsmen that was the cause of the debacle east of the Ardennes. Yet there was more to it than even this. While I Corps's and First Army's heavy artillery was instructed to not fire closer than four miles from the front lines, the relevant commanders had but to ask to pull their fire in closer. Robert H. Ferrell, in his exhaustive study of the 35th Division's performance in the Meuse-Argonne battle, notes that, inexplicably, the ninety-five available 155mm cannons (forerunners of World War II's "Long Toms") were still firing on targets far in the German rear instead of saturating the forest with steel "because the 35th had not asked for artillery assistance." [17]

At least from that point on, the 35th's own artillery was allowed to engage in "observed fire" in the 28th Division's sector, but the damage had already been done by allowing the German guns to deploy unhindered and in force. And it also appears that Traub was able to put a rosy enough face on the situation to convince his boss that once his division's artillery could return fire into the Ardennes, the German guns could be adequately dealt with. The request for I Corps and First Army artillery support close to the battle lines would only come the following day, after the morning thrust into Exermont and Hill 240 was repulsed with terrible losses and the division's front was threatened with collapse. Even then the actions of the division commander and artillery chief are ambiguous. "Presumably," wrote Ferrell, "either Traub or Berry could have asked corps for support. In the event, it is unclear who asked." [18]

What all this had to do with Truman, aside from the tasks at hand—killing Germans, keeping his own men alive, and doing his duty for God, country, and the 35th Division—was that the same chain of command that on Friday, D-plus-1, was threatening to send him home in disgrace, was on Sunday, D-plus-3, using the out-of-sector firing of his and Captain McGee's batteries as a shield to help ward off criticism by both the corps headquarters above and the regimental commanders below. This was to become a stock defense, recited by both Traub and Berry in response to queries by everyone from inquisitive congressmen to newspaper reporters to skeptical officers. The Regular Army men, investigating and investigated alike, were all graduates of the U.S. Military Academy and charter members of what Truman derisively called the "West Point Protective Association," and, from his and the other guardsmens' point of view, the regulars had swiftly closed ranks to shift virtually all blame to the National Guard.

This went on for many months after the armistice, and Traub testified before Congress in January and February 1919 while the 35th Division remained in cold, drafty French barracks awaiting their return to the United States. Even after Truman got back home, he still could not escape the sad fact that the division was being used as a scapegoat for others failings and that he personally was being ill used by both Traub and Berry, who referred, both directly and indirectly, to Truman's activities to bolster their arguments. On one remarkable occasion, Truman even found Traub embellishing his role in the battle, and must have wondered just how much of this was going on that he didn't see.

Addressing the severe criticism that the division's infantry had received no fire support on D-day after the opening bombardment, Traub countered in the *Kansas City Post* that on D-day, "The battery under Captain Harry Truman was in action before noon, and continued in action throughout the day, wiping out machine-gun nests and anti-tank guns on the slopes."[19] Battery D, however, while certainly arrayed for action, never fired a shot during this period. This and Colonel Klemm's erratic behavior did not leave a good impression with the captain, who, when he became president, briefly explored doing away with the "The Point" and spreading its functions among the schools at Fort Leavenworth, Fort Sill, and other locations, explaining to his staff that he had "been thinking about it for thirty years."[20]

CHAPTER 15

Counterattack at Exermont

TRUMAN LATER RECORDED that "the night of September 28th and 29th was quiet." Heavy rains followed by a cold, continuous drizzle put the damper on activity along both sides of the line, leaving only the distant rumbling of heavy artillery fire and an occasional burst from nervous machine gunners. Just down the slope to the left of Truman and Gates's position, though, men were on the move. Trudging north in the opposite direction of the ambulances and ammunition trucks bearing wounded, Colonel Edward Stayton's 110th Engineers were passing through the mist. Prisoners being taken by the regiments along the front revealed that the two divisions the 35th Division had been battling since D-day had suddenly become five, including two elite guards divisions. A German offensive was clearly in the offing, and the engineers were to build and defend a trench line across the muddy high ground a little over a mile behind the forward line of own troops (FLOT) in the Montrebeau Woods. The 35th Division's depleted infantry regiments would carry out their own planned advance in the dubious hope that it might disrupt whatever the Germans were planning.

As things stood on the cold wet morning of September 29, 1918, Truman's battery was now so far behind the advancing doughboys that it could barely reach the ground beyond the infantry's initial objective, the road running east from Pleinchamp *ferme* (farm), with Exermont at the center. If the D-plus-3 effort was successful, it would be the 2nd Battalion's turn to leapfrog ahead, this time to the ground east of Montrebeau Woods. If the attack failed, they might stay where they were or move to a location north of Very. If a serious German counterattack erupted, they would remain in place while trying to blunt it and, if the worst came to pass, cover the withdrawal of the infantry and forward batteries. There was also a certain tactical limitation that Battery D shared with virtually all the 75mm batteries on the battlefield that day: not a one of them was in a position to provide anything approaching adequate fire support during the time between the jump-off and attainment of the initial objective.

It was a matter of terrain and the nature of the 75mm gun itself, as its rounds traveled a much more direct path to their target than those of a howitzer, which could travel higher and plummet at a steep angle. The bulk of the Americans on the left and center would be attacking down the reverse slope of Hill 224 crowning Montrebeau Woods, a descent of roughly 330 feet over a distance of 1,100 yards at the closest point between the FLOT and Exermont in the valley. If the ground had been relatively flat, it would have been a simple matter for the light batteries to walk a barrage ahead of the infantry at a distance averaging roughly four hundred yards. But the reverse slope combined with the relatively flat descent of rounds to point of impact in the final seconds of their trajectory made this a highly risky advance for any infantryman following the barrage. This was plainly evident to any artilleryman looking at the locations of the objective and the various units on a terrain map. The howitzers of the 130th Field Artillery theoretically could have laid down an effective fire on the reverse slope, but the unit was not trained for this type of close-in work with the infantry, and if there was any consideration by the conservative Berry in employing them in such a manner, it is not recorded.

For purposes of morale and to encourage the troops to carry out their mission vigorously, the men must see that they are not acting alone; that they are being supported. The division's guns had to fire even if they would have little or no effect on the enemy. Consequently, Berry's headquarters ordered what was then termed "harassing fire"—a single round per minute per gun—instead of the six or more common in the support of an infantry assault—a rate of fire so slow that all four guns in each battery were allowed to shoot instead of three at any one time. The battery commanders knew very well that they were firing in support of a dawn attack, but had no knowledge of its details other than the coordinates and times that were given as a basis to compute their firing data. Still, the orders calling for such a low rate of fire would have been perplexing and more than a little unsettling. Battery D's records bear this out. Normally, if looking strictly at battery-generated paperwork during this era, one would only find the rate of fire if there happens to be enough detail in the daily ammunition report to allow a correlation with firing times in the daily operation report. In Truman's case, he found this rate of fire so questionable that he specifically noted the rate for this mission, and it alone, in his comments on the twenty-one fire missions outlined in his operations report covering the Meuse-Argonne battle.

This was the best that the infantry, and the cannoneers tasked with supporting them, could do with the hand that was dealt them, "due to consideration of the safety of our own infantry."[1] If considerably more time had been available, a tightly choreographed movement of troops down the slope at a safe but militarily useful distance behind the fall of shot could have been painstakingly worked out. Such a task was utterly impossible on the night of September 28–29. As it was, the infantry received no morale benefit at all from the artillery's effort because the extremely slow rate, spread across a wide frontage and impacting down in a narrow valley, was essentially invisible within the larger battle erupting all around them.

Curiously, a basic error also crept into the orders the 60th Field Artillery Brigade issued the previous night and corrected hours later at half-past midnight. The correction, received at Truman's battery around 3:30 a.m., had no effect on his battery's operation but is indicative of the kinds of mistakes that can happen among soldiers engaged in nonstop movement and combat over a period of days or weeks. In spite of the fact that the minimalist fire plan was structured around the brigade's inability to safely conduct a rolling barrage during the planned attack, the initial orders inexplicably called for the few rounds fired to fall along a line where a rolling barrage close to the FLOT would normally start. This error was discovered and corrected by readjusting the barrage an additional six hundred meters (or a length equivalent to six and a half football fields) farther from the troops.*

Truman's battery was at first kept in reserve but was brought to action when German units moved to the attack. A confused situation had developed in which "the American advance on the right and the German counter-advance on their own right [the Americans' left] overlapped each other to some extent."[2] Battery D was engaged in this fight on the left, shelling German elements along the point 650 yards north of the woods where the reverse slope begins to descend sharply to the then American-occupied Exermont. The battery fired a bare 641 rounds between 8:45 and 11:00 a.m., with a short break at 10:15. Truman was likely tempted to shoot at a higher rate than ordered, but, with no "eyes on," he found it more prudent to obey orders. Still, records show that Dizzy D had to work hard to restrain itself, as its gun crew kept creeping up past the prescribed round-per-minute schedule.

Between 11:30 and 12:30, Truman's fire moved to the valley area immediately west of town to interdict German troops and cover the American withdrawal ordered just after noon. It was then shifted 550 yards north to Hill 240 in a weak effort—his and the other batteries had never been directed to increase the rate of fire—to engage the German 77s raining high-explosive and gas shells on the retreating soldiers.

---

*Although this incident may have been caused by a simple typing or transcription error, resulting in the intended coordinate of "X-line 80.6" appearing as "X-line 80.0," Robert Ferrell speculates in *Collapse at Meuse-Argonne*, p. 88, that General Berry may have misread the 35th Division's field order. He also notes the intriguing possibility that confusion in the orders may have been due to the division's assistant chief of staff, Walter V. Gallagher, "not thinking at all straight" due to illness (Gallagher had contracted pneumonia and would die later that week on October 4). The 129th's regimental history (Jay M. Lee, *The Artilleryman: 129th Field Artillery, 1917-1919, the Experiences and Impressions of an American Artillery Regiment in the World War*, p. 153) implies that the error occurred in Berry's headquarters.

Throughout the confused fighting, German artillery in the area of this hill and the surrounding woods (the Bois de Boyon), together with the ever-present batteries to the west in the 28th Division's sector, and 105mm guns farther to the rear, had continued to play on the exposed American infantry. It took roughly an hour for the 137th Infantry and part of the 139th at Exermont to retire south to the 110th Engineers' line as Truman's battery dropped a paltry 101 undirected rounds on the hill.

Other 35th Division troops to the northeast held their ground until ordered out in midafternoon, and a deep penetration by the 91st Division to their right at Gesnes was also forced to withdraw, largely because of the severe losses inflicted by the Germans' "terrific artillery support . . . from the east edge of the Argonne, [which] enfilded our lines with gas and HS shells."[3] Meanwhile, the American artillery placed well forward—Captain Marks's C Battery at Baulny and the 1st Battalions of both the 128th and 129th Field Artilleries just south of Charpentry—could actually *see* the German infantry pressing in against them and lent direct, effective—and furious—support to the engineers and reforming infantry. In turn, the Germans handled them roughly, with some batteries suffering heavy casualties.

It was during this period that the battalions near Charpentry were treated to the sight of the forward French batteries of the 219th Artillery Regiment pulling out of their positions east of town and galloping to the rear. Truman and Gates saw them as well, probably when they crested Hill 202 on their way south before reaching the Route Nationale. According to "Squatty" Meisburger, this did not look good to Major Gates, and it was unlikely that the officers immediately recognized who these artillerymen were. A steady stream of foot and truck traffic had been moving in surges back and forth past the battalion all day as the battle raged to their front, but what was going on now? Had the engineer line collapsed or been flanked? Were the Huns hot on the heels of the horses, men, and guns making haste right toward the 2nd Battalion? In the absence of any information whatsoever, Gates ordered Truman (and presumably Captains Salisbury and Allen) to remove the antiaircraft machine guns mounted on the fourgons and deploy them to defend the guns.

The battalion was also being targeted by the Germans and shelled—heavily shelled. Or at least their old gun line was. Incremental advances by the 28th Division had by now pushed German artillery spotters back to the Apremont area, effectively removing the 2nd Battalion from easy observation. The Germans still had, or thought they had, the unit's coordinates, and its gun flashes seemed to confirm that it hadn't moved. The result? "German shells fell in front of the battery position at half hour intervals all day."[4] Truman's battery was directly south of what had been Battery F's location, yet the highly efficient 77mm and 105mm gunners sent not one "over" crashing into Truman's position during the course of these bombardments, and none of his men received even a scratch. However, it was the sorry lot of a Battery D private away from the unit on detached duty with the 110th Ammunition Train to be caught by a German barrage. Adolf F. Anderson, one of several Texans transferred to D while at Camp Doniphan, was badly wounded the day before, evacuated to Neuvilly, and essentially forgotten by the Missourians he had served with for nearly a year. His captain did not learn until much later of his death, and the regiment, never notified of his passing, carried Anderson as "wounded in action."[5] Corporal Joseph Coyle was also wounded while serving with the ammunition detail but returned to the battery.

After a lengthy period where Battery D was not called upon to fire, Truman and the rest of the battalion received orders to lay a barrage on the Espêrance Road and then move their fire south on a rise four hundred meters (437 yards) closer to the engineers' line. Whether Truman was directed from above or acted on his own initiative, he abandoned the agonizingly slow rate of fire from earlier in the day in favor of four rounds per minute per three guns during the bombardment that started at 3:50 p.m. and lasted twenty-five minutes. The range was then increased two hundred meters, and a lazy, harassing fire laid down until a cease-fire order was given at 4:53. The last shooting of the day came later that rainy and increasingly cold evening in answer to a "rocket call" from the engineers. Whenever a battery was not engaged in firing at targets directed by higher command or targets of opportunity, they were kept "laid" on one or more areas of potential trouble, just in case an immediate response was needed to counter some enemy move. Flares of different coded combinations could be fired by soldiers along the front to signal which portion of the front needed a barrage, and this is what Truman was responding to when three of his battery's guns fired 117 rounds in ten minutes against the road again between 7:33 and 7:43 p.m.*

Both sides were pretty well spent after the fighting of September 29. The Germans had succeeded in throwing back assaults of the 35th and 91st Divisions, and the outpost line of the Kansas-Missouri men on D-plus-4, September 30, fell along the same ground that they had seized by the night of D-plus-2. Other American divisions suffered grievously in the war, with some losing even more than the 35th Division during individual battles. But the loss of eight thousand men in just four days' combat was a record that no one envied. The AEF command ordered the 1st Division to hurry forward and effect the relief of the 35th over the night of September 30–October 1. The Germans were also forced to pull out two of the 35th's foes, including the decimated 1st Guard Division. Truman's men and the rest of the 60th Field Artillery Brigade were to remain in place to cover the relief and support the "Big Red 1" until all of its artillery could be brought forward and positioned.

As 1st Division units began to form up near Battery D's horse line and to the east around Cheppy, Truman's gunners kept up a steady harassing fire on D's slice of the Espérance Road, its first 125 yards extending east from the Route Nationale. A perceived massing of Germans behind the rise separating the road and the engineers' outpost line—for a counterattack, perhaps?—prompted Truman's and every other battery in the 129th to drop shells into the area at four rounds per minute (three guns) between 8:15 and 8:25 a.m. Whatever the Germans were contemplating, the sudden surge of between 350

---

*Within the five documents or accounts referencing this rocket-call response, it is listed as occurring on three different dates. I have chosen September 29 because it corresponds with statements and data on the relevant daily operation report and the operations report for the Meuse-Argonne battle. On the other materials, produced at times further removed from combat, it appears to simply be included out of chronology as an afterthought on one memo, and similarly squeezed in near the bottom of both drafts of an assessment of battery ammunition expenditures. The earlier of the two drafts says that 120 rounds were fired.

and 400 shells persuaded them to forget it, and Truman returned his men to the plodding pace that they had followed since first light. Throughout, the Germans were not letting the 129th's efforts go unchallenged, and Truman recorded:

> German shells fell constantly in front of the battery and to the right toward Cheppy. The road [250 yards] in advance of the battery position was shelled constantly. No doubt the German observers mistook this road for the battery positions, which was very lucky for us.[6]

The American artillerymen watching the clockwork eruption of German shells directly to their front couldn't agree more. They were profoundly relieved that the German gunners had repeatedly missed them but fearful that their luck could change in a heartbeat. And every round that fell reinforced the notion that Truman "saved a lot of lives."[7] Seemingly alone among the Battery D soldiers interviewed many decades later, Sergeant Meisburger appeared to be the only old soldier to clearly realize that it was Major Gates, not their captain, that ordered the battery—along with the rest of the battalion—to displace to a parallel road. The rest, like chief mechanic Wooden, credit Truman with their survival:

> If he hadn't moved us out, there probably wouldn't have been a one of us left. . . . Yes. He probably saved the whole damn battery's life right there. The main thing of the artillery is getting the location. You locate them, and they're just about a dead duck. Now that's all there is to it.[8]

Twenty minutes after completing the sustained shelling of Germans concentrating near the engineers, Battery D resumed its standard harassing fire, but soon received orders to drop the total from four rounds per minute to the just-to-let-you-know-we're-here rate of one round per gun every four minutes, with all weapons firing. The bone-tired solders could practically take a nap between shots with this fire program, but almost immediately the men were jolted to the fullest attention by an extremely unwelcome event. "At 9:45," reported Truman, "No. 2 gun got H.E. normal with long fuse lodged in bore. Could not remove it. Continued firing with 3 guns."[9]

Private John Gordon,* to the right of the piece, had pulled the lanyard as he had done 1,359 times since 4:20 a.m. on D-day, but instead of the barrel hurtling back four feet as a fiery tongue leaped from its muzzle, only a dull, metallic "TAK" drifted over the gun line.

This small sound got the attention of everyone within earshot. Chief mechanic Wooden and Lieutenant Housholder made beelines to the gun as Sergeant William Tierney waited a few seconds and instructed Gordon to try again—"TAK." And again—"TAK."

Nothing.

Procedures for dealing with a misfire called for one minute to pass before the breech block was gingerly opened, exposing the fully-fused shell. The soldier acting as the gun's loader was ready to receive the live round if the weapon's extractor mechanism tugged it from the breech, but the round held fast. Since the battery was in the midst of carrying out harassing fire that a single cannon could easily maintain, the gun crews on either side were ordered to evacuate while Sgt. Ralph Thacker's No. 4 section, furthest from No. 2, kept up a slow fire on the road.

---

*This is the same John Gordon whom Truman had promoted from private to sergeant because of his actions during the "Battle of Who Run" on August 29, 1918. Gordon earned and shed stripes faster than any soldier in Dizzy D, having been reduced from private first class to private a week before the battery's opening engagement because he was caught lying to Truman and then missed reveille. He was busted back down from sergeant to private on September 10 when caught riding on a carriage during the long march from the Vosges. Instead of receiving a "nonjudicial" punishment to coincide with the demotion, he was brought up on charges and sent to trial at a regimental or brigade summary court (probably at the insistence of Colonel Klemm) and was acquitted. Gordon was promoted to corporal sometime in November and apparently retained the extra stripe for the duration of his time in the service. "Battery D Roster and Reference Book" and "Battery D Extra Duty Roster," HSTL.

Careful hands started to work at the rim of the live round, but it wouldn't budge, refusing to be either rotated or levered out. Housholder knew what needed to be done, but as this was the first (and only) misfire that D would experience, he likely consulted page eighteen of his dog-eared and very heavily annotated *Provisional Drill Regulations for Field Artillery, 75mm Gun*, before he and the others proceeded any further. Gently tapping around the edge of the shell's base produced no results. The last thing to try was pushing or, heaven forbid, knocking the round back through the breech with a rammer, a procedure only to be done "under the commander's supervision and with extreme caution."

Ironically, the breakdown of the tasks performed by the individual crew members meant that Gordon himself would be the man to handle the rammer, and everyone held their breath as he slid the end with the cup-shaped devise, opposite the long, cylindrical sponge, carefully down the barrel. Pushing didn't work, and, although it was permissible to "strike the fuse," it is unlikely that this was done with much vigor. Unwilling to press their luck further, the matter was turned over to the division's ordnance section. Tierney's men carefully disengaged the barrel from the carriage and placed it suspended in an ordnance *fourgon*'s rope cradle to minimize the bouncing and jostling of the round during its short journey to the ordnance repair shop. With luck, a replacement barrel would be delivered before the battery left to rejoin the rest of the division. The 1st and 3rd sections went back to work (what little of it there was), and the three remaining guns continued shooting until a cease-fire was called at 11:45.

The rest of the day and all through the evening, Truman's guns remained silent but were trained one thousand meters (nearly 1,100 yards) to the north, on a line running from the ravine jutting into the bluffs from the Route Nationale and extending east through the crest of Hill 224 and surrounding Montrebeau Woods. With the exception of some German harassing fire, the night of September 30–October 1 was exceptionally quiet, and Major Gates was pleased to see that in spite of two gas alarms, both of them false, his men were able to get a good night's rest. The next morning, both sides began to grope their way through where they believed their opponent's light artillery might be located. Truman's men joined in for two fast barrages between 9:30

and 9:46 a.m. against a perceived concentration of German infantry at the southeast corner of the woods, and from 2:30 to 2:38 p.m. against artillery a mile and a half northwest of Le Chêne Tondu and a mile west of Apremont. Battery D fired sixty-six and thirty-two rounds respectively. The newly arrived 7th Field Artillery headquarters was briefly—and heavily—shelled northwest of Very, but the battalions up by Charpentry remained the focus of German artillery spotters' attention, and the Germans threw no counterbattery fire the 2nd Battalion's way. Things changed after dark.

North of Truman's position that day, many German rounds had played up and down the Route Nationale and road over Hill 202 that split off toward Charpentry—and would have even if the Germans had not been tipped off to the 35th Division's relief by the long, single-file lines of doughboys stretching past Truman to the southern horizon. Directly to the captain's west, the 130th Field Artillery received some sporadic shelling (it was never the target of a heavy barrage despite its high visibility), but it soon became clear that the Germans had finally figured out that the 129th's 2nd Battalion was not where they'd though it was. Still, the same factors that had hidden its move now made the location of the new gun lines highly ambiguous. Rounds fell between, but not on, Batteries D and E, with more landing "on all four sides" of Captain Salisbury's very lucky cannoneers.[10] Farther east, outside Cheppy and less than a half-mile from D, Allen's Battery F bore the brunt of the barrage, which incorporated the standard German mix of gas and high-explosive rounds. The sudden barrage swept from front to back through the battery position, blowing the feet off one man who soon died, and wounding a half-dozen others before creeping on to the horse line, where thirteen animals were either killed outright or so badly wounded that they had to be shot.

WHEN NOT FIRING, Truman's and the battalion's guns had remained "laid on" and ready to strike along the same line as they had since noon on September 30. Throughout October 2, D-plus-6, Gates's men had sat cooling their heels, although the arrival of a replacement barrel for D Battery's No. 2 gun at 3:00 p.m. gave Sergeant Tierney's section and chief mechanic Wooden plenty to keep them busy. The sudden arrival an hour later of a stream of caissons carrying one thousand deadly phosgene gas shells to each battery immediately turned the entire road from Truman's left flank position to Cheppy into a frenzy of activity. Although orders had yet to arrive, the 2nd Battalion was to fire a massive barrage of persistent gas into the ravine sheltering the German ammunition dump northwest of Montrebeau Woods. The rounds, enough for each gun section to make a stack as long as a gun carriage and high as a 75's barrel when braced with wooden boxes on the ends, were placed on scrap wood and old shell cases to keep them off the wet earth. The empty caissons were sent back the way they had come, and the men looked out on the stacks of gleaming brass and steel that hadn't been there seemingly just moments before. Excited cannoneers speculated loudly about the target of the coming shoot as they began to queue up for the evening chow, when the Germans struck out of the blue—literally:

> Seven German planes flew from west to east over the 2nd Battalion position. They met a warm reception from the ground from machine guns, rifles, and every form of anti-aircraft weapon within range or seeming range; but unaffected by them they sailed deliberately over us several times, firing their machine guns and dropping bombs. The American fire had the effect, however, of sufficiently disconcerting them to prevent accurate direction of their fire; and their missiles for the most part did little damage. Almost the last one that dropped, however, fell near the cross-roads at the wayside shrine on the right end of the battalion.[11]

The enemy had decided to use their airpower to deliver a blow against the American gun lines below Hill 240 and Exermont. Despite the planes (one of which was shot down) making multiple passes along the center of their target area, only one Battery F man was badly wounded. Other aircraft that swept in low to attack the artillery's flank positions did considerably more damage. On the right, a trio of bi-planes overshot the guns and decimated an engineer outfit adjacent to the 7th Field Artillery's Battery A, with bombs hitting right among "the mass of men and animals" as they set up camp.[12] On the left, down the hill from Truman and Gates, a long line of 130th Field Artillery soldiers at Battery C's field kitchen were struck without warning in the opening seconds of the 5:30 p.m. attack, leaving "dead and dying men everywhere."[13] Five soldiers including the cook were either killed instantly or died soon after, with twenty-one more wounded.

The 2nd Battalion had emerged almost completely unscathed, and the din of the air strike had barely abated when orders arrived at 6:00 p.m. for the night's two-hour "special mission" against the ravine near Montrebeau Woods.* Shrapnel rounds would have been useful against this target if they had been available at the battery when needed, and the effort to drop high-explosive shells into this site on D-plus-2 had been completely futile because of the 75mm's flat trajectory. But it was a perfect target for the No. 5 special shell's heavy phosgene gas, which would settle and thicken all along the bottoms, thoroughly contaminating everything it touched, including the contents of the Germans' forward supply dump. The 35th Division's rapid advance had prevented the enemy from using the supplies and munitions that lined the ravine's deep recesses, but now that the front had "stabilized"—a situation the Germans would work hard to preserve—they could draw on this ready source when defending the woods from the 1st Division.

The clock was ticking, and Truman worked feverishly from map overlays drawn by Captain Fouilhoux on Klemm's staff in order to have his fire plan completed and briefed to the gun sergeants by the 8:00 p.m. H-hour. Operating under the expectation that some portion of the Germans in the area of the dump would likely flee to progressively higher portions of the feature to escape the gas, Truman planned to shift fire three hundred meters (325 yards) to the northeast after some specified amount of time—in effect, to chase the Germans onto less-sheltered ground. Salisbury's men were to drop their gas along the western crest of Hill 224 and Allen's along the southeast portion of the woods: both likely spots for a German defense of the area.

All of this was done in preparation for a quick assault by the 1st Division which intended to seize the area before the Germans could

---

*Major Gates reported receiving the orders substantially later, at 7:30, but the two officers were likely referring to different things: Truman, for example, a verbal "warning order" of some sort, and Gates, the published 60th Field Artillery's Special Mission No. 4.

consolidate any further: an assault in which the 2nd Battalion would likely pummel much of the same ground a second time, only with high-explosive shells. The 2nd Battalion was prepared for action and was only moments from starting its fire program when it was notified that the shoot was suddenly called off. Not only that, but they were to gather up their gear, retrieve their animals from the horse line, and be ready to vacate their position by 10:00 p.m.!

Somewhere along the chain of command, the attack had been ordered postponed. Perhaps the 1st Division's commander, the old artil-leryman Maj. Gen. Charles P. Summerall, wanted his own guns in the fight. But with many of its elements still struggling to get into position, it is more likely that he simply did not feel the division was ready. Whatever the reason, the 1st Artillery Brigade assumed responsibility for the 60th Field Artillery Brigade's mission at 9:00 p.m. sharp. And as for getting out, while certainly not as bad as getting in, it was not a trouble-free affair, particularly for the battalions near Charpentry that were forced to withdraw piecemeal while under heavy fire and could not move all the guns and caissons that night because so many horses were killed.

The gas shells just delivered to the 2nd Battalion, as well as the other munitions under camouflage in the field behind the various battery positions, would all be left in place for the 1st Artillery Brigade's use. Ironically, Truman's unit, which had ended up leading the entire brigade north seven days earlier, would lead it back out again, this time via Varennes to the 2nd Battalion's left. At the appointed hour, Battery D was harnessed, hitched, and ready to go, but had to hold up for more than an hour as enemy shells wracked the town (without inflicting any additional casualties on the 130th). Finally, the MPs opened the road, and D was off with the rest of the 129th Field Artillery's elements closed up a bit more tightly than "The Book" called for in their hurry to get through Varennes. The last fourgons of the regiment's supply train were on the move by midnight. Truman passed the spot where he and Major Gates had searched in vain for Colonel Patton, then marched south past the massive crater which now boasted a wide, two-lane, gravel road skirting its perimeter. He and his men hurried south and were beyond the reach of even the longest-range German artillery before dawn.

Chapter 16

"Frenchmen Buried in My Front Yard and Huns in the Back"

Truman and his men pulled into Signeulles, located west-southwest of the Saint-Mihiel battlefield, at 10 p.m. on September 5. The regiment had trudged through the town during the long march north, but in the aftermath of the Meuse-Argonne fighting, they would be billeted here for a week's rest. The drumbeat of the big guns supporting the First Army's second lunge toward Sedan provided an almost seamless rumble, but for the 129th Field Artillery there was no more D-day "D" plus the addition of some ever-larger numeral, it was simply a rainy Thursday night. And the men found that the rumor was true; they'd have roofs over their heads for the first time in almost a month.

Battery D's guns and rolling stock were in very good order despite having fired 8,385 rounds since July 17, plus having traveled more than two hundred miles on their own wheels, much of it through the rain and on muddy secondary roads, and then across shattered trenches and shell holes. The guns were so well maintained that the division's ordnance section judged them to be in "superior condition to that of any other battery of the two [75mm] regiments, [which] evidenced the fact that unusual care had been exercised by the commissioned and enlisted personnel of this battery."[1] The men, however, were all "nervous wreck[s] and we'd all lost weight until we looked like scarecrows."[2] Truman, who had shrunk from 160 to 135 pounds, didn't mention this to his fiancee Bess until after the war, but in his first letter to her in two weeks, he understandably assured her, "I am as fat, healthy, and look as well as I ever did, so don't worry about me because there is no German shell with my name on it."[3] Two days later he wrote, "I came through absolutely unscathed—didn't even lose a man in the Battery, although every other Battery had from one to a half-dozen fatalities." Unaware that Private Anderson's condition was turning out be mortal, he added, "A couple of my men who were on special duty with the ammunition train were slightly wounded and that's all."[4]

GOOD LEADERSHIP AT THE BATTALION and battery levels—and considerably more luck than any of the artillerymen could have dared hope for—meant that although they had been well within the German cone of fire that had inflicted 50 to 80 percent casualties among the 35th Division's line units, losses had been comparatively light among the field artillery. The 27,000-man division entered the Meuse-Argonne with just over 26,000 soldiers and reported to First Army the loss of 8,023 of them during five—really four—days of fighting. The post-battle sorting out of the division's losses resulted in a total of 1,130 killed, died of wounds, or missing/unidentified and later declared dead, plus 5,656 severely wounded; with the balance of 1,237 either lightly wounded or suffering from mild combat fatigue and returned to duty. This latter number includes 68 men known to have been taken prisoner. A portion of the severely wounded also returned to their units, but judging by the fact that the division received 10,605 replacements before returning to the United States, the number couldn't have been very large.

The 35th Division's average of 2,000 casualties every twenty-four hours represents one of the highest daily loss rates of any U.S. division during the war, virtually all occurring within a couple hundred yards to four miles of Truman's artillery battery as it pushed forward through the battlefield and went about its deadly work. By contrast, the loss rate of formations on its flanks was under 400 men per day. The 28th Division suffered 2,916 casualties in eight days of combat (September 26—October 3), and the 91st Division on the 35th Division's right experienced 4,735 over twelve days (September 26—October 7). The Germans' firm determination to block the drive up the Aire Valley was made painfully evident by their shifting of more and more forces, including guards divisions, to its defense. Moreover, the same artillery that wracked the 35th Division was still active when the 1st Division took over its sector, and the nearly unimpeded use of these guns on the Big Red 1's left flank inflicted most of its dead and wounded. The 1st Division initially reported 9,186 men lost before being pulled out on October 12, and although this number was later adjusted down to 6,629, the 1st and 35th Divisions' 14,000 to 17,000 casualties make the few miles from the Varennes-Cheppy area through Exermont and Hill 240 the AEF's most bloody ground of the war. The 1st Division's totals include 146 of the 35th Division's artillerymen who were assigned to it through October 2.

Fresh new uniforms, good food and plenty of it, and the certitude that they had soundly thrashed the dreaded Hun all gave the 129th a tremendous boost. Battery D and its captain were on top of the world. "We'll go in again when our turn comes," wrote Truman. He boasted, "The Prussian Guards simply can't make their legs stand when they get word that the Yanks are coming."[5] Even the frequent inspections did little to dampen the men's enthusiasm and conviction that they were the toughest doughboys in France.

Much time and energy was spent in attempting to coax their tired horses back to health. The poor beasts, in spite of their condition, had done all that was asked of them and were honestly in not much worse shape than the new allotment of animals sent as replacements for those that died during the march. Every man in the battery could be found doing one of four things during off-duty hours: catching up on letter writing, participating in discrete poker games, sleeping, or just lounging around with their buddies. Disciplinary problems were *almost* nonexistent. Days were considerably fuller for the sergeants and officers, but even they received more time off than they were used to. This was not so for their captain, his executive officer, and the battery clerk.

While Lieutenant Housholder worked on satisfying the battalion's and regiment's daily requirements, Truman and Corporal (Acting Sergeant) Keenan waded into the paperwork that had been building throughout the month, as only the most pressing items had been brought to Truman's attention. Truman made inquiries into why Battery D wasn't getting its copies of *Stars and Stripes* and wrote commendations; requisitions; general correspondence (including dealing with a Kansas City optical company trying to bill him for goggles purchased by another unit); recommendations for promotions; requests for his personnel records so that he could find out why he was still receiving only a lieutenant's pay; reports of every description; and of course, more letters to his dear Bess.

Among the chit chat, accounts of daily activities, and the most up-to-date information he had on the various officers and men she knew in the division, Truman also expressed his deep satisfaction at recommending a young private in his BC detail for an appointment to the U.S. Military Academy: "I sent one of my bright kids out of the battery to West Point yesterday. If he makes the grade on the examination he'll get in all right. I think he'll make it because he's a very bright boy. His name is John Uncles."[6] According to Truman, Pfc. John J. Uncles was "one of seven in AEF to make it"[7] to the academy, and he was not yet one month past his twentieth birthday when Truman recommended him. Uncles graduated in June 1922, commanded field artillery brigades in the 7th and 9th Armored Divisions during World War II, and ultimately became chief of staff, U.S. Army Europe, then commanded VII Corps in Germany during the late 1950s. Apparently it was a very good pick on the part of his proud captain.

Truman's relationship with the 129th's resident West Pointer, Colonel Klemm, was a bit strained, however. This situation was not unique to our captain, as cryptic references to problems between Klemm and the men pepper his letters to Bess. "[Lieutenant Charles]

Bundschu is in Headquarters Company and seems to be in bad with K.D.K [Klemm]," wrote Truman on October 11, "but that is nothing to worry about because we are all in that fix."[8] Several days earlier, the colonel, perhaps as part of an effort to mend fences with the officers, invited Truman and Captain Marks to accompany him to nearby Bar-le-Duc, where they had dinner together. Uncharacteristically, Truman did not mention the event in one of his gossipy letters but noted it in his calendar book for Tuesday, October 8.

Like the rest of the 35th Division, the 60th Field Artillery Brigade's elements moved to their new piece of the line in stages from October 12 to 16. The division was headed for the Sommedieue Sector just east of Verdun, where it would be arrayed from north to south in expectation of the coming drive, which, for the first time in four long years of war, would carry the war into the German heartland. A sign of the Allies' changing fortunes was that, until they got within range of enemy long-range artillery, they made most of their approach during the day, inviting observation by German aircraft in spite of the weather. Lieutenant Lee describes the move:

> The Meuse River, like the Missouri, meanders lazily hither and yon in a broad valley, frequently overflowing its banks, and never of certain channel. For water traffic a well dredged canal has been constructed along the east edge of the bottom-land. In places the range of hills known as the Meuse Heights comes so close to the canal that there is just room between the two for the National Highway which during the war constituted one of the main traffic roads from the direct south and from the rail-head at Rattentout, to the chain of forts which constituted the permanent defenses of Verdun on the east, and to the front lines which were strung out in the valley below the eastern slope of the hills. This road and canal, though not visible from the enemy's lines, except possibly at certain points from balloons, were yet more or less constantly under fire; for the Germans of course realized their importance as an avenue for supplies, and it was easy to lay on them with their long range guns.

Riding along this road toward the front, after a week's freedom from any fear of hostile shells, our men could hear, but paid little attention to, the never-ceasing but gradually more distinct roar of distant artillery. As they rode, away off to the right, five or six miles away, sounded the muffled "boom" of some German large calibers. A few moments of indifference as before— then—a sudden thrill of realization as out of the atmosphere comes that wicked "Br-r-r-r," and—"Bang!" a shell bursts on the hillside above them. Another moment of silence, then from one of them: "Gee! I swallowed my chew!"[9]

The Sommedieue Sector was located between the territory seized during the Saint-Mihiel offensive and the current American drive toward the critical double-tracked rail link above Sedan that fed the bulk of the German armies in France. The 35th Division's line of contact generally ran as little as a half-mile from the most eastern bastions, which were arranged in depth across the entire area. These forts bore names that virtually every officer was familiar with because of the epic struggle that had raged there only two years before, and the carnage which still defies imagination—434,000 German and 542,000 French casualties, almost half of which were killed or died of wounds. The positions of the batteries were shifted several times over the next two weeks but ultimately came to rest with, north to south, Pete Allen's Battery F located in an uncomfortably exposed position near Fort de Souville, then Battery D and Salisbury's E astride the southwest portal of the Paris-Metz railroad tunnel bored 1,200 yards through a ridge that offered them at least a degree of protection. Fort Tavannes, protecting the tunnel, lay only about 300 yards east of the battery, while 1,500 yards north of the tunnel's opposite portal, and 2,300 yards northeast of Battery D, lay Fort Vaux.

Battery D's location in relation to the ridge was such that it had a narrower field of fire than either Major Gates or Truman liked. They were stuck with the location for the time being, however, and Gates's extensive efforts to locate better positions for all his guns were largely futile, because for every potential advantage the alternate sites secured, new disadvantages were immediately apparent. But at least his efforts provided Truman's battery with a place it could scoot to if things should get too hot near the tunnel, and few if any days saw fewer than 250 German shells of up to 150mm fall within the battalion area. As if to emphasize the point, Gates passed on to Truman a message from Captain Paterson at headquarters which warned, "In view of the fact that French Batteries were shelled out the positions now occupied by your Battalion, it is advisable that you reconnoiter the new positions if possible."[10]

The 2nd Battalion's horses and rolling stock, excluding those detailed to the kitchen, were sheltered in a deep ravine more than four miles to the south with other regimental equipment at Camp la Beholle. Major Gates's headquarters group was located in a series of well-maintained dugouts just off Truman's left flank, and the captain was more than satisfied with his *poste de commande*.

There is an old Battery of 155 long guns across the road from me whose date of manufacture was so long ago that no one knows it. They shoot gas at the Hun every time he fires this way and it seems that their work is very effective because the Hun usually ceases to fire when this antique outfit starts. The Frenchmen say that the old guns shoot very accurately. I have paper windows in my dugout and the concussion from the guns has completely ruined it.

You should see the palace I live in. It is a different one from that in which I was when I wrote you last. I have a very large arched room which contains the Battery kitchen. On one side I have a small room with a stove, a table, a chair, some boxes, a lot of maps and firing tables and other necessary Battery commander junk. On the other I have a sleeping apartment with room for myself and two lieutenants and a stove. The Battery is up the road a couple of hundred meters and so well hidden that I can't find it myself after dark sometimes. I have a telephone right at my bedside and one on my desk so that when barrages and things are called for I can be immediately informed. I have all the comforts of home except that I'll have such a habit sleeping underground that I'll have to go to the cellar to sleep when I get home.[11]

At the other end of the tunnel, Acting Sgt. (and later Col. when the army next fought its way through France and Germany) William Triplet of the 140th Infantry found life was not so sweet:

> Before the war the area had been largely wooded, but an average of three shells had plowed into each square yard of soil and the low, rolling hills had been scalped of vegetation. Now and then one would see a splintered stump of the original trees, none over ten or twelve inches high. Dugouts were everywhere along the trench lines ranging from one-man niches [dug into the trench walls] to large, deep, and commodious underground palaces capable of housing a section or small platoon. Some of the latter were collapsed and all were badly flooded by ground seepage, unusable unless pumps kept them clear, and with rotting roof timbers that could not be trusted.[12]

When Sergeant Triplet's company unexpectedly received fifty replacements during broad daylight (the unit had suffered 86 percent casualties during the fighting from Cheppy to Exermont), he refused the temptation to herd the youths quickly into two unused—and dangerously deep—dugouts in his area. The sergeant and every other soldier on the front knew the chilling story of the French company buried in a collapsed trench near Fort Douaumont, with only a line of bayonets poking above the mud to mark where the soldiers had stood in life.

> In case of a hit or near miss, they'd be buried a lot deeper than those forty Frenchmen who had been standing for over a year in the collapsed *Tranchée des Baionettes* a couple of miles to our left. And I wasn't going to have them dig new niches. Somebody'd spade out a Frenchman or German or pieces thereof, and the morale of this lot was low enough now. Then I remembered this little cut-and-cover hut snugged up under the reverse slope two hundred yards to the rear, on the way to the kitchen. It should hold twenty men. The roof was thin, just planks sagging under a

layer of sandbags. But it would stop splinters[,] and nothing short of Fort Vaux would protect them from a direct hit anyway.[13]

Truman's men on the other side of the ridge were generally quartered in shelters of this "cut-and-cover" type that had been built into the reverse slope long before their arrival, and were high enough to remain dependably dry during their stay in what they could tell had once been a lush forest. Truman wrote Bess:

> I am sure that this desolate country was cultivated and beautiful like the rest of France and now, why Sahara or Arizona would look like Eden beside it. When the moon rises behind those tree trunks I spoke of awhile ago you can imagine that the ghosts of the half-million Frenchmen who were slaughtered here are holding a sorrowful parade over the ruins. . . . Trees that were once most beautiful forest trees are stumps with naked branches sticking out making them look like ghosts. The ground is simply one mass of shell holes.[14]

Triplet's ground had changed hands thirteen times, and though the bodies had long since been removed, it was impossible to not step on some form of remains:

> This muddy moonscape was crisscrossed by fire and communication trenches and lines of rusting barbed wire entanglements resembling the disorderly web of a black widow spider. Every trench had had a purpose when it was dug but with the flood and ebb of the tide of battle most of them had fallen into disuse. These had been blocked with sections of concetina wire to hinder their use as covered lines of approach by the enemy. The soil was littered with moldy scraps of *feld grau*, African mustard, and French horizon-blue cloth, bones, unexploded shells, bullet-riddled helmets, cast-iron shards, and boots of rotten leather containing bone and gristle.[15]

But it was what was hidden beneath the fragile covering of earth that was most unnerving. Truman wrote Bess, "There are Frenchmen buried in my front yard and Huns in the back yard and both litter up the landscape as far as you can see. Every time a Boche shell hits in a field over west of here it digs up a piece of someone. It is well I'm not troubled by spooks."[16] It came as no surprise when one poor doughboy, a runner named Richardson, approached Sergeant Triplet, wide-eyed and frantic after finding that he had company in his trench-wall niche:

> I gotta have another slot to sleep in—goddamn Frenchman. I'm movin' out. . . . Was diggin' that wall out for a little more elbow room and this goddamn arm fell out, right on my bunk, and there he was. I tell you I ain't gonna sleep there. I'll sit up all night before I raise that flap again.[17]

Said Triplet, "We soon learned to dig cautiously and to stop digging when our shovel brought up cloth or bone fragments."[18]

The 35th Division quickly discovered that the German use of poison gas was also far more prevalent in the Verdun area than it had been in either the Vosges or the Argonne, although if the Kansas-Missouri soldiers had stayed along the Aire River several more days—and the artillerymen just one more—they would have found out first hand what the Germans were capable of doing. While the 35th's medical personnel reported 382 gas casualties (others were affected to varying degrees of severity but were more seriously wounded by such things as shrapnel or bullets), the 1st Division logged fully 1,603 as gassed, excluding those that were killed outright by the weapon, principally by phosgene. Regimental historian Lee, who was also the 129th's gas officer, oversaw preventive measures for the batteries, headquarters, supply, and ordnance elements:

> Anti-gas guards were constantly maintained at all positions, with Klaxon horns and gongs for warnings, and where possible, dug-outs were made gas-proof, all under the immediate direction

of the Gas Non-Commissioned Officers of the respective batteries, and with the aid of the battery mechanics. . . . They were responsible, in their respective organizations, under the supervision of their captains, for seeing that every man had a well-fitting mask, in good order; for training the men in their use and care; for looking after the gas defense in each position, such as gas-proofing of dugouts, installation of gas alarms, keeping on hand a supply of lime for neutralizing mustard gas and of gas-proof gloves for handling gas protection; and lastly, the highly important duty of constantly, night and day, maintaining gas guards, who would give the alarm when occasion demanded it.[19]

Wearing gas masks for lengthy periods of time was hard on the men and, with gas so prevalent in the sector—really a continuous presence—it required constant and close monitoring. False alarms at night were particularly bothersome and robbed the men of badly needed sleep. Truman's gas NCO, Harry Murphy, related that on one occasion the Germans were dropping gas shells dangerously close to the battery but that the wind was pushing most of the killer fumes past its position.

One night that we were in Verdun, we were being shelled by mustard gas and I stayed up at Captain Truman's headquarters. In fact we stood out under the stars and discussed whether we should call a gas alarm or not. We stayed there for several hours and decided it wasn't a sufficient concentration to justify a gas alarm. . . . They weren't close enough. We were getting just a faint smell of gas, but not enough to justify an alarm. . . . We had gas alarms a good many times, but it just did not necessitate putting on masks.

One day I was out walking around and most of the men were in the dugouts, French dugouts east of Verdun, and all of a sudden they came rushing out with their gas masks on. There had been a gas barrage forward of our position, but the gas that was used was chlorine gas and it lays very low on the ground. And due to the fact that I was walking around, I never smelled any of it, but it floated right down and went into the dugouts and the men all came out with their eyes watering, grabbing their masks and getting them on. That just shows how that gas lays right down on the ground, it's heavy.[20]

This part of France was enjoying a brief dry spell that partially mitigated the effect of gas when the division first moved into the Sommedieue Sector, but it was not going to last forever. "Then this drizzling rain set in," said Triplet. "Jerry took advantage of the favorable weather and dropped a number of mustard gas shells where they would do the most good—the cold rain would keep the gas effective in liquid form for days until we searched out and sprinkled lime on every burst." In theory, all of the dugouts used as living quarters were to have been gas-proofed, and they generally were against German harassing fire. But when heavy concentrations were dumped on the area, there was more persistence, leading to increased seepage and higher concentrations within the shelters. The simple act of going and coming when performing one's duties would allow fumes or contaminated clothing inside, no matter how quickly and careful a soldier's exit and entrance. Whether one was inside or out, when the klaxon sounded, a wise doughboy put on his mask. "My sleeping apartment is practically bomb proof," Truman told Bess. "So I sleep soundly and well—unless there's gas, and I've almost gotten so I can sleep with a gas mask on. Next time I send you a picture it will be with a gas mask on."[21]

CHAPTER 17

"It's Over, Over There"

Fʀᴏᴍ ʟᴏɴɢ ᴇxᴘᴇʀɪᴇɴᴄᴇ, the Germans knew the location of every past and present battery site on the Verdun front. The object of the artillerymen when camouflaging their positions—a task at which Lieutenant Housholder was *the* acknowledged expert in the 2nd Battalion—was to keep the enemy guessing as long as possible as to precisely which of the old French positions were in use. The time finally came when they had to risk being spotted, and Truman's gunners started firing for registration on potential trouble spots on Friday, October 18th. Guns were kept trained on specific areas at all times so that they could fire in support of Triplet's regiment, the 140th, or its neighbor to the north, the 138th Infantry, on a moment's notice. The battalion responded to three back-to-back false alarms called by the infantry the following Monday, and another several days later on Wednesday.

Concurrent with these protective barrages was a disagreement pitting the battalion and battery commanders on one side versus the regimental leadership on the other, although there is some evidence that the other battery commanders did not stick their necks out as much as did Truman. The crux of the matter is that the firing unit commanders believed that the rate of fire dictated in their headquarter's field orders could wreck the guns. Colonel Klemm and his exec, Elliott, called for barrages of eight rounds per gun per minute for five minutes, followed by four rounds each for five minutes, then two rounds for ten minutes to keep the barrel temperatures from climbing too high. Although the normal procedure during such a fast rate of fire was to have a gun held out of action for ten minutes, followed by others in rotation to allow their barrels to cool, the report by Truman is written from the standpoint that the 129th's leadership intended to have *all* guns firing. Klemm and his staff must have reasoned—correctly, if narrowly—that a protective barrage of this duration, coupled with a decreasing rate of fire, would not generate any risk. But what would happen if several protective fires were called in quick succession, effectively preventing the barrels from cooling?

This is precisely what happened on October 21, and there's not a word about it in the regimental history. As evidenced by Captain Allen's response to the problem presented by the field orders and his commander's intent, Allen carried out the initial barrage in the manner ordered. Then, when the additional calls for fire started coming in, he shut F Battery down for ten-minute periods in the middle of the mission. Yet even this was insufficient time to cool for the pace ordered. Allen reported, "Guns heated after completion of first barrage so that guns were almost unsafe to load projectiles." He neglected to give a total for the rounds expended in this report, yet pointedly added that he had eight misfires. Earlier that evening, Captain Marks's C Battery, which was temporarily attached to the 2nd Battalion, attempted to perform a similar mission in the time allotted, but Marks clearly cut back on the rounds fired, reporting 820 expended instead of 960, and offered no criticism or opinion. In Captain Truman's report, he let it be known that the rate of fire called for in the field order, and commander's intent for all guns to be used simultaneously, were wholly unworkable if the batteries should find themselves in a rapidly developing situation:

At 20:00 hour rocket was reported for barrage. Before this barrage was finished a repeat was sent up. Firing was continued at two (2) rounds per minute until 20:25 when barrage was repeated. Rockets were going up continually. Tried to get confirmation by phone, and could not.

Flare was dropped in front of battery position #22* at 21:25.

Started third barrage at a rate of two (2) rounds per minute because of shortage of ammunition, at 21:40 when order to cease firing was given by Battalion Commander.

The rate of fire could not be maintained on account of the guns over-heating. It is impossible to fire 32 rounds per minute with three (3) guns and allow one to cool.[1]

Truman made a clumsy attempt to provide himself with some cover by claiming that there was a shortage of ammunition—there was no less at D's position than at any other battery site that evening—but ultimately could not hold back. If he suffered any immediate consequences for his impertinence, it is not recorded. Future field orders from headquarters, 129th Field Artillery, contained instructions covering overlapping calls for fire: "Hereafter whenever there shall be successive calls for normal or eventual barrages, and sufficient time shall not have elapsed between the completion of one barrage and the call for the next to permit the guns to cool, the rate of fire as fixed by paragraph 4, F.O. No. 11, these Headquarters, 18 October, 1918, shall be changed to the following:[2] eight rounds per minute during the initial call's opening segment, dropped back to five rounds in successive calls after the guns were given ten minutes for cooling and cleaning."

TRUMAN AND THE FIRING UNIT COMMANDERS had made their point and ensured that their weapons could continue do their job even during sustained German attacks, yet Truman's response was arguably more effective at protecting the infantry than what headquarters came up with. It was better to fire a continuous eight rounds per minute per battery until a situation was clarified than to provide no fire support at all for a mandated—and agonizingly long—ten minutes during a frontline brawl. That the calls for fire were false alarms was a separate

---

*Position #22 was one of the unoccupied alternative battery sites scouted by Major Gates on October 20.

issue, and officers from the 140th Infantry's 2nd and 3rd Battalions sent letters denying that their units had anything to do with the signals or that any were even seen by their troops. It should be noted, however, that the mistakes are more likely to have originated from nervous fingers in the trenches than the artillery spotters, since the combinations of colors, numbers, and types of flares calling in the artillery were very specific and frequently changed for security reasons. For example, two red flares followed by two green might signal a request for a barrage all along the front, while a white burst followed by a single red might signify the need for a box barrage on three sides of some forward outpost. What is known is that the number of false alarms fell to almost zero after these initial incidents.

"The mission of troops in this sector had been heretofore primarily a holding one," said Lee. "In some respects it was more trying than an actual advance; for the fixedness of the positions, more or less known to the enemy, or always within the range of search of his aeroplanes, made constant vigilance imperative. No lights at night, resort to cover from observation at the approach of any hostile aeroplane by day, the never-ending 'searching' or 'harassing' fire by enemy artillery over our area." These aircraft were used almost exclusively for reconnaissance, but also dropped some propaganda leaflets much to the delight of the battalion's souvenir-hungry artillerymen. One night, one of these snoopers circled over an alternate battery site near Batteries D and E. When it "continued to hang above the position," Truman became suspicious, and an "investigation was made to see if any lights were visible at this position."

Extremely few aircraft were brought down by ground fire, but one pilot of a two-seater tried unsuccessfully to bring his shot-up plane in for a safe landing on the deceptively flat-looking ground immediately west of Truman's guns:

> One of their aviators fell right behind my Battery yesterday and sprained his ankle, busted up the machine, and got completely picked by the French and Americans in the neighborhood. They even tried to take their (there were two in the machine) coats. One

of our officers, I am ashamed to say, took the boots off of the one with the sprained ankle and kept them.

The French, and Americans too for that matter, are souvenir crazy. If a guard had not been placed over the machine, I don't doubt that it would have been carried away bit by bit. What I started to say was that the German lieutenant yelled *"La guerre fini"* as soon as he stepped from the machine. He then remarked that the war would be over in ten days. I don't know what he knew about it or what anyone else knows but I am sure that most Americans will be glad when it's over and they can get back to God's country again. It is a great thing to swell your chest out and fight for a principle but it gets almighty tiresome sometimes. I heard a Frenchman remark that Germany was fighting for territory, England for the sea, France for patriotism, and Americans for souvenirs.* Yesterday made me think he was about right.[3]

Other than the barrages in response to false alarms, Battery D shot at nothing at all between the firing for registration on October 18 and the shelling of a crossroads on the 29th. From Truman's vantage point, it was clear that the problem was incompetence in the echelons above his battalion. On October 26, the exasperated captain wrote in his calendar book, "The Brigade operations officer orders barrages at 11 p.m. that we can't fire. Some operations officer! Ditto for Handlebars [General Berry]."[4] Orders that would change this state of affairs arrived on the 27th instructing the artillerymen to prepare for the 60th Field Artillery Brigade's biggest operation since the opening of the Meuse-Argonne. The November 1 bombardment, part of a series of preparatory moves ahead of a drive directly into Germany, would cover the relief of the

---

*One of the French scavengers presented Major Gates with a cap relieved from one of the aviators, while cannoneers gleefully pulled "a large swatch of camouflaged fabric" from the aircraft's frame and gave it to their captain who, despite his comments here, didn't mind holding on to the occasional souvenir. Decades later, he passed the wing component on to his presidential library in Independence, Missouri.

35th Division (minus its artillery) by the new 81st Division. No surreptitious easing-in and easing-out of forces, it was to be completed in one day, and the entire sector of the front would be vulnerable when this occurred. The objective of the artillery was to erect a virtual curtain of steel and fire in front of the movement, and Truman's regiment alone was scheduled to fire more than ten thousand rounds on "J-day."

Battery D immediately set to work preparing individual, camouflaged ammunition bunkers and further strengthening its position for the expected counter-bombardments. It was in the midst of this feverish activity that the men got to watch a floor show prompted by the arrival of a young officer from one of the headquarters up the chain. But first, some background.

Truman had the knack of always looking sharp, no matter what the conditions. "After a couple of weeks in the trenches without any chance to take a bath or to change clothes," recalled Harry Vaughan of the 130th, "the rest of us would look like bums with mud sticking all over us." One time, the two artillerymen were riding about the Verdun moonscape on horseback, looking for new gun positions for their respective units, when they ran into each other. Vaughan became acutely embarrassed by his appearance: "[Truman] always looked immaculate. . . . I couldn't see myself, but I imagined I looked like a buck private in the Mexican Army, but Truman looked like he just stepped out."[5] On this particular day, however, the captain's efforts with the gunners had left him somewhat worse for wear. And it was at this point that the hapless junior officer arrived. Truman's friend, Sergeant Jacobson from F Battery on the left flank, had the good fortune of being present for the fireworks:

A young second lieutenant, from the administrative offices far behind the lines, came up for a quick look at the preparations. He was all shined and polished and he seemed to be horribly shocked by the weary and grimy men of Battery D. When a group of them failed to salute, he gave them a dressing down and demanded to see their commanding officer. Captain Truman, busy, tired and just as grimy as his men, was in no mood to be bothered. He gave the lieutenant a "chewing" that must have curled his hair and chased him back to his headquarters with orders never to return.[6]

When J-day arrived, it almost seemed like a nonstop training exercise. The Germans to the front had seen major American offensives on both their flanks and, understandably believing that they were next, left only light forces which hunkered down during the pummeling. The German artillery response was also less than expected, but despite the crushing weight of counterbattery fire from the big guns to Truman's rear, the enemy artillery left its mark on E Battery, where two soldiers were wounded and one killed. Battery D's part in covering the 35th Division's relief was the firing of 944 high-explosive rounds between 3:30 and 6 a.m.

During the run-up to this mission, Truman and his men were cheered by the praise of division commander Traub, which Truman likely read to them when assembled for reveille. (The rows of asterisks indicate information that had been deleted for brevity.)

Headquarters, 35th Division
American Expeditionary Forces
29th October 1918.

From: Commanding General, 35th Division.

To: Commanding Officer, Battery D, 129th Field Artillery
(Through Commanding General, 60th F. A. Brigade)

Subject: Commendation.

1. The following extract from the report of the Commanding Officer, 110th Mobile Ordnance Repair Shop, is quoted for your information—********* "The materiel of Battery D, 129th Field Artillery, was found to be in a most excellent condition; ********* The materiel of this battery was in superior condition to that of any other battery of the two regiments, and evidenced the fact that unusual care had been exercised by the commissioned and

enlisted personnel of this battery, resulting in the highest state of efficiency in the care of its Ordnance Materiel."

2. The above report is of a kind that the Commanding General of this Division expects, but too infrequently receives. I take great pleasure in commending you and the officers and enlisted men of your battery for this excellent showing which I consider a standard for the other organizations of this Division to reach and to hold.

(signed) Peter E. Traub

PETER E. TRAUB
Major General, U. S. Army
Commanding[7]

Immediately after the J-day shoot, Truman told Bess all about the citation.

I got a letter of Commendation, capital C, from the commanding general of the 35th Division. The ordnance repair department [commander] made a report to him that I had the best-conditioned guns after the drive that he had seen in France. The general wrote me a letter about it. My chief mechanic is to blame, not me. He knows more about guns than the French themselves. As usual in such cases, the C.O. gets the credit. I think I shall put an endorsement [Army: indorsement] on the letter stating the ability of my chief mechanic and stick it in the files anyway. I am going to keep the original letter for my own personal and private use. It will be nice to have someday if some low-browed north-end politician tries to remark that I wasn't in the war when I'm running for eastern judge or something. I'll have the "papers" and can shut him up.[8]

True to his word, Truman responded the next day in an endorsement that Corporal Keenan must have taken great pleasure in typing:

3rd Ind.

C.O. Battery D, 129th F. A., APO #743, A.E.F., 2 November 1918.

To C. G. 35th Division. (thru channels)

1. The Commanding General's letter of October 29th commending this organization on the excellent condition of its Ordnance Materiel is the result of the untiring efforts of Chief Mechanic McKinley Wooden and the enlisted personnel of the Battery to whom all credit belongs.

(signed) Harry S. Truman

Harry S. Truman
Captain 129th Field Artillery,
Comm'dg.
HST/k⁹

RUMORS OF AN ARMISTICE had been circulating for weeks; sometimes setting off uproarious, drunken celebrations among the French *poilus,* and only increased in frequency. Truman later recalled:

On Oct. 27, 1918, we were moving along the road in France from one front line zone to another when a French newspaper was distributed along the line. Headlines in black letters informed us that an armistice was on. Just then a German 150[mm] shell burst to the right of the road and another to the left. One of the sergeants remarked, "Captain, those G—— D——— Germans haven't seen this paper." . . . On Nov. 7 Roy Howard [of United Press International] sent a message to the USA announcing a false armistice. Such false newspaper reports are terrible things. [10]

Rumors, though, were just rumors, and from what the men could see, the fighting was going to intensify, not suddenly screech to a halt. How was Truman to know that his Battery D had just received its last call-sign, and would end the war as "Jolley B60"—"Jolley" for the regiment, "Bravo" for the battalion, and "Six Zero" for the battery?

Firing for registration on the morning of November 4 was followed by preparations for the next big push, scheduled for Saturday, November 9, and the unofficial word circulating among the officers was that the ground seized this weekend would serve as the launching point for a full-blood thrust toward Fortress Metz on the 14th.

Battery D's role in the Saturday morning festivities was to provide a steady, methodical barrage of two rounds per minute per gun, zeroing in on known and suspected machine-gun positions that hugged the woods to the west which had largely escaped the shredding of the Verdun battles. A more extensive bombardment had been planned for D and the regiment, but at the last minute, verbal orders had been received from the headquarters over the 81st Division, the 2nd Colonial Corps, to switch to the more limited fire program beginning at 7:30 a.m. Truman's men and batteries A, E, and F worked over the tree lines along the west edge of Bois de Moranville as well as the northeast and southern woods of Etang du Moulin in support of the 322nd Infantry while Batteries B and C kept the road southwest of Blanzée under fire. Batteries E, F, and C were then pushed forward at midmorning with the expectation that the others would leapfrog them within the next few days.

Truman's guns were ordered trained on Grimaucourt overnight, and the advance continued the next day with D conducting a steady harrassing fire on the Montricelle woods southeast of Hautecourt between 8 and 10 a.m. When the barrage was lifted, the 332nd stormed into Grimaucourt, with Housholder keeping tabs on the situation as an artillery observer for the battalion. The 332nd was not able to hold onto the town, however, and withdrew during the early afternoon because of heavy shelling as the 130th Field Artillery traded counterbattery fire with German 150mm guns and D fired into the town itself to cover the withdrawal. Truman, with time on his hands that evening, wrote Bess about the day's fighting but saw no reason to mention the beating that the infantry took.

This has been a beautiful Sunday—the sun shining and as warm as summer. It sure made me wish for *Lizzie* and five gallons of gas with her nose pointed down Blue Ridge Boulevard and me stepping on the throttle to get there quickly. I wonder how long it will be before we do any riding down that road. Easter? Maybe, if not sooner. Heine seems to be about finished. Just to make the day interesting one of their planes came over and shot down one of our sausage balloons and came near getting shot down himself. I shot away about five hundred rounds of high explosive shells myself. Not at the plane but at some Hun machine guns about seven miles away [and Grimaucourt]. I don't know if I hit them, but I have hopes as I laid the guns very carefully. A Hun plane dropped some bombs not far from my back yard last night and sort of shook things up. They made him run home in a hurry too. There is a big railroad gun about a kilometer behind me that shoots about every fifteen minutes and I heard one of the boys remark that "There goes another rolling kitchen over to pulverize Jerry." The projectile makes a noise like a wagon going down the road when it goes through the air, so the remark was very good.[11]

The plan for Monday, November 11, was to have the fresh 321st Infantry take and hold the town, and Battery D to repeat the previous day's mission between 5:30 and 6 a.m., then engage in other barrages as the situation developed later in the morning. The men were policing the line and cleaning the guns after the opening shoot of the day when a runner from the battery command post, apparently told to lasso the first NCO he found, poked his head into Sgt. Eddy Meisburger's dugout:

It must have been 7 o'clock or something, a runner came and said, "The captain wants you to come and report to his headquarters at once;" and I went down there, and he was sitting at a table, and one of the lieutenants. I don't remember whether it's Housholder or Jordan. Well, they were sitting there eating breakfast and the captain was grinning, and the lieutenant of course was grinning. I went in and the captain had a sheaf of papers and he said, "Sergeant," he said, "why don't you take this, go back and read it to the battery?" And I said, "Yes, sir." I looked at it and all those words there, kind of made them out. It said, "Effective November 11, 1918 firing will cease on all fronts at 11 a.m. November 1918," signed by—it wasn't signed by General Foche, it wasn't signed by Pershing, it was signed by I don't remember his name, the chief executive officer of the division. I don't remember his name.* But anyway, that was the message and I went back up to the battery positions and finally got them quieted down and read it and it didn't create a whole lot of excitement. It created some Bronx cheers and I think a few shoes were thrown at me if I remember right.

I think the United Press put out a story a few days before, that an armistice had been signed. . . . It was about midnight or 1 o'clock in the morning. We were aroused by a lot of uproar and noise, and we found some French troops in position over the roadway down the gully beyond us had got that message from Paris or something; and they got the wine bottles out and they stuck candles in the neck of them and lighted them and put their hands on each other's shoulders and came marching into where we were bedded down and woke us up and were all singing, *"Fini Le Guerre, the war is over,"* and they carried on for an hour or two; and then this next day they found out it was a false alarm. Then when we got the real one, it was kind of hard to make them believe.[12]

Truman had actually known about the cease fire since 5 a.m. when a call came in from Major Paterson, the regimental operations officer. But with so many false alarms raising and dashing the men's hopes, he and the other officers were instructed "not to tell anyone,"[13] and their lips stayed zipped until a piece of paper arrived from headquarters. Besides, German shells were falling with increasing intensity, and the left wheel of one of Marks's guns was struck by shrapnel as late as 10:45, just fifteen minutes before the fighting was to cease. Battery D, which had sent 68 rounds in the general direction of Germany at dawn, fired off a final barrage of 164 rounds. "But an old French 155 (6-inch) Battery

---

*A similar warning order issued later at 8:21 a.m. from Headquarters, 129th Field Artillery, was signed "Roberts, Chief of Staff."

behind me kept right on right up to 11:00 a.m.," said Truman, "shooting as hard as they could just to be shooting. The commander said because they had *beaucoup* ammunition."[14] Three decades later, Truman remembered that eventful Monday as if it had been yesterday:

> I fired the Battery on orders until 10:45 when I fired my last shot on a little village—Hermaville—northeast of Verdun. The last range was 11,000 meters with the new D shell. Eighty-eight hundred meters was the extreme range of the 75mm. guns with regular ammunition, but with the streamlined D shell it would reach 11,500 meters.
>
> We stopped firing all along the line at eleven o'clock, Nov. 11, 1918. It was so quiet it made your head ache. We stayed at our positions all day and then crawled into our pup tents that evening.
>
> There was a French battery of old Napoleon six-inch guns just behind my battery position. Three old Napoleon guns had wheels six feet in diameter and no recoil mechanism. They'd run back up tall wooden contraptions built like a carpenter's sawhorse and then run down into place again. If a gunner got in the way either going or coming he'd lose an arm or a leg or any other part of his anatomy that happened to be in the way of the old gun. It was a good gun, though, and would hit the target if laid by an expert.
>
> Along in the evening all the men in the French battery became intoxicated as result of a load of wine which came up on the ammunition narrow gauge [railway]. Every single one of them had to march by my bed and salute and yell, *"Vive President Wilson, Vive Captain, Artillerie American."* No sleep all night, the infantry fired Very pistols, sent up all the flares they could lay their hands on; fired rifles, pistols and whatever else would make noise all night long.
>
> Next day we had orders to leave our guns in line and fall back to the [regimental] echelon. After that we spent our evenings playing poker and wishing we were at home.[15]

The men were moved almost immediately out of their rude dugouts and into long, frame storage sheds at Camp la Beholle that would serve as barracks through the winter after the addition of double-deck, plank bunks. A Battery D muster on November 13 was a significant enough event that Truman recorded its results in his private calendar book, as, possibly for the first time since he took command, all 194 soldiers, including officers, were present. (On a few occasions, special details to other units had reduced the number of men at his battery position to fewer than seventy men.) The artillerymen found that, while not "unpleasantly situated, as camps go," as Jay M. Lee said, "mud there was, in plenty, and time to kill."[16] Of paramount importance, now that the unifying fear of imminent death had melted away, was to keep the men busy beyond the frequent treks to the nearby battlefield for firewood and care of the horses.

Daily drills and marches were instituted, as were frequent inspections. Unfortunately, bored officers at virtually every stratum above the battalion also ordered even more inspections, much to the irritation of not only the men, but also Truman and the other battery commanders. Amusements such as athletic events and target shooting were also initiated, but were not set up on a systematic basis until an increase in disciplinary problems drove the issue of "idle hands" to the forefront among commands from regiment all the way up to AEF Headquarters. Not surprisingly, this also spurred an increase in the against-the-regulations betting that usually accompanies such things, Truman himself losing one thousand francs when "a Gorilla named Hamby" from E Company beat Sergeant Meisburger in a boxing match. Soldiers from the 35th Division were sent in organized detachments for week-long stints in the Savoy Leave Area, while officers received two weeks leave and could roam unsupervised throughout France. Truman and numerous other officers of the 129th Field Artillery received notice that they would be granted leave commencing November 26. The captain visited Paris, the Riviera, and the Italian border region, usually in company with Major Gates and, on one jaunt or another, various other officers, including Klemm, Elliott, McGee, Marks, and Housholder. In all, it was a memorable trip, which he recounted extensively in a series of letters to Bess. What Truman found upon his return to la Beholle, however, was best left unsaid, and he recorded not a word on it in any of his letters or numerous postwar accounts.

Battery D tried. Tried very hard. But they were, after all, Dizzy D. Lieutenant Jordan was left in charge when Truman and Housholder headed for Paris. Lieutenant Eagleton had transferred out earlier, and Lieutenant Zemer left that day for temporary duty at General Berry's headquarters. Guarding the chicken coop with Jordan (a good-natured fellow who knew his horses quite well, but whom some of the men apparently thought of as a pushover) was a fresh addition to the outfit, Lt. Lawrence J. Baldwin. Would some of "Truman's Irish" take advantage of the situation now that the cat was away?

The very night Truman left, a large portion of the battery went on a drinking spree in nearby Dugney-s-Meuse, making a nuisance of themselves in the process. Excluding the revelers who escaped capture or were let go with just a warning, nine cannoneers ended up with honorable mentions in the extra-duty roster. Soldiers with a degree of rank or authority could not be given the consideration allowed some of the privates, and the list of miscreants was headed by Sergeants Murphy and Tierney, and Corporals Donnelly and Reilly. After this, the men seemed to settle down briefly, with only scattered infractions judged serious enough for extra duty, such as missing reveille or retreat, but seven not already confined to barracks missed formation or reveille on December 2 after an apparently hard evening.

Throughout the rest of D Battery's time in France, Truman would deal with a steady series of discipline problems—far more than when the unit was in combat—but it would never approach the raw quantity of monkey business that occurred when he was away. The captain found that if he did not act firmly on seemingly small matters—whether it be the "dirty shoes at inspection" on Pvt. Hilbert Nease, or Pvt. Alfred Breen's being late for guard duty, or Pvt. James Walton's dirty belt, or Pvt. Roy Percintina's "snapping gum" during formation—discipline as well as pride in themselves and the unit would almost imperceptibly begin its downward slide. One of the Sunday mounted inspections, done by either Captain Allen or Captain Salisbury in rotation, particularly raised Truman's ire:

Battery "D"
129th. Field Artillery
Mounted Inspection.
Sunday Morning at 9:30.

1. You had the rottenest inspection in the Battalion this morning.

2. Your rolls were not of uniform size.

3. The rolls of the horses, especially the sergeants and single mounted men were not properly put on.

4. The strap ends were not in the keepers.

From the above reasons and because it was evident that you did not try to have a good inspection, there will be another at 9:30 A.M. Sunday morning.

If that one is not the best ever put on, there will be another at 2:30 P.M. and then another at 4:30 P.M.

Drivers rolls will be carefully made 44 inches long, strapped to the cantle of the saddle on the off horse and turned over into the saddle.

Cannoneers rolls will be uniformly made 22 inches long, and placed in the luggage racks lying down. There will be three on each carriage including the American caissons.

All men who are not mounted will make dismounted rolls and fall in at the rear of the battery. No one except Cooks, Stable Police, and the Guards on post will be excused from this inspection.

By Order of the Battery Commander.
Harry S. Truman

Capt. 129th F.A.
Comdg.[17]

Although the men grumbled, their opinion of their captain did not suffer, and the feeling was mutual.

> You know it is the hardest job a man ever undertook to be abso-
> lutely square and just to 194 men when you have good ones and
> bad ones (very few bad), smart ones and dull ones. I love 'em all
> and if anybody wants a fight or a quarrel with me he can get it
> suddenly and all he wants if he says anything derogatory about
> my Battery or one of my men. I wouldn't trade off the "orneriest"
> one I've got for any other whole Battery. While I'm not a braggart,
> I believe I can take my outfit and beat any other one in the A.E.F.,
> shooting or doing any other kind of Battery work (every Battery
> commander in the regiment says the same thing). . . . You know I
> have succeeded in doing what it was my greatest ambition to do
> at the beginning of the war. That is to take a Battery through as
> Battery commander and not lose a man.[18]

But what the Germans couldn't do, disease did. On January 17, Corporal Keenan noted in Battery D's correspondence book that he had transferred the unit's records of Francis L. Conboy to the army hospital at Bazeilles, where the private was being treated for either pneumonia and influenza. Three days later the handwriting in Battery D's correspondence book changed. Instrument Sergeant Fred Bowman, who had just returned from attending the artillery school at Saumur, told why:

> I went back [to the battery] and reported to Captain Truman . . .
> and I asked him what I could do and he said, "Well, the boy in the
> office there," a kid named Leo Keenan, was kind of a clerk, wasn't
> feeling too well and had been a little behind, and he said, "Maybe
> you can help Leo on some of his records."[19]

Keenan's condition worsened rapidly, and he was rushed to the Base Hospital 91 at Commercy. With no Huns to shell, and possessing typing skills, Bowman took Keenan's chair, working his way through D's paperwork, when barely a week later, on the 25th, a letter arrived from the chief surgeon at Commercy informing Truman of the death on January 22, 1919, of Cpl. L. P. Keenan. Truman was devastated and wrote that day that he felt as if he had "lost a son."[20] Private Conboy would finally succumb on March 30, but not before Pvt. William J. Robertson from the 2nd Gun Section died on February 11. More would be lost, with Truman formally requesting information on the deaths of his young corporal and others when it wasn't immediately provided, but the letter he wrote to Mr. Jack Keenan of Kansas City, Missouri, on the last day of January was the only condolence letter that is recorded in the battery correspondence book.

CHAPTER 18

"Full and Immediate Separation"

Truman had plenty of time for thinking now that the fighting was over and pondered his place in the army:

> There is never any prospect of my ever being anything in the military line beyond a captain, although had the war continued, which God forbid, I should eventually have had another promotion. . . . All promotions ceased in the A.E.F. on November 11, 1918, the greatest day in history. Personally I'd rather be a Battery commander than a brigadier general. I am virtually the dictator of the actions of 194 men and if I succeed in making them work as one, keep them healthy morally and physically, make 'em write to the mammas and sweethearts, and bring 'em all home, I shall be as nearly pleased with myself as I ever expect to be.[1]

Truman continued his ruminations on the army in a subsequent letter to Bess Wallace:

> I can't see what on earth any man with initiative and a mind of his own wants to be in the army in peacetimes for. You've always

got some old fossil above you whose slightest whim is law and who generally hasn't a grain of horse sense. For my part I want to be where I can cuss 'em all I please when I please, and you can bet there are some in this man's army who are going to get cussed and more if they fool around me when I get out. I'd give my right arm to be on the Military Affairs Committee of the House. It's not an impossibility, is it? You've no idea how the attitude changed when there was no more chance of promotion. It's right laughable sometimes. . . .

We have rumors of going to Hunland and rumors of going to Brest and rumors of staying where we are till the peace is signed. I told you I'd sign up for *"full and immediate separation from the army."* We call ourselves the F & I's, and we kid the life out of those who signed up to stay in. Major Gates, Major Miles, Sermon, Marks, McGee, the colonel, and myself are all F & I's. Salisbury, Allen, Paterson, [and] Dancy signed up to stay in. The rest signed up for the reserve. . . . But we'll all probably come home together.[2]

Yet, they didn't all "come home together." The officers and men of the regiment had never felt close to their commander, Klemm. They showed deference and respect to his rank but never really trusted him after his repeated instances of odd behavior during the march from the Vosges, including the genuine glee that he displayed when riding along the line, snatching caps from their heads. That very few men of the 129th had even seen him during the Meuse-Argonne battle had not added to his luster. When it turned out that their colonel had maneuvered an early ticket home, leaving his men behind in the "mudhole" of Camp la Beholle, what little tolerance that remained for Klemm vanished overnight, as he left quickly—almost like a thief in the night—without even addressing the regiment, and leaving behind a syrupy, meaningless General Order No. 17 praising the men and expressing his "Elation at the prospects of returning to loved ones, and sorrow at leaving you after such eminently satisfactory service as we have enjoyed together."[3]

Good riddance, for now at least, and the battery went about the tiresome rounds of drills and inspections and finally the turning-in of their guns, caissons, and even the officers' mounts, on a snowy Friday morning five days after Klemm's exit. And it was a sad day when the men said goodbye to their guns. Truman did his best to try to explain to Bess how every one of them felt:

> You've no idea how I hate to give up my guns, my French 75s, those implements of destruction which the Hun has said were weapons of the devil. You know I told you in a letter from Coetquidan that if I could only give the command that fired one volley at the Hun I would go home willingly and be satisfied. Well there were some ten thousand rounds—or if fired in volleys, over two thousand volleys— fired by those guns at Heine, and they did it all at my command. They are the same guns that I learned to shoot with and, with the exception of one barrel which I had to leave in the Argonne with a shell lodged in it, there have been no repairs on them.
>
> If the government would let me have one of them, I'd pay for it and pay the transportation home just to let it sit in my front yard and rust. Men you know—gunners and section chiefs especially— become very much attached to their guns. They name 'em Katie, Lizzie, Liberty, Diana, and other fantastic and high-sounding names, and when they fire them they talk to them just as if they were people. French gunners even cry when their guns are taken away from them. Guns do have an individuality. No two of them shoot alike and weather conditions will affect each of them differ-ently. Two of mine would shoot short of the range table, one over and one almost exactly. . . .
>
> I don't suppose I'll ever fire another shot with a 75 gun and know I won't with these I'm so attached to and it makes me rather sad. It's like parting with old friends who've stood by me through thick and thin and now I have to give 'em to some ordnance chap to put away and maybe later some fop out of West Point will use 'em for target practice and declare they're no good because he don't know how to shoot 'em. . . .

At least a few men couldn't "let go" quite as gracefully as Truman, and succeeded in getting their captain into a very considerable amount of trouble. The worst culprit was Pvt. Floyd T. Rickets, from Sergeant Meisburger's 1st Gun Section, who practically field stripped their weapon in an effort to take as much of it home as possible.

> Before we turned the guns in there were several things on that gun I thought might be pretty good souvenirs to take home and one was the lanyard, that was a little wooden knob and cord that you pulled to fire the gun; so, I took that off of the gun. Then I thought, "Well, I'll take the firing pin," and I took the firing pin off, and that led to another piece. So, before I got through I had a bag full of parts off of this gun, and I kept them under the straw tick that was my mattress. Several weeks after we turned the guns in, apparently the French Government questioned our act and wanted these parts returned. I suppose some of the other fellows had taken souvenirs also.
>
> So, one evening Captain Truman asked us if we had any of these parts and to turn them in. Well, there was complete silence and none were turned in.
>
> About a week went by and one morning after reveille we stood formation and instead of releasing us for the day, they gave us squads right and took us up on a little hill nearby; and they marched us back and forth for about an hour or two and finally back. Well, it so happened my sergeant, Sergeant Meisburger, was the sergeant of the day, and the story I get from Sergeant Meisburger was that Captain Truman made the rounds of the different billets and when it came to mattresses, all mattresses had to be turned over and looked under; and when they came to mine, why, here was this little bag, and Captain Truman asked Sergeant Meisburger, "What is that?"
>
> He said, "Well, that's just a few souvenirs that I think Private Rickets has collected to be taken home." Truman then said, "Dump it out." So Sergeant Meisburger had to open the

sack and dump it out. The first thing Truman said, "My God, he's got everything but the barrel."

But, I'll tell you this, nothing was ever said to me, I wasn't disciplined. I just lost my souvenirs and I've always regretted it. Many years later I asked Truman about that and he said, "Well, you just don't know how much hell I caught from headquarters about those parts being missing." He said, "I would have liked to have had you take them home with you, but I was under orders to find those parts and get them back to the French Government or else."[4]

Shortly after the equipment and animals—seventy-six horses and forty-nine mules—were turned in, General Pershing, with the young Prince of Wales in tow, performed a farewell inspection in which one of Battery D's cheeky Irishmen in the rear ranks nearly gave Truman a heart attack. Sergeant Bowman relates that after working for hours to make everything "spic and span" for the inspection, a sudden downpour turned the entire area into a muddy quagmire:

> They were slow in coming. . . . And finally they did come along and they opened ranks for them, for the Prince to come down there and it was just as he got by us, this little Higginbotham [Pvt. John J.] in the back end says, "Captain, ask that little son-of-a-bitch when he's going to free Ireland." You could hear that all over. Here was General Pershing, and here was the major general of the division, and the colonel of the regiment, and finally poor old Captain Truman along with them, when this guy blurted that out.[5]

Prince Edward, who'd probably heard much worse during his time as a midshipman in the Royal Navy, kept his approving inspection smile intact, and Pershing offered his hand to Truman:

> You have a fine looking bunch of men, Captain. And I hope you will take them home as clean morally and physically as they were when they came over so that the people at home can be as proud of them as I am.[6]

Truman took great pride in Pershing's words, and had certainly done his best (even following, albeit uncomfortably, the AEF's "Outline of Talk on Venereal Disease to be Given Soldiers by Line Officers"),[7] but at this point he was probably growing more concerned with getting all of his men home alive. Sickness continued to spread throughout the army in France—it was little better in the States—and word had reached the unit that former battery 1st Sgt. Giles Eggleston had died, probably from influenza or pneumonia. The situation grew worse as the regiment waited in the port of Brest to ship out, and numerous battery members contracted lung ailments. Although Truman and the other officers were quartered in the luxurious Chateau la Chesnaye, a former home of Ferdinand de Lesseps, the men found the embarkation camp "a mudhole, a pesthole," said Private Leigh. "We got to Brest and I got pneumonia."

> We came back on the *Zeppelin*. They wanted to put me in a hospital, but I got these two friends of mine. They carried me on board. One on each side, and we go up the gangplank, and they've got a doctor there checking, there was a good deal of sickness at Brest; and I could hardly breathe, but I wasn't going to the hospital. And the three of us went up and they were holding me one on each arm.
>
> We had a guy die in the hospital there of pneumonia. The second day out, in the morning, I went to the bow. You know on a vessel how that bow goes up and down. I threw up my guts and do you know the next day I felt like a new man and the congestion was gone. I was afraid to ask for any medicine. I just wanted to get out. . . . I'd heard too many stories about Brest.[8]

Private Harry J. Dabner, who helped get communications up and running between Truman's observation post and the guns, was the soldier who died at Brest's Camp Pontanezen Base Hospital on Monday, April 28, three weeks after the German-crewed *Zeppelin* sailed for New York.

Truman, indeed most of the 129th Field Artillery, was miserably seasick all the way, as the rough seas and dearth of cargo failed to create an adequate ballast resulted in a hard passage. They awoke on April 20, Easter Sunday, to find themselves in New York Harbor. Truman sent Bess a telegram the next day to let her know that he was back, and a letter several days later to describe the hearty welcome they received:

> I have been in America just four days and I have been so busy just lookin' at the place and getting some honest-to-goodness food under my belt that I haven't had time to do anything else.
>
> I had the most miserable ten days coming over that I've spent in this war. We had a fine boat, brand new and never used before, but she was empty except for our baggage and ourselves and she did some rolling. I am not a good sailor and you can guess the harrowing details. Of course I could get no sympathy. Even my own Battery laughed at me. I lost about twenty pounds (and I can afford to lose it). For a time I wished most sincerely that I could go back to the Argonne Forest and at least die honorably. I am bravely over it now and I fear that I am gaining in weight.
>
> I've never seen anything that looked so good as the Liberty Lady in New York Harbor and the mayor's welcoming boat, which came down the river to meet us. You know the men have seen so much and been in so many hard places that it takes something real to give them a thrill, but when the band on that boat played "Home Sweet Home" there were not very many dry eyes. The hardest of hard-boiled cookies even had to blow his nose a time or two. Every welfare organization in America met us and gave us something. The Jews gave us handkerchiefs; the Y.M.C.A. chocolate; the Knights of Columbus, cigarettes; the Red Cross, real homemade cake; and the Salvation Army, God bless 'em, sent telegrams free and gave us Easter eggs made of chocolate. They took us off the boat at Pier No. 1 in Hoboken, fed us till we wouldn't hold any more, put us on a ferry, and sent us to Camp Mills, where they gave us a bath and lots of new clothes, the first some of the men have had since they joined.

Then we made a raid on the canteens and free shows. I'll bet ten barrels wouldn't hold the ice cream consumed that first evening. I was so busy that I didn't connect until the next day but I've been going strong ever since.

I was down on Broadway night before last with Major Miles and Major Wilson and stopped in at an ice cream joint and who do you suppose asked me if I belonged to the 35th Division? Stella Swope. She asked me where I was from, what regiment I belonged to, and then if I knew you, before she told me who she was. I was somewhat embarrassed but managed to tell her. She was with a sailor but didn't introduce him.[9]

The only dark cloud on the horizon was that Colonel—now "Mr."—Klemm might try to take part in the May 3 parade planned for the 129th Field Artillery's passage through Kansas City on its way to Camp Funston, Kansas, where the men would be discharged. A delegation from the city had arrived in New York to make arrangements, and Majors Gates and Miles informed them that it was far more than a matter of Klemm simply being unwelcome. The delegation quickly wired back, warning organizers in Kansas City "to exert precautions that Colonel Klemm shall not participate in the program lest a demonstration among the troops ensue," which immediately spilled into the pages of the *Kansas City Star*. Making sure that there were no misunderstandings, Gates telegraphed the mayor of Independence "to keep Klemm out of any parade of this regiment to prevent an unpleasant situation."[10]

Truman likewise wrote Bess, who was an active member of local patriotic organizations (and whose brother's wife was the daughter of *Independence Examiner* owner William Southern) that "They'd better keep Klemm out of that parade."[11] Klemm stated that he would witness it as a private citizen and that "the representatives of the committee who went to the port to meet the troops had gone with the intention of digging up such a feeling against him."[12]

Truman's relationship with the men was a world apart from that of Klemm's. It would remain a closely guarded secret from Truman for another couple weeks that, while on the *Zeppelin*, the men held aside a certain percentage of each poker game's pot so that the battery could purchase a silver loving cup in tribute to its commander. The nonstop nature of the games resulted in a $400 kitty, which was used to purchase a striking cup, sixteen inches tall, which the men had inscribed to "Captain Harry S. Truman. Presented by the members of Battery D in appreciation of his justice, ability and leadership."

Truman and the men of Battery D, with whom he had shared so much, would remain friends for the rest of their lives. Yet, his relationship with the army and its generals would be a rather more complex affair, particularly when he became president of the United States. Riding the train back to Kansas City from Camp Funston with hundreds of other former soldiers on that Tuesday afternoon of May 6, 1919, Truman believed that his army days were done with and looked forward to his long-delayed marriage to his dear Bess—with Ted Marks as the best man and not a few of his old Battery D buddies in attendance. With him was his blue denim duffel bag containing all the possessions that he hadn't already shipped to the Grandview farm separately, his prized honorable discharge, and a thick folder of other paperwork.

While he would have laughed it off as an absurd suggestion that he should stay in the army, and perhaps even joked about it with Marks on the train, a part of Truman likely took very seriously that he was recommended for promotion to the rank of major before the regiment sailed for home, and that he was recommended again for promotion and a commission in either the Regular Army or Officers' Reserve Corps upon his discharge. Not even a year would pass before he would take the army up on its offer.

Notes

The citations below for documents at the Harry S. Truman Library and Museum (hereafter cited as HSTLM) reflect where I originally found documents in that archive, but reorganizations of the Truman Papers since I began working there twenty-five years ago have shifted the locations of where a portion of these materials are located. As an example, the folder "Military Service: Longhand Notes of Harry S. Truman Regarding," which was in box 21 of the subfile "Military File, 1914–1936 (MF)," of the "Family, Business, and Personal Affairs File" (FBP), is now in that file's box 30. I have updated the revised locations as I have come across them, but researchers are encouraged to check with the archive staff before requesting materials for examination.

—D. M. G.

Chapter 1

1. Edward P. Meisburger, from locally televised interview with Battery D veterans, Kansas City, Missouri, circa December 26–31, 1972.

2. *History of the Original Company "A" 110th Engineers, 35th Division, A.E.F., from June 21, 1917 to May 3, 1919,* (no imprint: circa 1935), unpaginated, fifth page.

3. "Report of Investigation by Lieut. Col. R. G. Peck, Inspector General, First Army Corps: Taken October 15, 1918," in Robert H. Ferrell, *Collapse at Meuse-Argonne: The Failure of the Missouri-Kansas Division* (Columbia, Missouri: University of Missouri Press, 2004), 51.

4. Harry E. Murphy, oral history interview, 14, HSTLM.

5. Vere C. Leigh, oral history interview, 24–25, HSTLM. Since American and Allied batteries were composed of four guns, Leigh, and likely others, incorrectly assumed that four guns were destroyed. German batteries, however, were six-gun formations. That the one in question was of the standard configuration was confirmed by the U.S. Army engineers

repairing the bridges along the Aire River, as mentioned in *History of the 27th Engineers, U.S.A., 1917-1919* (New York: Association of the 27th Engineers, 1920), 32.

6. Alonzo L. Hamby, *Man of the People: A Life of Harry S. Truman* (New York: Oxford University Press, 1995), 19.

7. *The Service of the Missouri National Guard on the Mexican Border under the President's Order of June 18, 1916* (Jefferson City, Missouri: Headquarters, Missouri National Guard, 1917), li.

8. *The Autobiography of Harry S. Truman*, Robert H. Ferrell, ed. (Niwot, Colorado: University Press of Colorado, 1980), 27.

9. "Battery B is Mustered In: It Starts with Sixty Men, with George R. Collins as Captain," *Kansas City Times*, June 15, 1905, 1; untitled notice, *Kansas City Star*, June 15, 1905, 6.

10. Harry S. Truman, "Two Years in the Army," FBP, General File, box 30, "Military Service, Longhand Notes by Harry S. Truman Regarding," HSTLM.

11. Harry S. Truman, remarks to members of the National Guard Association, Mayflower Hotel, Washington, D.C., October 25, 1950, Public Papers of the Presidents, HSTLM; *Memoirs by Harry S. Truman, Vol. 1, Year of Decisions* (New York: Doubleday & Company, 1955), 125.

12. Harry S. Truman, "The Military Career of a Missourian," box 168, folder "Personal Correspondence, 1938," Senatorial and Vice Presidential Files, HSTLM.

13. Ibid.

14. *Autobiography*, 27.

15. Meyer Berger, "Mother Truman—Portrait of a Rebel," *New York Times Magazine*, June 23, 1946, 14-15; Robert H. Ferrell, *Harry S. Truman: A Life* (Columbia, Missouri: University of Missouri Press, 1999), 4, from Jonathan Daniels' notes taken during a November 12, 1949, interview with Truman.

16. Jonathan Daniels, *The Man of Independence* (Philadelphia: J. B. Lippincott, 1950), 39.

17. *Autobiography*, 28. Strictly speaking, this was a different "house" from the original structure, which had been allowed to stand after the issuance of Orders No. 11 probably because of Solomon Young's work for the Union, but accidentally burned down shortly after the war.

Chapter 2

1. Postcard to Battery B members, March 27, 1909, box 30, folder "Military Service: Records, Harry S. Truman," FBP-MF, HSTLM.

2. H. H. Halvorsen, oral history interview, 55, HSTLM.

3. Truman, "Military Career"; Truman, remarks to National Guard

Association, October 25, 1950.

4. Truman, "Two Years in the Army."

5. Truman, "Military Career."

6. Boyd L. Dastrup, *King of Battle: A Branch History of the U.S. Army's Field Artillery* (Fort Monroe, Virginia: Training and Doctrine Command, 1992), 147.

7. Truman, "Military Career."

8. Harry S. Truman, longhand notes on Pickwick Hotel stationery (one of several sets of notes collectively referred to as the "Pickwick Papers"), December 3, 1930, box 334, "Longhand Notes—County Judge File, 1930–1934," President's Secretary's Files, HSTLM.

9. Truman, "Military Career."

10. "Pickwick Papers," December 3, 1930.

11. Truman, "Military Career."

12. Ted Marks, oral history interview, 8, HSTLM.

13. Ibid., 12.

14. Truman, "Military Career."

15. Ibid.

16. *Service of the Missouri National Guard*, liii.

17. Truman, "Military Career."

18. "Pickwick Papers," May 14, 1934.

19. Truman, "Military Career"; *Autobiography*, 41.

20. Harry S. Truman to Bess Wallace, July 14, 1917, HSTLM.

21. *Memoirs*, 1:127–28.

22. Edward D. McKim, oral history interview, 5, HSTLM.

23. Report of Physical Examination, June 22, 1917, box 30, folder "Military Service: Records, Harry S. Truman," FBP-MF, HSTLM.

24. David McCullough, *Truman* (New York: Simon & Schuster, 1992), 105.

25. Individual Equipment Record, June 22, 1917, box 30, folder "Military Service: Records, Harry S. Truman," FBP-MF, HSTLM.

26. Jay M. Lee, *The Artilleryman: 129th Field Artillery, 1917–1919, the Experiences and Impressions of an American Artillery Regiment in the World War* (Kansas City, Missouri: Press of Spencer Printing Co., 1920), 16–17.

27. *Memoirs*, 1:128.

28. Daniels, *Man of Independence*, 89–90.

29. Harry S. Truman to Bess Wallace, July 4, 1918, HSTLM.

30. Lee, *Artilleryman*, 16–17.

31. Harry S. Truman to Bess Wallace, July 14, 1917, HSTLM.

32. Arthur W. Wilson, oral history interview, 3, HSTLM.

33. Leigh, oral history, 3–4, HSTLM.

34. Lee, *Artilleryman*, 16.

35. "I Knew Him When: Eddie Jacobson on Harry Truman," prepared by Joe Whitley, Edward Jacobson Papers, box 1, "World War I File, 1917–1933," HSTLM.

36. "I Knew Him When."

37. McKinley Wooden, oral history interview, February 12, 1986, 18–19, HSTLM.

38. National Guard Annual Report of Physical Examination, Adjutant General's Office, August 9, 1917, in Department of the Army, Personnel Records, Military, Harry S. Truman, COL, FA, ORC, Medical Records, 1915–1955, (Official Records, closed until 2030 [rescinded]), RG 407, National Archives and Records Administration (NARA), HSTLM.

39. Lee, *Artilleryman*, 17.

Chapter 3

1. Harry S. Truman to Bess Wallace, September 27, 1917, HSTLM.

2. Harry S. Truman to Bess Wallace, September 29, 1917, HSTLM. "Petticoat Lane" was the nickname for 11th Street east of Main Street in downtown Kansas City, a fashionable shopping area near the Convention Hall.

3. Ibid.

4. Harry S. Truman to Floyd Clymer, February 9, 1953, in *Floyd Clymer's Historical Motor Scrapbook, No. 7* (Los Angeles: Floyd Clymer Publications, ca. 1958), 217–19.

5. Harry S. Truman to Bess Wallace, September 29, 1917, HSTLM.

6. Lee, *Artilleryman*, 19–21.

7. Harry S. Truman to Bess Wallace, October 4, 1917, HSTLM.

8. Harry S. Truman to Bess Wallace, October 4, 1917, HSTLM.

9. Lee, *Artilleryman*, 24–25.

10. December 1917 statement attached to Office of Quartermaster General Form 697, "Military Service Misc.," box 22, HSTLM. The army reimbursed him these expenses in December 1917.

11. Harry S. Truman to Bess Wallace, September 30, 1917, HSTLM.

12. Harry S. Truman to Bess Wallace, October 3, 1917, HSTLM.

13. Lee, *Artilleryman*, 25.

14. Ibid., 28.

15. Ibid.

16. Harry S. Truman to Bess Wallace, October 11, 1917, HSTLM.

17. Harry S. Truman to Bess Wallace, September 30, 1917, HSTLM.

18. Ibid.

19. Harry S. Truman to Bess Wallace, October 28, 1917, HSTLM.

20. *Memoirs*, 1:128.

21. Harry S. Truman to Bess Wallace, October 3, 1917, HSTLM.

22. Harry S. Truman to Bess Wallace, October 5, 1917, HSTLM.

23. Leigh, oral history, 9, HSTLM.

24. Harry S. Truman to Bess Wallace, October 5, 1917, HSTLM.

25. Ibid., October 17, 1917.

26. Lee, *Artilleryman*, 21.

27. Harry S. Truman to Bess Wallace, October 5, 1917, HSTLM.

28. Harry S. Truman to Bess Wallace, October 11, 1917, HSTLM.

29. Ibid.

30. Lee, *Artilleryman*, 26.

31. Harry S. Truman to Bess Wallace, October 15, 1917, HSTLM.

32. W. P. MacLean, *My Story of the 130th F.A., A.E.F.* (Topeka, Kansas: The Boy's Chronicle, 1920), 6. It was very shortly after this incident that Truman purchased $10,000 in life insurance from the Bureau of War Risk Insurance, U.S. Treasury Dept.; see insurance certificate dated November 1, 1917, FBP, box 22, folder "Mrs. Martha E. Truman, Grandview, Mo.," Military File, World War I, HSTLM.

33. Harry S. Truman to Bess Wallace, October 9, 18, and 19, 1917, HSTLM.

34. "I Knew Him When."

35. Harry S. Truman to Bess Wallace, September 30, 1917, HSTLM.

36. Harry S. Truman to Bess Wallace, October 5, 1917, HSTLM.

37. Harry S. Truman to Bess Wallace, March 10, 1918, HSTLM.

Chapter 4

1. Lee, *Artilleryman*, 27.

2. Harry S. Truman to Bess Wallace, November 17, 1917, HSTLM.

3. Lee, *Artilleryman*, 27.

4. Eugene Donnelly, oral history interview, 9–10, HSTLM.

5. *The 35th Division: 1917–1918* (Carlisle Barracks, Pennsylvania: U.S. Army War College, 1922), 9–10. Caldwell stated flatly that the "Infantry instruction was poor."

6. Ibid., 10.

7. Lee, *Artilleryman*, 29.

8. "Safety First for 129th," *Kansas City Star*, September 30, 1917, 4.

9. Michael Dean, "Repeal of Prohibition 1959," *Oklahoma Journeys*

podcast, week of April 6, 2008, http://www.okhistory.org/okjourneys/prohibition.html.

10. McKim, oral history, 49, HSTLM.

11. Harry S. Truman to Bess Wallace, November 3, 1917, HSTLM.

12. Edward P. Wilson, "Eleven Dogs, One Gideon, and E Battery," *Kansas City Times,* June 5, 1962, Liberty Memorial Museum.

13. Harry S. Truman to Bess Wallace, October 20, 1917, HSTLM.

14. Harry S. Truman to Bess Wallace, November 21, 1917, HSTLM.

15. Harry S. Truman to Bess Wallace, November 2, 1917, HSTLM.

16. Harry S. Truman to Bess Wallace, November 24, 1917, HSTLM.

17. Harry S. Truman to Bess Wallace, December 12, 1917, HSTLM.

18. Harry S. Truman to Bess Wallace, December 14, 1917, HSTLM.

19. Harry S. Truman to Bess Wallace, December 12, 1917, HSTLM.

20. "I Knew Him When," Jacobson Papers, HSTLM.

21. Harry S. Truman to Bess Wallace, October 15, 1917, HSTLM.

22. Harry S. Truman to Bess Wallace, November 11, 1917, HSTLM.

23. Harry S. Truman to Bess Wallace, November 12, 1917, HSTLM.

24. Ibid.

25. Roger T. Sermon, Jr., "Captain of Battery D Succeeded in Winning Approval of His Men," *Independence Examiner Centennial Edition,* May 1984, HSTLM.

26. *The 35th Division,* 9–10.

27. Harry S. Truman to Bess Wallace, December 26, 1917, HSTLM.

28. *Notes on the French 75-mm Gun,* Army War College, (Washington: Government Printing Office, October 1917), 5.

29. Harry S. Truman to Bess Wallace, December 14, 1917, HSTLM.

30. Wooden, oral history interview, February 12, 1986, 26–27, HSTLM.

31. Lee, *Artilleryman,* 23.

32. Harry S. Truman to Bess Wallace, October 21, 1917, HSTLM.

33. Harry S. Truman to Bess Wallace, January 27, 1918, HSTLM.

34. Harry S. Truman to Bess Wallace, December 25, 1917, HSTLM.

Chapter 5

1. Harry S. Truman to Bess Wallace, December 26, 1917, HSTLM.

2. Marks, oral history, 19–21, HSTLM.

3. McKim, oral history, 7, HSTLM.

4. "I Knew Him When," Jacobson Papers, HSTLM.

5. "Pickwick Papers," May 14, 1934, HSTLM.

6. Lee, *Artilleryman,* 32.

7. Harry S. Truman to Bess Wallace, January 10, 1918, HSTLM.

8. Harry S. Truman to Bess Wallace, February 23, 1918, HSTLM.

9. Harry S. Truman to Bess Wallace, November 8, 1917, HSTLM.

10. Harry S. Truman to Bess Wallace, February 16, 1918, HSTLM.

11. MacLean, *My Story of the 130th F.A., A.E.F.*, 10–11.

12. Harry H. Vaughan, oral history interview, March 20, 1976, 4, HSTLM.

13. Harry H. Vaughan, oral history, January 14, 1963, 3–6.

14. Harry S. Truman to Bess Wallace, February 23, 1918, HSTLM.

15. "Pickwick Papers," May 14, 1934, HSTLM.

16. Harry S. Truman to Bess Wallace, February 23, 1918, HSTLM.

17. Harry S. Truman to Bess Wallace, February 16, 1918, HSTLM.

18. Harry S. Truman to Bess Wallace, December 2, 1917, HSTLM.

19. Harry S. Truman to Bess Wallace, February 11, 1918, HSTLM.

20. Harry S. Truman to Bess Wallace, February 26, 1918, HSTLM.

21. Harry S. Truman to Bess Wallace, March 5, 1918, HSTLM.

22. Harry S. Truman to Bess Wallace, March 10, 1918, HSTLM.

23. Colonel Robert M. Danford to Harry S. Truman, October 7, 1919, box 28, folder "Correspondence, 1918–1919, FBP-MF, HSTLM.

24. Harry S. Truman to Bess Wallace, March 10, 1918, HSTLM.

25. Harry S. Truman to Bess Wallace, March 27, 1918, HSTLM.

26. Harry S. Truman to Bess Wallace, March 10 and 17, 1918, HSTLM.

27. Harry S. Truman to Bess Wallace, March 19, 1918, HSTLM.

28. Harry S. Truman to Bess Wallace, March 13, 1918, HSTLM.

29. Harry S. Truman to Bess Wallace, March 8, 1918, HSTLM.

30. Harry S. Truman to Bess Wallace, March 10, 1918, HSTLM.

31. "Pickwick Papers," May 14, 1934.

32. William Hillman, *Mr. President* (New York: Farrar, Straus & Young, 1952), 171, from the third set of longhand notes handed over to Hillman during a series of interviews at the Blair House.

33. Harry S. Truman to Bess Wallace, March 21, 1918, HSTLM.

34. Harry S. Truman to Bess Wallace, December 25, 1917, HSTLM.

Chapter 6

1. Wilson, oral history, 13, HSTLM.

2. Lee, *Artilleryman*, 34.

3. Harry S. Truman to Bess Wallace, March 24, 1918, HSTLM.

4. Harry S. Truman to Ethel and Nellie Noland, March 26, 1918, Mary Ethel Noland Papers, HSTLM.

5. Harry S. Truman to Bess Wallace, March 27, 1918, HSTLM.

6. Harry S. Truman to Bess Wallace, March 28, 1918, HSTLM.

7. Truman, "Military Career."

8. "Pickwick Papers," May 14, 1934, HSTLM.

9. Truman, "Military Career."

10. Harry S. Truman to Bess Wallace, April 13, 1918, HSTLM.

11. Ibid.

12. "Peace Flag Greets New German Liner: Unfurled as the George Washington Arrives on Her Maiden Trip from Bremen," *New York Times,* June 21, 1909, 7.

13. Harry S. Truman to Bess Wallace, March 10, 1918, HSTLM.

14. Harry S. Truman to Bess Wallace, April 14, 1918, HSTLM.

15. Harry S. Truman to Bess Wallace, April 23, 1918, HSTLM.

16. Truman, "Military Career."

17. Harry S. Truman to Bess Wallace, April 23, 1918, HSTLM.

18. Harry S. Truman to Bess Wallace, May 5, 1918, second letter, HSTLM.

19. French ledger book Truman labeled "Fire & Orientation," box 31, "Training Course, Harry S. Truman Longhand Notes for," FBP-MF, HSTLM.

20. Harry S. Truman to Bess Wallace, May 12, 1918, HSTLM.

21. Harry S. Truman to Bess Wallace, May 5, 1918, first letter, HSTLM.

22. Harry S. Truman to Bess Wallace, May 12, 1918, HSTLM.

23. Harry S. Truman to Bess Wallace, June 27, 1918, HSTLM.

24. Harry S. Truman to Bess Wallace, May 5, 1918, first letter, HSTLM.

25. Harry S. Truman to Bess Wallace, May 19, 1918, HSTLM.

26. Harry S. Truman to Bess Wallace, June 19, 1918, HSTLM.

27. Harry S. Truman to Bess Wallace, May 26, 1918, HSTLM.

28. Ibid.

29. Major Richard C. Burleson, "Some Observations Concerning the Use of Accompanying Batteries," *Field Artillery Journal* 11 (November–December 1921): 523–34. Major is the "permanent rank" Burleson reverted to after the war. He was a lieutenant colonel at Montigny, a colonel when Truman met him during the Meuse-Argonne battle, and rose again to colonel in the 1930s.

30. Harry S. Truman to Bess Wallace, June 2, 1918, HSTLM.

Chapter 7

1. Harry S. Truman to Bess Wallace, June 2 and June 14, 1918, HSTLM.

2. Wilson, oral history, 8–9, HSTLM.

3. Harry S. Truman to Bess Wallace, June 14, 1918, HSTLM.

4. Harry S. Truman to Bess Wallace, June 19, 1918, HSTLM.

5. Harry S. Truman to Bess Wallace, June 27, 1918, HSTLM.

6. Harry S. Truman to Bess Wallace, June 14, 1918, HSTLM.

7. Ibid.

8. Lee, *Artilleryman*, 48.

9. Donnelly, oral history, 20, 27, HSTLM.

10. Harry S. Truman to Bess Wallace, June 27, 1918, HSTLM.

11. Lee, *Artilleryman*, 49.

12. "Pickwick Papers," May 14, 1934, HSTLM.

13. Ibid. Scholarly purists have noted correctly that more of the men were
    from another Catholic high school, De LaSalle Academy, than Rockhurst,
    and that three captains preceded Truman (still a very high turnover for
    a battery in existence for little more than a year), but Truman's comment
    certainly captures the essence of what he faced. Besides, if one counts
    Lt. Walter Teasley, who served as interim commander between the second
    and third captains, there were, as Truman states, "four commanders"
    before him. Although known within the regiment as the Irish—and
    by implication, Catholic—battery, Truman's notations next to a list of
    soldiers at the battery position on October 21, 1918, indicate that at least
    ten of its privates belonged to Protestant denominations. Since more than
    a third of the privates were detailed to the regiment that day to assist on
    supply matters, the number of Protestants would likely be significantly
    larger. No fewer than a dozen men were Texan draftees who filled out the
    battery's ranks in the fall of 1917.

14. Donnelly, oral history, 14, HSTLM.

15. Papers of John H. Thacher, box 1, letter of July 20, 1918, in summary,
    "Excerpts from letters of Captain John H. Thacher," HSTLM. Klemm and
    Elliott wanted to send Thacher home for "inefficiency" but thought better
    of it because of the captain's acquaintanceship with President Wilson,
    whom he knew from his Princeton days. It was felt that he would perform
    adequately if in a position that did not require the command of combat
    troops. Thacher was later promoted to major.

16. Bowman, oral history, 12–13, HSTLM.

17. Truman, "Military Career," HSTLM.

18. McKim, oral history, 4, 16, HSTLM.

19. Leigh, oral history, 6, 8, HSTLM.

20. Albert A. Ridge interview in Merle Miller, *Plain Speaking: An Oral
    Biography of Harry S. Truman* (New York: Berkley Publishing, 1974),
    94–95.

21. Murphy, oral history, 7, HSTLM.

22. Daniels, *The Man of Independence*, 95.

23. Leigh, oral history, 10, HSTLM.

24. Ibid., 19.

25. Edward P. Meisburger, oral history interview, 10–11, HSTLM.

26. Murphy, oral history, 20, HSTLM.

27. Leigh, oral history, 19, HSTLM.

28. Floyd T. Rickets, oral history interview, 7, HSTLM.

29. McKim, oral history, 6, HSTLM.

30. Harry S. Truman to Bess Wallace, June 23, 1918, HSTLM.

31. Ibid.; Harry S. Truman to Bess Wallace, June 22, 1918, HSTLM.

32. Harry S. Truman to Bess Wallace, July 14 and 31, 1918, HSTLM.

33. Harry S. Truman to Bess Wallace, HSTLM.

34. "Handwritten Account by Vic Housholder of his Experiences as a Member of Battery D, 129th Field Artillery in France during World War I," Victor H. Housholder Papers, box 1, HSTLM.

35. Lee, *Artilleryman*, 53.

36. Truman, "Military Career," HSTLM.

37. Lee, *Artilleryman*, 52–53.

Chapter 8

1. "Handwritten Account by Vic Housholder of his Experiences as a Member of Battery D," HSTLM.

2. Ibid.

3. Lee, *Artilleryman*, 53.

4. Henry H. Haven, *Battery "C" 129th Field Artillery: Their Participation in the Great World War, 1914–1918* (St. Louis, Missouri: 1920), 16.

5. Lee, *Artilleryman*, 54.

6. MacLean, *My Story of the 130th F.A., A.E.F.*, 45.

7. "Roster, Extra Duty—Battery D," box 31, FBP-MF, HSTLM.

8. "Handwritten Account by Vic Housholder of his Experiences as a Member of Battery D," HSTLM.

9. Harry S. Truman to Bess Wallace, November 23, 1918, HSTLM.

10. Lee, *Artilleryman*, 56.

11. Harry S. Truman to Bess Wallace, November 23, 1918, HSTLM.

12. Ibid.

13. Ibid.

14. Lee, *Artilleryman*, 58.

15. Thacher letter, August 31, 1918, HSTLM.

16. MacLean, *My Story of the 130th F.A., A.E.F.*, 45.

17. Ibid., 49.

18. Lee, *Artilleryman*, 58.

19. Harry S. Truman to Bess Wallace, November 23, 1918, HSTLM.

20. Ibid.

21. Ibid.

22. "Handwritten Account by Vic Housholder of his Experiences as a Member of Battery D," HSTLM.

23. Harry S. Truman to Bess Wallace, November 23, 1918, HSTLM.

24. Ibid.

25. "Handwritten Account by Vic Housholder of his Experiences as a Member of Battery D," HSTLM.

26. Harry S. Truman to Bess Wallace, November 23, 1918, HSTLM.

27. Ibid.

28. Bowman, oral history, 15, HSTLM.

Chapter 9

1. Harry S. Truman to Bess Wallace, November 23, 1918, HSTLM.

2. Bowman, oral history, 16, HSTLM.

3. Harry S. Truman to Bess Wallace, November 23, 1918, HSTLM.

4. "Handwritten Account by Vic Housholder of his Experiences as a Member of Battery D," HSTLM.

5. "Roster and Reference Book—Battery D," and "Roster, Extra Duty—Battery D," box 31, FBP-MF, HSTLM.

6. Ibid.

7. "Handwritten Account by Vic Housholder of his Experiences as a Member of Battery D," HSTLM.

8. "Addenda to Division Code," box 28, folder "Field Orders and Reports: January–August, 1918," FBP-MF, HSTLM.

9. "Handwritten Account by Vic Housholder of his Experiences as a Member of Battery D," HSTLM.

10. Ibid.

11. Harry S. Truman to Bess Wallace, November 23, 1918, HSTLM.

12. Ibid.

13. Lee, *Artilleryman*, 59.

14. Ibid., 56.

15. "Handwritten Account by Vic Housholder of his Experiences as a Member of Battery D," HSTLM.

16. Lee, *Artilleryman*, 60.

17. "To commanding officer of 'D' Battery" and HST response, box 28, folder "Field Orders and Reports: January–August, 1918," FBP-MF, HSTLM.

18. "Roster and Reference Book—Battery D," box 31, FBP-MF, HSTLM.

19. Harry S. Truman to Bess Wallace, November 23, 1918, HSTLM.

20. MacLean, *My Story of the 130th F.A., A.E.F.*, 51.

21. "Handwritten Account by Vic Housholder of his Experiences as a Member of Battery D," HSTLM.

22. Ibid.

23. Harry S. Truman to Bess Wallace, November 23, 1918, HSTLM.

24. Ibid.

25. Ibid.

26. Ibid.

Chapter 10

1. Harry S. Truman, notes on Glen F. Woolridge, box 31, "Roster and Reference Book—Battery D," FBP-MF, HSTLM.

2. Wooden, oral history interview, February 12, 1986, 29, HSTLM.

3. Harry S. Truman to Bess Wallace, November 23, 1918, HSTLM.

4. Bowman, oral history, 11, HSTLM.

5. Harry S. Truman, "Soldier's Diary and Note Book," August 28, 1918, box 30, FBP-MF, HSTLM.

6. Truman, "Military Service: Longhand Notes of Harry S. Truman Regarding," box 30, FBP-MF, HSTLM.

7. Harry S. Truman to Bess Wallace, November 23, 1918, HSTLM; HST longhand notes, HSTLM.

8. Wooden, oral history interview, August 31, 1988, 24, HSTLM.

9. Wooden, oral history, February 12, 1986, 28, HSTLM.

10. Meisburger, oral history, 17–18, HSTLM.

11. Truman, "Military Career," HSTLM. Later in life, Housholder would expand on this role in interviews with various local newspapers in towns where he was living, saying that he had saved Truman's life: "After considerable artificial respiration I was able to revive him" (1950), and "gave him mouth-to-mouth resuscitation and heart massage and he finally came to" (1971), and other stories, such as that Truman rode "piggyback" on Housholder's horse all the way back to the original battery positions—a highly unusual thing for Truman, a former swing driver, to do, as there were ample saddled horses available. Since other BC and gun crew personnel who were on the scene did not recall such details—which certainly would have become a topic of conversation and part of the battery lore—and Housholder was not one of the three soldiers put in for commendations for their activities that night, historians have disregarded his later accounts. See clippings in Housholder Papers.

12. Harry S. Truman, "Military Service: Longhand Notes of Harry S. Truman

Regarding," box 30, FBP-MF, HSTLM; Truman, "Military Career";
oral histories of McKim (p. 18), Wooden, February 12, 1986 (p. 29),
and others, HSTLM. Variations exist on what exactly the first sergeant
shouted, but participants generally agreed upon these words from the
earliest Truman accounts.

13. Harry S. Truman, "Military Service: Longhand Notes of Harry S. Truman
Regarding," box 30, FBP-MF, HSTLM; Truman, "Military Career," HSTLM.

14. Daniels, *The Man of Independence*, 97–99.

15. Harry S. Truman to Bess Wallace, July 14 and 22, 1918, HSTLM.

16. Harry S. Truman to Bess Wallace, September 1, 1918, HSTLM.

17. Ibid.

18. Ibid.

19. Truman, "Military Career," HSTLM.

20. Harry S. Truman to Bess Wallace, September 1, 1918, HSTLM.

21. *Kansas City Post,* undated clipping, General File, 1876–1971, box 23
"Newspaper Clippings," HSTLM. Although this quote is from an undated
clipping, Bess Wallace's mention of the article in a letter to Truman
indicates that it was published sometime before mid-November 1918.

Chapter 11

1. Major Marvin H. Gates, "Report on operations August 29 & 30," August
31, 1918, box 28, folder "Field Orders and Reports: January–August,
1918," FBP-MF, HSTLM.

2. Daniels, *The Man of Independence*, 97.

3. Lee, *Artilleryman*, 70.

4. Truman, "Soldier's Diary and Note Book," September 11, 1918, HSTLM.

5. MacLean, *My Story of the 130th F.A., A.E.F.*, 64.

6. Haven, *Battery "C" 129th Field Artillery*, 17.

7. MacLean, *My Story of the 130th F.A., A.E.F.*, 71.

8. Lee, *Artilleryman*, 75–76.

9. Ibid., 72.

10. Truman, "Soldier's Diary and Note Book," September 7, 1918, HSTLM.

11. Thacher letter, September 14, 1918, HSTLM.

12. Truman, "Soldier's Diary and Note Book," September 11, 1918, HSTLM.

13. Truman, "Military Career," HSTLM.

14. McKim, oral history, 20, HSTLM.

15. MacLean, *My Story of the 130th F.A., A.E.F.*, 68.

16. Rickets, oral history, 14–15, HSTLM.

17. McKim, oral history, 25, HSTLM.

18. Meisburger, oral history, 26–27, HSTLM.

19. McCullough, *Truman*, 126.

20. Leigh, oral history, 15, HSTLM.

21. Ibid., 17.

22. Truman, "Soldier's Diary and Note Book," September 20, 1918, HSTLM.

Chapter 12

1. Truman, "Soldier's Diary and Note Book," September 22, 1918, HSTLM.

2. Lee, *Artilleryman*, 83.

3. Edward P. Meisburger, "20 Years Ago K.C. Men Made Argonne History," *Kansas City Journal Post*, September 25, 1938, 1.

4. Wooden, oral history, August 31, 1988, 30, HSTLM.

Chapter 13

1. Ferrell, *Collapse at Meuse-Argonne*; Clair Kenamore, *From Vauquois Hill to Exermont: A History of the Thirty-Fifth Division of the United States Army* (St. Louis: Guard Publishing, 1919); Charles B. Hoyt and Charles B. Lyon Jr., *Heroes of the Argonne: An Authentic History of the Thirty-fifth Division* (Kansas City, Missouri: Franklin Hudson Publishing, 1919); and Lee, *Artilleryman*.

2. Kenamore, *From Vauquois Hill to Exermont*, 147.

3. *History of the Original Company "A" 110th Engineers*, unpaginated, fifth page.

4. Meisburger, "20 Years Ago," HSTLM.

5. Harry S. Truman notes on Sergeant Harry Kelley, box 31, "Roster and Reference Book—Battery D," FBP-MF, HSTLM.

6. Truman used the word "east" in the longhand draft that forms the basis of this text. For whatever reason, Truman had a propensity to use the word "east" in a variety of notes, drafts, letters, and reports when he meant to say "west." In this case, "east" would have resulted in the "heavy caliber" guns being located well within the range of Truman's guns and in the same general area of the 28th Division sector where he successfully called down fire three times. Incorrect usages of "east" were sometimes left uncorrected in the longhand texts and even in one undated, typed memorandum where the stated map coordinates are clearly west of the reference point given, the town of Montblainville. However in both the draft and the October 7, 1918, final copy of "Operations Report of Battery D, 129th F.A. From Morning of Sept. 26, 1918. To: Evening of Oct. 3, 1918," the correct direction, "west," is given for the same target near Montblainville, and an incorrect "east" is scratched out and corrected in an undated letter to the regimental historian.

7. Joseph R. Younglove, from a December 8, 1944–December 19, 1944,

exchange with then Vice President Truman, box 168, folder "Personal Correspondence, 1944," Senatorial and Vice Presidential Files, HSTLM.

8. Lee, *Artilleryman*, 128.

9. *Pennsylvania in the World War*, vol. 2, (Pittsburgh: States Publication Society, 1921), 643.

10. Major Herman von Giehrl, "The Battle of the Meuse-Argonne," part 1 of 3, *Infantry Journal* 19, no. 2 (August 1921): 131–38.

Chapter 14

1. Harry S. Truman to Bess Wallace, November 23, 1918, HSTLM.

2. *Pennsylvania in the World War*, 2:700.

3. Hillman, *Mr. President*, 167.

4. Wooden, oral history, February 12, 1986, 50, HSTLM.

5. Lee, *Artilleryman*, 130.

6. Truman, *Memoirs*, 1:130.

7. Hillman, *Mr. President*, 166.

8. From a newspaper account read into the record by Governor Henry J. Allen of Kansas during hearings before the Committee on Rules, House of Representatives, *Losses of Thirty-Fifth Division during the Argonne Battle*, February 18, 1919 (Washington, D.C.: U.S. Government Printing Office, 1919), 67, in Ferrell, *Collapse at Meuse-Argonne*, 120. The House Rules Committee had before it a resolution to investigate the alleged lack of artillery support of the 35th Division. Governor Allen had served in the 35th Division during the Meuse-Argonne battle.

9. Meisburger, "20 Years Ago," HSTLM.

10. Lee, *Artilleryman*, 135.

11. Ibid., 135.

12. Ibid., 135–36.

13. *28th Division Summary of Operations in the World War*, Field Orders No. 58, I Corps, September 27, 1918 (Washington: American Battle Monuments Commission, U.S. Government Printing Office, 1944), 47; *35th Division Summary of Operations in the World War*, Field Orders No. 59, I Corps, September 27, 1918, (Washington: American Battle Monuments Commission, U.S. Government Printing Office, 1944), 17.

14. Lee, *Artilleryman*, Appendix S, 303.

15. *Pennsylvania in the World War*, 2:643

16. Kenamore, *From Vauquois Hill to Exermont*, 229.

17. Ferrell, *Collapse at Meuse-Argonne*, 104, 148 n. 22. In addition to a compelling analysis of the battle, the grim story of the subsequent finger-pointing and excuses is also covered in this work.

18. Ferrell, *Collapse at Meuse-Argonne*, 148.

19. "Real Story of 35th Relates Authentic Details of Argonne," *Kansas City Post*, undated, 1919, HSTLM.

20. *Truman in the White House: The Diary of Eben A. Ayers*, Robert H. Ferrell, ed. (Columbia, Missouri: University of Missouri Press, 1991), 40–41.

Chapter 15

1. Major Thomas C. Bourke, unpublished May 18, 1927, letter to *Liberty Magazine*, Liberty Memorial Museum, Kansas City, Missouri.

2. Lee, *Artilleryman*, 159.

3. Colonel Conrad H. Lanza, "The End of the Battle of Montfaucon," *Field Artillery Journal* 23 (July–August, 1933): 360–61.

4. Harry S. Truman to Jay M. Lee, undated letter circa 1919, box 30, folder "Military Service: Records, Harry S. Truman," FBP-MF, HSTLM.

5. Lee, *Artilleryman*, 348.

6. Harry S. Truman to Jay M. Lee, undated letter, HSTLM.

7. Rickets, oral history, 10, HSTLM.

8. Wooden, oral history, February 12, 1986, 50–51, HSTLM.

9. Draft and October 7, 1918, final copy of "Operations Report of Battery D, 129th F.A. From Morning of Sept. 26, 1918. To: Evening of Oct. 3, 1918," box 29, "Field Orders and Reports: October, 1918," FBP-MF, HSTLM. Truman indicated in his calendar book for September 30 that the shell was lodged in the No. 3 gun, but the daily and cumulative ammunition reports, which indicate that no rounds were fired from the No. 2 gun, substantiate the "Operations Report." The error in the calendar book and the fact that Truman did not mention the unusual and dangerous event in a letter to his fiancee Bess may indicate that he was not at the battery position when the event took place. Since Truman was not involved in any battalion observation post at this time, he could well have been at the regimental or brigade command post, meeting officers of the newly arrived 1st Infantry Division headquarters or artillery brigade.

10. Major Marvin H. Gates, "Operations Report Sept. 25th to Oct. 2nd," October 8, 1918, box 29, folder "Field Orders and Reports: October 1918," FBP-MF, HSTLM.

11. Lee, *Artilleryman*, 183.

12. *History of the Seventh Field Artillery (First Division A.E.F)*, with foreword by Maj. Gen. Charles P. Summerall, (New York: privately printed, 1929), 94–95.

13. MacLean, *My Story of the 130th F.A., A.E.F.*, 102.

Chapter 16

1. Major Gen. Peter E. Traub to Harry S. Truman, October 29, 1918, box 29, folder "Field Orders and Reports: October, 1918," FBP-MF, HSTLM.

2. Harry S. Truman to Bess Wallace, November 23, 1918, HSTLM.

3. Harry S. Truman to Bess Wallace, October 6, 1918, HSTLM.

4. Harry S. Truman to Bess Wallace, October 8, 1918, HSTLM.

5. Ibid.

6. Harry S. Truman to Bess Wallace, October 6, 1918, HSTLM.

7. Harry S. Truman notes on John J. Uncles, box 31, "Roster and Reference Book—Battery D," FBP-MF, HSTLM.

8. Harry S. Truman to Bess Wallace, October 1, 1918, HSTLM.

9. Lee, *Artilleryman*, 203–04.

10. Captain N[ewall] T. Paterson, memorandum to Commanding Officer, 2nd Battalion, 129th F.A. October 27, 1918, box 29, folder "Field Orders and Reports: October, 1918," FBP-MF, HSTLM.

11. Harry S. Truman to Bess Wallace, October 30, 1918, HSTLM.

12. William S. Triplet, *A Youth in the Meuse-Argonne: A Memoir, 1917–1918*, Robert H. Ferrell, ed. (Columbia, Missouri: University of Missouri Press, 2000), 255.

13. Ibid., 259.

14. Harry S. Truman to Bess Wallace, October 30, 1918, HSTLM.

15. Triplet, *A Youth in the Meuse-Argonne*, 255.

16. Harry S. Truman to Bess Wallace, November 1, 1918, HSTLM.

17. Triplet, *A Youth in the Meuse-Argonne*, 257.

18. Ibid., 255.

19. Lee, *Artilleryman*, 60, 148.

20. Murphy, oral history, 9–10, HSTLM.

21. Harry S. Truman to Bess Wallace, November 5, 1918, HSTLM.

Chapter 17

1. Untitled October 22, 1918, report on operations during the night of October 21–22, 1918, box 29, folder "Field Orders and Reports: October, 1918," FBP-MF, HSTLM.

2. Field Order No. 13, Headquarters, 129th F.A., October 24, 1918, box 29, folder "Field Orders and Reports: October, 1918," FBP-MF, HSTLM.

3. Harry S. Truman to Bess Wallace, November 5, 1918, HSTLM.

4. Truman, "Soldier's Diary and Note Book," October 26, 1918," HSTLM.

5. Vaughan, oral history, January 14, 1963, 6, HSTLM.

6. Jacobson, "I Knew Him When," 4–5, HSTLM.

7. "Commanding General, 35th Division, to Commanding Officer, Battery D, 129th Field Artillery. Subject: Commendation," October 29, 1918, box 29, folder "Field Orders and Reports: October, 1918," FBP-MF, HSTLM.

8. Harry S. Truman to Bess Wallace, November 1, 1918, HSTLM.

9. "C.O. Battery D, 129th F. A., APO #743, A.E.F. To C. G. 35th Division,"

November 2, 1918, box 29, folder "Field Orders and Reports: November–December, 1918," FBP-MF, HSTLM.

10. Hillman, *Mr. President*, 171.

11. Harry S. Truman to Bess Wallace, November 10, 1918, HSTLM.

12. Meisburger, oral history, 28–30, HSTLM.

13. Harry S. Truman to Bess Truman, November 11, 1926, HSTLM.

14. Ibid.

15. Hillman, *Mr. President*, 171–72. This narrative, written for Hillman's book in 1951, was later used almost word-for-word by Truman in his 1955 *Memoirs*, 1:131.

16. Lee, *Artilleryman*, 233.

17. Battery "D" 129th. Field Artillery Mounted Inspection, undated, box 30, folder "Military Service: Records, Harry S. Truman," FBP-MF, HSTLM.

18. Harry S. Truman to Bess Wallace, November 15, 1918, HSTLM.

19. Bowman, oral history, 22, HSTLM.

20. Harry S. Truman, January 22, 1919, entry in notebook, "Agenda, Souvenir Journalier, 1919," box 30, FBP-MF, HSTLM.

Chapter 18

1. Harry S. Truman to Bess Wallace, December 1, 1918, HSTLM.

2. Harry S. Truman to Bess Wallace, December 19, 1918, HSTLM.

3. Lee, *Artilleryman*, 241.

4. Rickets, oral history, 17–19, HSTLM.

5. Bowman, oral history, 39, HSTLM.

6. Harry S. Truman, February 17, 1919, entry, "Agenda, Souvenir Journalier, 1919," HSTLM.

7. Special Memorandum, Headquarters, 35th Division, January 27, 1919, box 29, folder "Field Orders and Reports: January, 1919," FBP-MF, HSTLM.

8. Leigh, oral history, 45, HSTLM.

9. Harry S. Truman to Bess Wallace, April 24, 1919, HSTLM.

10. "Klemm out of the Parade: Some of the 129th Men have Feud with Their Colonel," *Kansas City Star*, April 27, 1919, 3.

11. Harry S. Truman to Bess Wallace, April 24, 1919, HSTLM.

12. "Klemm out of the Parade."

Index